THE SNAKE-OIL SYNDROME
PATENT MEDICINE ADVERTISING

THE SNAKE-OIL SYNDROME
PATENT MEDICINE ADVERTISING

By A. Walker Bingham

Founded 1910
THE CHRISTOPHER PUBLISHING HOUSE
HANOVER, MASSACHUSETTS 02339

Library of Congress Catalog Number 93-72216
ISBN: 0-8158-0484-9

PRINTED IN THE UNITED STATES OF AMERICA

CONTENTS

Acknowledgments

It was fifteen years ago that Professor James Harvey Young of Emory University first encouraged me to research and write about patent medicines. William H. Helfand, for many years Senior Vice President of Merck Sharpe and Dohme and a pre-eminent collector of pharmaceutical images, has befriended me with advice and materials. A number of other collectors, curators and librarians have graciously added to my education and inventory of illustrations. I am grateful to all of these individuals, named and unnamed, for their kindnesses. I salute the courage and perseverance of my editor and publisher, Harold F. Walsh, and most of all I give thanks for the confidence and patience of my wife, Nicolette.

Preface

For the cure of his ailments, real and imagined, the man in the street has always been drawn to the promised magic of exotic substances. Nothing is more closely bound up with human hopes and fears than the recapture or preservation of health. In nineteenth century America, this syndrome was fed and exploited by a fascinating parade of sincere doctors, hopeless charlatans, bewildered pharmacologists and acute businessmen.

Robber baron ethics were not solely to blame for a patent medicine industry that resembled a vast carnival. In the gas-light era, when modern medicine was just coming out of the shadows, genuine discoveries were as unbelievable as the pseudo-scientific nonsense with which they fought for recognition. Germs? Antiseptics? Inoculation? Would they have persuaded you, as new ideas, to abandon your faith in Balm of Gilead and Kickapoo Indian Sagwa?

Over the century, the selling of medicine passed from the face-to-face sales of the itinerant peddler and the local druggist to the mass merchandising of the millionaire nostrum manufacturer and publicity genius. He used the newspapers, billboards, traveling medicine shows, trade cards, almanacs and give-away novelties in great profusion. The patent medicine story is entwined with the emergence of national advertising, mass marketing techniques, and new public attitudes, in a turbulent period of economic and social development.

To appreciate fully how America was sold its nostrums, the story must be told not only with the accents of scholarship and the precision of statistics but also with the actual words and images that moved the public at the time. Most of the surviving artifacts of medicine advertising fall into the category of paper ephemera — printed matter that was made to be thrown away in a short space of time — and the historian must become a sort of ragpicker, a hundred years late.

The examples of patent medicine advertising that have come down to us are infinitely varied and cover the broadest range of visual subjects. They depict social history in a very direct and poignant manner, dispensing in capsule doses the romance and excitement of bygone days. We catch with freshness and immediacy, the dress and manner of speech, the architecture, the technology, and some of the popular concerns of the moment. There is color and action to attract the eye of the uninitiated and sophistication to satisfy the most accomplished connoisseur.

The purpose of this book is to open a door for those who are intrigued by the snake-oil syndrome — the appeal of the patent medicine — and the way in which it was developed, refined and exploited in nineteenth century America. Beyond this door lies a wealth of fascinating material of which I have provided only a small glimpse.

New York, NY
November 5, 1993

A. Walker Bingham

PART ONE

The Patent Medicine Industry

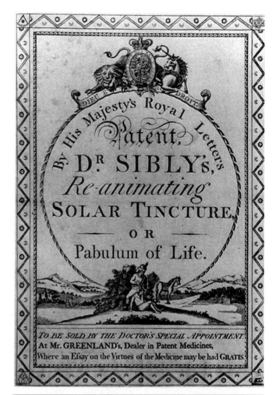

1.

What is a Patent Medicine?

A "patent medicine" is any dubious remedy, in the colloquial sense in which we use those words today, but it was not always so. At the turn of the century, these words distinguished a ready-mixed nostrum that was self-prescribed, from a medicine prescribed by a doctor whose ingredients were compounded by the pharmacist for the individual patient. The notion of a "patent" medicine goes back to early English beginnings. In the sixteenth century, patents were monopolies granted at the pleasure of the sovereign, to encourage various skills and manufactures. In return the proprietor was required to make his secret "open" or "patent." Patent rights were refined and restricted as English law developed. Today the monopoly involved in a patent lasts for a fixed but short time, and its scope is limited by the written description of the product accepted by the Patent Office.

The magic of the word "patent" persisted well into the nineteenth century and indeed the Industrial Revolution gave it further emphasis in the public mind. Patent status was featured in the advertising of humble items like washboards and hand pumps as well as more sophisticated inventions, to convey a sense of importance and exclusivity. Notwithstanding the American Revolution and seventy years of independence, one American remedy popular in the 1850s actually bore the words "By the King's Royal Patent Granted to Robert Turlington for His Invented Balsam of Life."

One can only obtain a patent on an invention or a method of manufacture that is unique, or a combination of ingredients that is novel. Today the Patent Office is reluctant to recognize that any invention is present in a new mixture of well-known

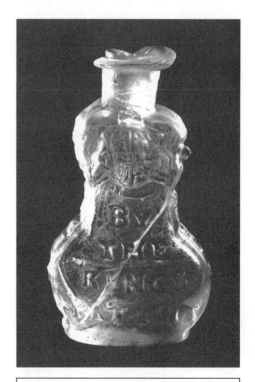

3

Above, a washboard patented in 1886, named The Northern Queen. Above right, a comic trade card poking fun at the emphasis that some advertisers placed upon their patents.

A pair of metallic tractors patented by Elisha Perkins (1741-1799), the first medical patent issued in the United States. Their alleged benefit was based upon Anton Mesmer's theory of animal magnetism. *Courtesy Mutter Museum, College of Physicians of Philadelphia.*

drugs, which is the most favorable description that could be given to the patent medicines of the last century. The early Patent Office was more liberal. Then, as now, a patented invention did not need to work. The first medical patent was awarded, in 1796, to Perkins' Metallic Tractors, "for drawing out disease". As one writer has said about those early days, ". . . patenting a product does not preclude telling fairy tales about it. In fact, therapeutic claims contained in the description of some of the patents for medicines are grossly false and fraudulent. "[1]

The important thing to note is that, even when it was easy to get a patent on a medicine, very few of the nostrum manufacturers did it. For all of the hundreds of remedies offered in the forty years following Mr. Perkins, an average of two per year were actually patented. The explanation is very simple. When a patent issues, the ingredients become a matter of public record, and the right to use them becomes public property in seventeen years. The composition of a patent medicine was a business secret of the highest order. Secrecy afforded some protection against close imitation and concealed the dangerous ingredients or, in other cases, the palpable simplicity of the remedy which would have destroyed its appeal. The nostrum manufacturer was well aware that when a patent expired, the public following attached to the product by years of advertising expenditure went up for grabs. Pitcher's Castoria was one medicine that was genuinely patented. Its principal ingredients were senna, Rochelle Salts, wormseed, sugar and water. In later years "Fletcher's Castoria," "Gray's Castoria," and others enjoyed a free ride on the coat-tails of the original proprietor.

New medicines, and new techniques for making medicines, are of course still patented today. Some of these patents are enormously important and valuable, but we do not think of the pharmaceuticals they cover as "patent medicines." Penicillin, the product of carefully nurtured microorganisms, were discovered in 1929 by an English bacteriologist named Alexander Fleming. The large-scale production of penicillin, achieved during World War II, began a new age in medicine, the Age of Antibiotics. Penicillin showed the way for terramycin, streptomycin, and tetracycline, to name just a few of the wonder drugs in what is now an industry measured in billions of dollars and countless saved lives. Alexander Fleming never patented his discovery and never received any significant financial reward for it.

In the case of most of the nineteenth century nostrums we are considering, the manufacturer's exclusivity rested, not on a patent, but on his trademark. Nearly every nostrum had a fanciful name, registered at the Patent Office, which it was his property alone to exploit. (For usual meanings of medicine names, see the Glossary.) The composition of the medicine could change, the effects claimed could change, but the ownership of the name remained intact. One writer has claimed that over the years almost every ingredient in Lydia Pinkham's Vegetable Compound

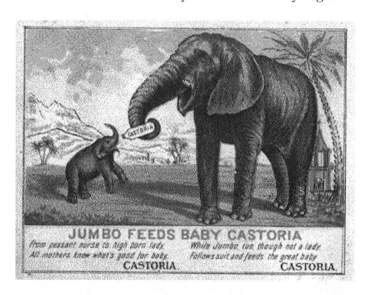

JUMBO FEEDS BABY CASTORIA
from peasant nurse to high born lady.
All mothers know what's good for baby.
While Jumbo, too, though not a lady,
Follows suit and feeds the great baby
CASTORIA   CASTORIA

was changed except the alcohol, but the Pinkham interests continued to use the same name and the famous picture of Lydia. Only they were entitled to do so, and it was the public image of this product and its proprietor, of course, that constituted the company's most valuable asset.

The professional did not generally speak of a "patent medicine." In place of this rather ambiguous lay term he would use the phrase "proprietary medicine," meaning a preparation to which sole manufacturing rights are claimed by virtue of owning the formula. This formula might or might not have been secret, and might or might not have been patented. The manufacturer was referred to as the "proprietor."

"Castoria" under three different flags. The trade card upper right capitallized on the public interest in the gigantic elephant named Jumbo, star of P. T. Barnum's circus.

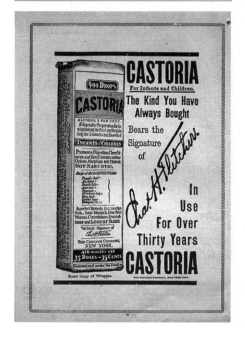

WORLD FAMOUS PITCHER'S CASTORIA.

THE OLD RELIABLE BRAND.

THE BEST REMEDY KNOWN FOR ALL STOMACH AND BOWEL COMPLAINTS OF INFANTS AND CHILDREN.

PROMOTES DIGESTION, CHEERFULNESS AND REST.
FREE FROM HARMFUL SUBSTANCES.

Castoria is truly a wonderful medicine for children. Doctors prescribe it, medical journals recommend it, and more than a million mothers are using it in place of Paregoric, Bateman's Drops, so called soothing syrups and other narcotic and stupefying remedies. Castoria is the quickest thing to regulate the stomach and bowels, and give healthy sleep, the world has ever seen. It is guaranteed to be perfectly harmless.

MORTALITY. Nearly every married couple have children and every infant and child is sick more or less during the first and second years. Infant mortality is something frightful, and we can hardly realize that 22 per cent. or nearly one-fourth of all born die from stomach and bowel troubles before the age of one year. This being true, it is very essential that their young bodies be closely watched and irregularities be quickly corrected. If now one remedy was to be selected which would cure all these ills, but one name would be on every tongue, Castoria, Castoria; nothing but Castoria. The best physicians of today prescribe it, recommend it, and even go so far as to state that if a child's stomach and bowels were kept in perfect condition with some harmless remedy like Castoria, that infants and children would be free from nearly all their more serious ills. Castoria it the one remedy that meets all the requirements of children, it is the one medicine that is known the world over as The Mothers' Blessing and the Babies' Friend.

OUR PRICE, ONLY
18c.
Regular Price, 25c.

CHILDREN CRY FOR IT. Children cry for Castoria because they like it. No trouble to give, it is beneficial and makes the child healthy and cheerful. We do not hesitate in saying that Castoria has done more for suffering children than all other remedies combined. The least irregularity in the food of the nursing mother upsets the stomach and bowels of the child, then comes indigestion, sour stomach, wind colic, constipation, loss of sleep, etc. The child becomes cross and feverish and sickness follows. Every mother then thinks of but one remedy, Castoria; only Castoria. The popularity of this wonderful remedy has so increased until it now stands alone among druggists and physicians as the only reliable and harmless regulator of children's complaints. It is being used more and more every week, until the sales of this beneficial remedy double every three years. This proven but one thing—Castoria is very beneficial, is harmless and does the work. "It is truly a Mother's Blessing, a Baby's Friend and a Father's Comfort.

WHAT IS IT? Dr. Pitcher's Castoria is composed of the medicinal properties of Pumpkin Seed, Alex. Senna, Rochelle Salts, Anise Seed, Peppermint, Bicarbonate of Soda, Worm Seed, Clarified Sugar and Wintergreen. A pure, vegetable preparation for assimilating the food and regulating the stomach and bowels of children and infants. Promotes digestion, cheerfulness and rest. Contains neither opium, morphine or any form of narcotic. A perfect remedy for constipation, sour stomach, diarrhea, worms, convulsions, feverishness and loss of sleep.

A FEW FACTS FOR MOTHERS.

1. No medicine should be given to children without knowing what you are giving. Castoria is purely vegetable, and the ingredients are given upon every package.
2. Castoria is harmless, is the standard prescription of Dr. Pitcher, and has been in constant use by thousands of mothers for over thirty years.
3. Castoria may be given to any one and at any time; it is superior in its effects to Paregoric, Castor Oil or any other cathartic or quieter. It is free from dangerous or nauseous properties.
4. Castoria keeps indefinitely and hence no danger of spoiling by age. The last drop is just as effective as the first one taken from the bottle.
5. Castoria is without doubt the best medicine for children and infants the world has ever known. In it mothers have something absolutely safe, pleasant to give, effective in results and perfectly satisfactory in every respect.
6. Castoria assimilates the food, regulates the stomach and bowels, and produces perfect and natural sleep. With this valuable medicine on hand, much sickness may be avoided, the child kept cheerful and robust and the parents obtain their needful sleep.
7. Castoria being the world's medicine for children, is grossly imitated and adulterated. Many castorias are on the market, but we handle only the well known and world famous Dr. Pitcher's Castoria. Do not allow anyone to sell you anything else on the plea that it is just as good. What you want is Dr. Pitcher's Castoria.
8. Castoria is usually sold for 25 to 35 cents per bottle; but now consider our exceptionally low price of 18 cents. Order now and obtain a supply. It should be in every home.
No. 8F345. Regular price, per bottle, 25 cents; our price, 3 bottles for 50c; each..........18c
Unmailable on account of weight.

[Image text: 900 DROPS / CASTORIA / CASTORIA / ALCOHOL 3 PER CENT. / AVegetable Preparation Cheerfulness and Rest Contains neither Opium, Morphine nor Mineral NOT NARCOTIC. / INFANTS ~ CHILDREN / CASTORIA / For Infants and Children. / The Kind You Have Always Bought / Bears the Signature of / In Use For Over Thirty Years / CASTORIA / THE CENTAUR COMPANY, NEW YORK CITY.]

[Image text: PITCHER'S CASTORIA / THE OLD RELIABLE BRAND / TRADE MARK REGISTERED / FOR INFANTS AND CHILDREN / A PURELY VEGETABLE REMEDY FOR REGULATING STOMACH AND BOWELS PROMOTES APPETITE AIDS DIGESTION CURES DIARRHOEA REMOVES WORMS OVERCOMES CONSTIPATION AND RELIEVES FEVERS / THE OLD RELIABLE BRAND / IS ABSOLUTELY GUARANTEED TO GIVE SATISFACTION / PRICE 25 CENTS / PREPARED ONLY BY CENTRAL REMEDY CO. ST. LOUIS, MO. U.S.A.]

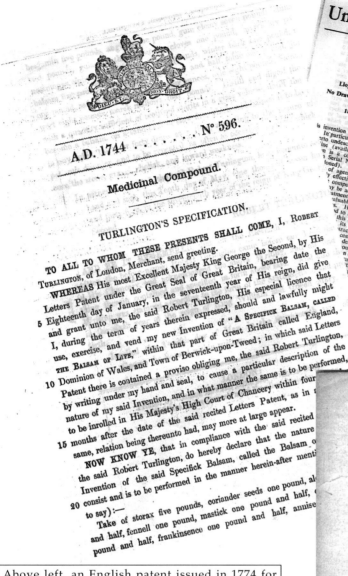

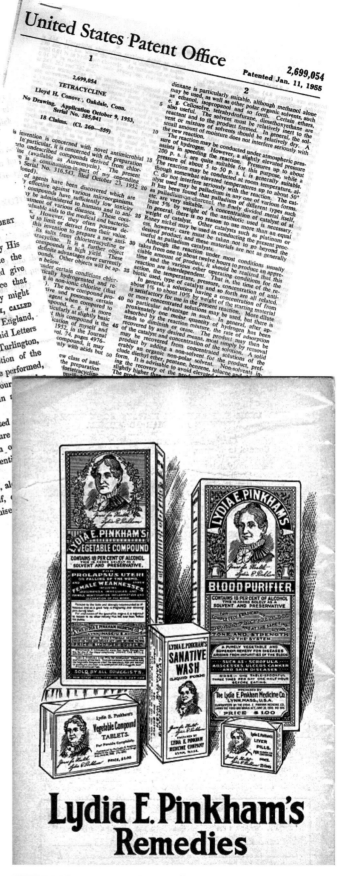

Above left, an English patent issued in 1774 for Turlington's Balsam. Above right, a modern U.S. pharmaceutical patent for tetracycline.

Pharmaceuticals compounded by the druggist, who followed a doctor's prescription, were referred to as "ethical medicines." Today the law specifies those medicines that require a prescription before they may be dispensed, and this category of medicines is based upon the danger of the substance and the care with which it must be used. A prescription drug can, of course, be proprietary and may be one that has been patented. As a matter of trade usage, the term "ethical medicine" also refers to one that is sold by the manufacturer to the druggist, doctor or dentist for use in his practice.

Packages for Lydia Pinkham's products that featured her famous trademarked image.

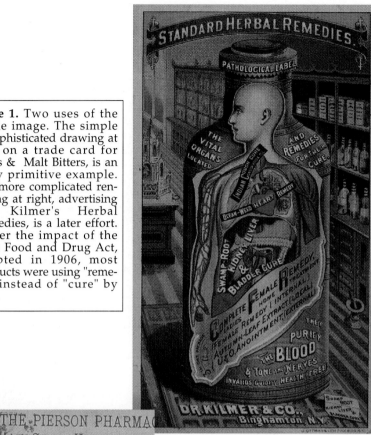

Plate 1. Two uses of the bottle image. The simple unsophisticated drawing at left, on a trade card for Hops & Malt Bitters, is an early primitive example. The more complicated rendering at right, advertising Dr. Kilmer's Herbal Remedies, is a later effort. Under the impact of the Pure Food and Drug Act, adopted in 1906, most products were using "remedy" instead of "cure" by 1912.

THE OLD-TIME DOCTOR

Plate 2. Doctor and druggist images were flattering to the prescriber and to the vendor of patent medicines. The scene above showing the doctor in his buggy bears a drugstore imprint in its upper right corner and an advertisement for Mellin's Special Formula for Babies on the reverse. Dr. McLane's scene at right shows us an upscale pharmacy of the 1890's. The customers are intended to be Mr. and Mrs. Cleveland, accompanied by the President's famous bird dog.

Plate 3. Today's landmarks were recent wonders in the patent medicine days. The Bartholdi Statue, later known as the Statue of Liberty, was completed in 1886 and became a favorite subject for advertisers. Voegler's St. Jacob's Oil has found an opportunity to call attention to its logo, a monk in red robes, on the trade card above.

Plate 4. Lydia Pinkham's Vegetable Compound, one of the most famous patent medicines of all time, might have liked to hang its sign on the Brooklyn Bridge, as shown in the equally fanciful drawing at right.

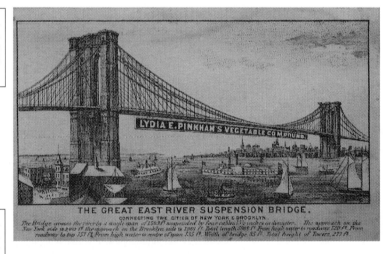

Plate 5. The Panama Canal is featured on the postcard shown below advertising Hostetter's Stomach Bitters. This historic engineering achievement was constructed during the period 1904 to 1914 under conditions requiring extraordinary medical efforts.

Plate 6. The patent medicine proprietors frequently associated themselves with patriotic themes. The makers of Burdsal's Arnica Liniment, on the cover of their Centennial Year almanac at left, show us Revolutionary War troops that the medicine may or may not have supported at that time.

Plate 7. Harter's Iron Tonic issued formal "cabinet photographs" on cardboard in 1888 of the Presidential candidates and their wives. At right are Mr. and Mrs. Cleveland who were married in the White House in 1886 during Cleveland's first term. The discreet advertising pin at Mrs. Cleveland's throat is, no doubt, the work of a retoucher.

Plate 8. The royalty of Europe are portrayed on the trade card at left, issued by the makers of Horsford's Acid Phosphate, a medicinal drink. Those identifiable are, left to right, King George V of England, Emperor Franz Joseph of Austro-Hungary, Kaiser Wilhelm of Germany, and the Sultan of Turkey.

Plate 9. American celebrities of the theater were natural subjects for trade cards. The portrait of the actor, Edwin Booth, at top left, was one of a series issued by Burdock Blood Bitters. Lillian Russell is the actress shown at top right advertising a hair preparation named Carboline. A different sort of celebrity was Henry M. Stanley, the newspaper reporter who went out to search for the missing explorer, Dr. David Livingston, in 1871. The cartoon at left shows Stanley, and Swayne's Ointment, in Africa.

Plate 10. A more crude form of humor was that directed at ethnic groups, particularly the newly emancipated blacks, who were frequently shown in an unsympathetic manner. The example at right, advertising the stomach preparation Biliousine, was one of the few with this subject matter that employed such elaborate lithography.

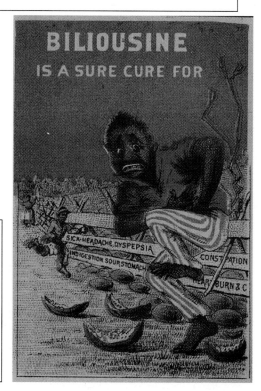

2.

What was in Them?

Sometimes, of course, a patent medicine was just a combination of flavoring, coloring and aromatics. The American Medical Association reported that Munyon's Kidney Cure consisted entirely of sugar and water and that no alkaloid or other active ingredient could be detected.[1] Advertising for this product featured the imposing Dr. Munyon with his finger upraised like a biblical preacher, and the slogan "If the sign of the cross were to be dropped, the next best sign would be 'The Index Finger Pointing Heavenward.' "

Frequently patent medicines contained a long list of herbs, most of which lacked any provable pharmaceutical efficacy. Dr. Kennedy's Medical Discovery was widely and handsomely advertised. According to a 1904 analysis it was composed of sugar, water, alcohol, wintergreen, licorice root, bitter root and sneezewort.[2] The same source tells us that the modestly named Seven Barks contained hydrangea, poke root, Culver's root, dandelion, ladies slipper, colocynth, bloodroot, blue flag, stone root, golden seal, mandrake, black cohosh, butternut, aloes, capsicum, sassafrass and ginger.[3]

It is probable that most of the nineteenth century patent medicines had no effect at all on the diseases that they were sold to cure. They were not even palliatives. Some sufferers may have been misled into taking patent medicines instead of more effective (and possibly more expensive) drugs prescribed by a doctor, but generally speaking, at that stage of medical learning there was often little that any doctor could do for a patient with a serious disease except to give emotional support. It has been suggested that the true opportunity for the nostrum vendor lay in the fact that eighty percent of all human ailments cure themselves regardless of what medicine the sufferer takes or does not take.[4]

On occasion the patent medicine probably helped. Quinine, digitalis, kaolin, ipecac and phenolphthalein were among the ingredients with genuine medical value. Many of the herbal medicines at least had a laxative or diuretic effect. This may not have been medically helpful in a particular case but at least it proved to the customer's satisfaction that the medicine was doing something.

Partial page from a 1902 pamphlet entitled "Munyon's Magazine". Dr. Munyon's advertising was heavy with portent but his medicine was a little light on medicament.

DR. DAVID KENNEDY,
OF RONDOUT, N. Y., U. S. A.

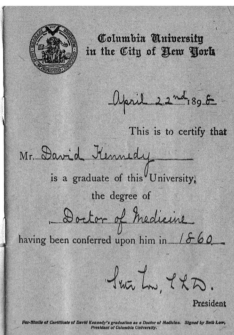

Columbia University
in the City of New York

April 22nd, 1896

This is to certify that

Mr. David Kennedy

is a graduate of this University,

the degree of

Doctor of Medicine

having been conferred upon him in 1860

Seth Low, LL.D.
President

Fac-Simile of Certificate of David Kennedy's graduation as a Doctor of Medicine. Signed by Seth Low, President of Columbia University.

Dr. Kennedy sought to establish his medical credentials by the most direct sort of proof, which in itself suggests some suspicion on the part of the public. At left, a page from a Kennedy almanac at the turn of the century.

SEVEN BARKS

COPYRIGHTED

Cover of an 1885 almanac that advertised Seven Barks, a representative nostrum crammed with a spectrum of herbal substances. One of them might work! Almanacs were frequently provided with a string to hang them in the kitchen or outhouse.

Some of the skin preparations of the nineteenth century, especially astringents, emollients, and soothing creams, are still in use. Aromatics such as wormwood, anise, eucalyptus, menthol, oil of cedar, wintergreen, and camphor had their uses in medicine. A pleasant smelling oil can alleviate an earache and the act of rubbing it in can ease sore muscles. A sweet syrup can comfort an inflamed throat. Some persons can obtain relief simply from what doctors call the "placebo effect" which stems from their faith in the medicine, their doctor, or some other non-therapeutic factor.

The real evil of the patent medicine lay in the indiscriminate use of substances inherently dangerous to take in uncontrolled amounts and in the substitution of self-dosage for effective medical care in serious cases. The "tonics," "bitters," and medicines for "female weakness" like Lydia Pickham's Vegetable Compound and McElree's Wine of Cardui, relied heavily on alcohol for their effect. The baby medicines like Mrs. Winslow's Soothing Syrup and Dr. Winchell's Teething Syrup, contained morphine (Plate 15). The headache powders like Koehler's and Orangeine contained acetanilid. The powders for relieving nasal congestion contained cocaine, which was originally hailed as a nonaddictive answer to pain (Plate 21). Cocaine was employed in a variety of products like Coca Wine and Vin Mariani, which were sold as general fortifying medicines (Plate 20).

There are recorded cases by the hundreds of the drastic effects of medicines like these on the unsuspecting, particularly the very young. No amount of nostalgia can gloss over the horrors that were committed knowingly and unknowingly by placing lethal preparations in the hands of an unsophisticated public. Not a few nostrum users became addicted to their medicines, either physiologically or by creating an emotional dependency.

Advertising materials for patent medicines that, when sold
over-the-counter, posed problems when over-used.
Clockwise: a flyer, a trade card, a label and a decorated
envelope.

There follows a list of some of the better known nostrums and the harmful ingredients they are said to
have contained at one time or another.[5]

Antikamnia—acetanilid
Ayer's Cherry Pectoral—heroin
Seth Arnold's Cough Killer—morphine
Birney's Catarrh Powder—cocaine
Bromo-Seltzer—acetanilid
Boschee's Syrup—morphine
Dr. Bull's Cough Syrup—opium
Capital DDD Remedy—chloral hydrate
Cephalgine—acetanilid
Doan's Kidney Pills—potassium nitrate
Fahrney's Teething Syrup—morphine and chloroform
Garfield's Powders—acetanilid
James' Soothing Syrup—heroin

Jayne's Expectorant—opium, digitalis
Dr. King's New Discovery—morphine, choloroform
Koehler's Headache Powders—acetanilid
One Day Cough Cure—cannabis indica
Orangeine—acetanilid
Dr. Pierce's Golden Medical Discovery—opium
Dr. Pierce's Favorite Prescription—digitalis, opium
Pike's Universal Vegetable Drops—chloroform, alcohol
Piso's Cure for Consumption—cannabis indica
Petit's Eye Salve—morphine
Smith's Consumptive Cure—chloroform, prussic acid
Taylor's Sweet Gum & Mullein Compound—morphine
Warner's Safe Cure—potassium nitrate
Mrs. Winslow's Soothing Syrup—morphine

The cheerfulness and innocent appeal of these medicine trade cards stand in marked contrast to the inherent dangers of the substances that they contained.

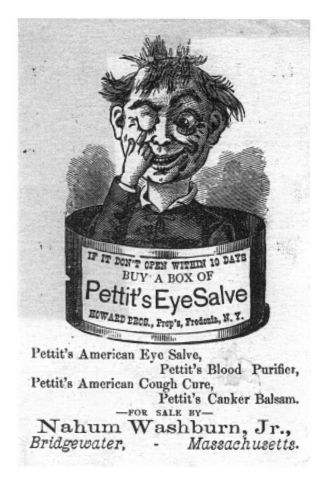

3.

One Born
Every Minute

Most of the patent medicines made extravagant claims of effectiveness with respect to a wide variety of ailments. Some of the earliest were advertised as "panaceas" or "cure-alls" for every ill known to man (Plates 22 and 23). Moffat's Life Pills claimed to cure fifty-one diseases, from night sweats to leprosy. The letterhead of Mrs. M. G. Brown, used as late as 1879, claimed thirty-four ailments and then added, at the foot of the list, "every disease of man, woman and child." It was noted specially that her scalp renovator also acted as a cathartic.

Other proprietors of patent medicines directed their assurances towards more vague problems like "dyspepsia" or "general debility." Anyone might diagnose these maladies in himself without a doctor, and the medicine could not be held accountable for failing to relieve this or that symptom. The famous Hartman's Peruna was a remedy for "catarrh." According to Dr. Hartman, pneumonia was "catarrh of the lungs" and Bright's Disease was "catarrh of the kidneys" (See Plate 17). If pressed, Dr. Hartman would assert that heart disease was "catarrh of the heart" and appendicitus was "catarrh of the appendix." In any case, the theory behind the cure-alls was much closer to the conventional medical view of that time than we are likely to appreciate today.

The claims made for the patent medicines suggest to us a limitless gullibility on the part of the public. There was a liniment, widely used in the past century, called opodeldoc. Its principal constituents were camphor and soap. It enjoyed official status in the U.S. Pharmacopoeia in 1850. In time, the name of this medicine was used to describe the sort of person who would put his faith in it. Fifty years ago, if you heard a joke about a man named Opodeldoc, you would have known that it referred to a "hick" or a "hayseed." But the problem was not gullibility nor was it the general lack of education. The problem was the state of medical knowledge.

The traditional view at the start of the nineteenth century was descended from Hippocrates' doctrine of the humors, that all illness stems from a single cause, the imbalance of the forces of Earth, Air, Fire and Water. In ancient times these forces were thought to be embodied in blood, phlegm, yellow bile and black bile. The notion was still in place in the early 1800s that the body was a single unified system and that good health was a matter of equillibrium

In this 1897 edition of a booklet advertising Peruna, Dr. Hartman continued to view all diseases as varieties of "catarrh".

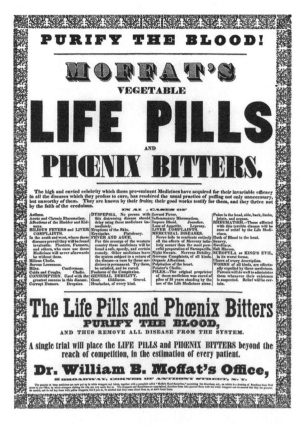

An 1860's poster for a typical panacea that promised to cure a long list of diseases. It measured 24 by 17 inches.

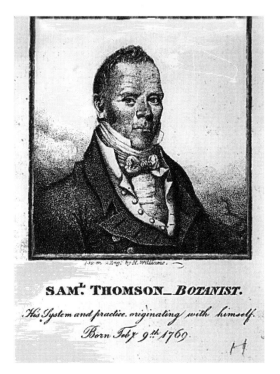

SAM.ᴸ THOMSON__ *BOTANIST.*

His System and practice, originating with himself.

Born Feb.ʸ 9ᵗʰ 1769.

H

Above, a contemporary engraving of Samuel Thompson, and below, one of the books of medical advice in which he urged that "Every man be his own physician".

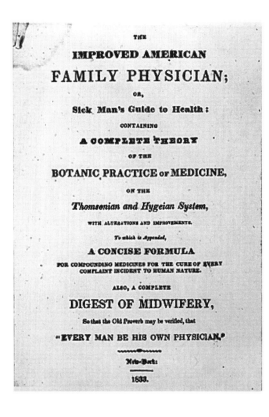

within it. It was thought that an imbalance of the human system could produce a variety of symptoms in various parts of the body because each part was inextricably interrelated.[1]

Doctors sought to control the balance of health by regulating the intake and the outflow of the body, which in practice meant controlling the secretions of the patient—urine, feces, sweat and menstrual flow. Drugs helped to adjust the internal equilibrium, as evidenced by their visible effect upon body processes, but to advocate a specific drug for a specific malady is what a regular physician would have considered quackery.[2] The notion of many distinct diseases, with their own particular causes and cures, was not generally accepted until the 1890s.

Success in controlling disease was measured by the relief of symptoms, of course. What we call symptoms was what the trouble was, wasn't it? The sufferer could be excused for thinking that the patent medicine was doing its job if the opiate or the alcohol made him feel better. Even in the middle of the century, the best of doctors could not explain the nature of many illnesses or be sure that this or that remedy might not alleviate them. By that time, competing philosophies waged war with each other in the medical journals and the medical colleges, as doctors groped for truth among new discoveries and new theories in an era of great change for the medical profession. There were marked differences in the treatments prescribed by doctors of various schools of thought.

Historically, the followers of Paracelsus believed in chemical drugs while the followers of Galen adhered to herbs and other natural substances. Medical opinion in the United States was dominated by the views of the eminent physician, Benjamin Rush, who had been a signer of the Declaration of Independence. He ascribed all disease to a morbid excitement in the blood, induced by capillary tension, and he endorsed the "depletive theory" which called for eliminating the offending agent from the body by strong measures. The standard treatments, which have been called collectively "heroic" therapy, were bleeding, blistering and purging. Medicines were designed to accomplish the latter two.

Bleeding can slow the pulse, change a flush to a pallor, and induce perspiration, all of which signal the natural end of a fever. Blistering was often followed by a local infection which produced what was called "laudable pus," apparently carrying off internal poisons. Purges were frequently helpful simply because the concept of a balanced diet was totally unappreciated. Of course, the relief of symptoms was not at all the same thing as the achievement of a cure.

The heroic remedies were challenged by new intellectual attitudes, an agressive empiricism among doctors who saw a need to evaluate the conventional methods of treatment. Some of them must have also felt the economic impact of competition from those who began to practice kinder, gentler therapies. New evidence, developed by certain European pathologists, demonstrated in particular the harm caused by bloodletting. The medical establishment came under attack at this point from Samuel Thomson, and his unique medical system which embraced pharmacology, medical practice and the distribution of medicines. His story furnishes an example of the extremes to which medical theory and public belief might be extended.

Thomson's bizarre theory was actually a limited replay of the humors according to Galen. "Air and fire, or heat, are the cause of life and motion," he said. ". . . Cold, or the lessening power of heat, is the cause of all disease . . ."[3] Medicine should, then, clean out the digestive tract, increase internal heat, and produce perspiration. Thomson's treatment involved several continuous rounds of steam baths, washing, wrapping in blankets and inducing extraordinary vomiting. There were six principal Thomsonian medicines, all of them herbal. Number 6, probably the most popular, was an aromatic concoction of pepper that actually made it into the U.S. Pharmacopoeia as Tincture of Capsicum and Myrrh. Thomson's favorite was Number 1, lobelia inflata, one of several herbs called "Indian Tobacco," an unfailing emetic of epic proportions.

Thomson managed to obtain two patents upon his medical practices and his medicines. He then peddled the right to use his system to members of the public through a network of agents and sub-agents. In 1839 he claimed that three million people had been treated under his system and that he had sold one hundred thousand Family Rights. Thomsonians set up their own depots and stores to compound and retail Thomson's medicines, and infirmaries where patients were treated. Holders of Family Rights were expected to boycott conventional pharmacies, which were not allowed to purchase these products. Thomson thus competed head-on with both the regular physician and the regular drug store. The doctors he called "quacks" and "ignorant pretenders." He believed in "The study of patients, not books — experience, not reading."[4] The druggists he referred to as part of the "Mineral Faculty." They in turn referred to the Thomsonians as "steam doctors" and "puke doctors."

Thomson began his working life as a farmer in New Hampshire. He lacked formal education and distrusted it, to the extent that he saw no need for formal training beyond furnishing his practitioners with a copy of his *New Guide to Health or the Botanic Family Physician* (price two dollars plus the purchase of one Family Right for twenty dollars). Apparently his personal rigidity produced hostile relationships with various of his medical followers, agents and dealers, engendering a succession of public disputes, splinter groups and commercial lawsuits. His campaign against traditional medicine was nonetheless remarkably well organized and effective.

Thomson's movement largely disappeared within ten years of his death in 1843 but, as a lasting contribution to American medicine, left a decreased reliance by traditional doctors upon bleeding and

Just bathe. It will help you as much as surgery. An anti-doctor view expressed in comic terms on a trade card for Good News Soap.

Frederick Humphreys M.D. (1816-1900) as he appeared on the cover of his Manual for 1897. Most of the Humphreys' Manuals, published from the 1860s to the 1950s, were mini-almanacs that measured $4\frac{1}{2}$ x3 inches and contained up to 144 pages.

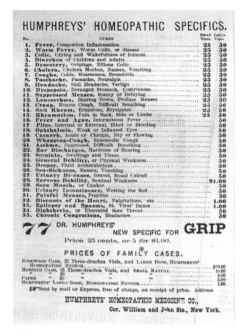

Price list of Humphreys' Homeopathic Medicines for 1895, and the large dollar-sized bottle that had a nickel-plated cap.

chemical drugs, and encouraged later botanists who made truly valuable additions to American materia medica.[5] It was a happy circumstance that herbal medicine increased in popularity during the nineteenth century. Not only did botanical substances, on the whole, do less damage to the human body, but also it was from plant substances that the very valuable drugs, quinine, morphine and digitalis were extracted.[6]

Other new medical theories challenged the preeminence of the heroic remedies.[7] There was the do-nothing school that believed the body itself can cure certain diseases if its own recuperative powers are allowed the proper conditions under which to work. This startling but perceptive theory was advocated in this country by Jacob Bigelow as early as the 1830s but became associated with the "Paris School," which concentrated on autopsies and pathology, to a degree that more activist doctors, and patient's families, found hard to accept.

Another brand of homeopathic remedies distributed by the C. N. Crittendon Company of New York, proprietor of a number of patent medicines. This advertisement pictures an elaborate sales rack.

Just a little later came the rise of homeopathy, which was also easy on the patient and did nothing for him, but appeared to do so. This school of medicine was originated by a German doctor, Samuel Hahnemann, in 1825. His appealing notion was that "like cures like"; nature provides a specific substance to cure each disease; and that this substance can be readily identified because it produces the same symptoms as the disease. Coupled to this was Hahnemann's belief that medicine gains potency by diluting it ("dynamization") and that the optimum prescription is the infinitesimal dose.

Oliver Wendell Holmes, and others, attacked this palpable nonsense in public lectures of pungent and humorous dimensions,[8] but homeopathic remedies remained in vogue well after the turn of the century and are still alive today. The man who made the most money out of this school of medicine was probably Frederick Humphreys M.D., the proprietor of Humphrey's Homeopathic Specifics. Dr. Humphrey's medicines bore numbers rather than names and looked rather like anemic bird shot intended for small wildfowl. Nevertheless, his little white pills and his hardcover book of 514 pages could still be found in the drugstores of the 1920s.

Other patent medicine manufacturers offered personal theories of medicine that explained the manner in which their products were supposed to work. While Dr. Hartman saw everything in

Dr. Carter Moffat was an English purveyor of "electric" body belts that promised to cure "nervous and organic derangements" in various parts of the body.

terms of catarrh, Dr. Jayne and others who sold sarsaparilla, believed that it was all important to purify the blood. Those who sold "tonics" focussed upon the fibers, nerves and particular organs of the body, which they promised to strengthen or tone up.[9]

The nineteenth century was a period of rapid discovery in many fields. Throughout history there have been charlatans who sought to profit from the public interest in various scientific developments and the lack of public understanding of them. This was certainly true of medicine in the 1800s. Perkins' Metallic Tractors "for drawing out disease" capitalized on the discovery of galvanism, which led to a wide variety of "galvanic" or "magnetic" belts, plasters, pads and rings. Most of them employed bits of flannel soaked in an irritating chemical that persuaded the wearer he was receiving electricity beneficial to his health. Medical devices using genuine electric currents to administer mild shocks were sold well into the 1900s, together with a second generation of instruments using expensive ultra-violet ray tubes of exotic shapes to irradiate various parts of the body.

The "liver pad" was another device that promised to exert a mysterious force on disease. This force was absorption. If disease was caused by evil substances in the body, why could they not be blotted up by an appropriate agent? This theory supported the sale of cloth bags, filled with sawdust or some equally efficacious medicament, scented perhaps with an aromatic oil. The sufferer wore them as close as possible to the affected organ. Liver pads were for some reason often kidney shaped.

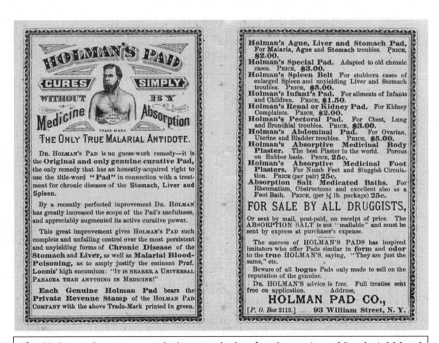

The Holman Company made liver pads for the absorption of "malarial blood poisoning", and a variety of other pads for specific purposes, listed in this two-page flyer.

Compliments of
MALTINE.

LOUIS PASTEUR,
Professor in the École des Beaux-Arts, Paris.

There were some genuine medical pioneers, like Louis Pasteur (1822-1885) among the prominent physicians celebrated in patent medicine advertising. Here, one of a series of handsome trade cards issued in the 1890's by the makers of Maltine, a health beverage.

"The Cure For All Diseases" is the modest claim of Radam's Microbe Killer. It appeared on this pamphlet containing testimonials dated 1892.

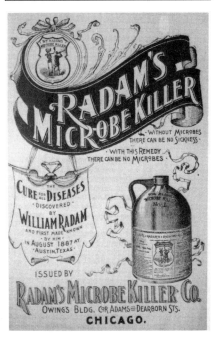

A bottle of Radithor, with captions, from an advertising booklet copyright 1926. Radithor was a genuine radium solution that produced disastrous effects in its faithful users.

An understanding of microbes, including pathogenic bacteria, pioneered by Pasteur, Lister and Koch among others, became widespread only in the last quarter of the nineteenth century. The germ theory was not even accepted by many physicians when William Radam began to capitalize upon popular gullibility with his Microbe Killer, a pink fluid composed of very weak sulfuric and hydrochloric acids, plus a trace of red wine.[10] This nostrum, which sold in the millions of gallons, could kill some germs in the test tube, but to take these acids internally for an extended period could be distinctly hazardous to your health.

In 1898, Pierre and Marie Curie isolated radium. They found that this extraordinary new element, even in minute quantities, emitted very powerful radiation that could burn the skin. It ultimately proved useful to medicine in the treatment of cancer and in a host of other ways. An understanding of radioactivity led an unprecedented advance in man's knowledge of matter and energy. Within a decade of radium's discovery, a quack named Dennis Rupert Dupuis was selling 7,800 treatments a year (as Dr. D. Rupert Wells) of "radium in liquid form," a medicine that he named Radol.[11] It contained no radium or radioactivity but was in fact an acid solution of quinine sulphate in alcohol, which exhibited a faint bluish fluorescence.

Within another two decades, the notion of infinitesimal dosage was joined to that of beneficial radiation. Traces of radon, the radioactive gas produced from the breakdown of radium, were found in various European hot springs noted for their supposedly curative waters. The idea of "mild radium therapy" surfaced with some reputable medical support and was applied with a vengeance by a dubious entrepreneur named William Bailey, who marketed an elixir named Radithor, a very dilute but all too real solution of radium and mesothorium in water. Bailey claimed that Radithor increased the intensity of the biological processes and, in addition to sexual rejuvenation, could correct more than sixty types of ailments. Frequent recourse to his half-ounce doses (at a dollar each) produced the same gruesome effects of radium poisoning that were discovered in the doomed girls who licked their brushes and applied radium paint to watch dials.[12]

The Modern Weapon
of Medical Science

This is the identical product described by Dr. Charles E. Morris in his epoch-making book "MODERN REJUVENATION METHODS"

SPECIAL NOTICE!

Do you handle Clark Stanley's Snake Oil Liniment? If not, you should, as it is a big seller, and gives the druggist a **Good Profit.**

The R. I. Drug Co., of Providence, R. I., sold 20 gross in 3 months.
The R. I. Drug Co., of Westerly, R. I., sold 10 gross in 6 months.
Wm. R. Greene, of Providence, R. I., sold 4 gross in 3 months.
C. E. Butler, of Lowell, Mass., sold 16 gross in 3 months' time in his two stores, all done through window advertising.

Can name hundreds of other Druggists who have sold a gross a week through using a window display. If you have a large show window and wish a new and novel window display, send a postal card to CLARK STANLEY SNAKE OIL LINIMENT CO., P. O. Box 1286, Providence, R. I., and same will receive attention.

Clark Stanley is the manufacturer of the following remedies, viz.:

Clark Stanley's Snake Oil Liniment,	-	$4.00 per doz.
" " Western Herbs,	-	4.00 "
" " Herbaline Ointment,	-	2.00 "
" " Worm Medicine for Children,	2.00	"
" " White Cactus Soap,	-	.75 "

TRADE SUPPLIED BY CHARLES N. CRITTENTON CO., NEW YORK.

The popularity of snake oil was not confined to the regions we usually consider reptile habitats, as this ad for the Rhode Island Drug Company illustrates.

4. Nineteenth Century Huckstering

In the 1800s there were many small entrepreneurs engaged in selling what passed for medicine. Some of them were no better than penny ante con artists who did a bit of doctoring without a license and peddled a bottle of some potion to receptive patients. One of these was William A. Rockefeller, a self-appointed cancer specialist who sold advice and elixirs at rural camp meetings in upstate New York.[1] His son, John D. Rockefeller, wisely chose fuel oil over snake oil as a career.

Other sellers of medicine were licensed doctors who found that sufficient popularity had attached to their prescriptions to permit them to become businessmen instead of practitioners. Still others were salesmen who picked up a formula and knew how to market it, or men of keen business sense who could acquire a small medicine business and make it bigger. In the latter days of the patent medicine era, products and firms were shuffled by millionaire entrepreneurs with a skill worthy of modern corporation takeover specialists.

It is fair to say that some of the patent medicine proprietors displayed the business ethics of the times at their worst, but it must be remembered that few nineteenth century businessmen in any industry showed much concern for the public interest or individual human welfare. The prevailing economic and social philosophy was one of laissez faire and showmanship, best symbolized in the methods of P. T. Barnum, that seemed to win more rewards than a reputation for integrity. The accepted rule of the market place was "let the buyer beware."[2]

CENTAUR LINIMENT is unquestionably the most nearly instantaneous cure of pains, burns, swellings, galls and lameness upon man and beast the world has ever known. "My equestrians and teamsters all say that Centaur Liniment is the best remedy for stiff joints, wounds and lameness they have ever used." P. T. Barnum, 488 Fifth Avenue, N. Y.

Phineas T. Barnum, the showman, has been called the "Emperor of Humbug". It is fitting to discover his name on a testimonial for a patent medicine.

In an age that esteemed the newly-created wealth of the industrial revolution, Compound Oxygen used a railroad magnate, suspiciously resembling Cornelius Vanderbilt, to give a man-of-distinction appeal to its trade card.

This was the era of the "robber barons" who established empires in railroads, steel, oil, sugar and cement. An enormous upsurge in consumer products took place during this period, increasing the role of the middleman who distributed the manufacturer's goods to the retailer. The general decline in business ethics is sometimes ascribed to the loss of contact between producer and public.[3] Those who worked in the nascent advertising industry admittedly ignored the merits (or demerits) of the products they handled, and regarded their services like those of a railroad carrying freight whose quality did not concern them.[4]

The successful patent medicines were those advertised by millions of newspaper ads, almanacs, trade cards, show cards, and mailing pieces. An 1881 article in *Scientific American* describes the facilities of the Charles A. Voegler Company in Baltimore, makers of St. Jacob's Oil.[5] Extensive space was provided for the company's own chromolithography department and for the answering of letters from customers. It appears that 4,500 square feet were devoted solely to the filing of newspaper advertising. In 1883, the year Lydia Pinkham died, her company was spending well over half its gross income on advertising.[6] Lydia's bold strategies were extended and refined by James T. Wetherall, the brilliant advertising man who served the Pinkham enterprise from 1889 until his death in 1926.

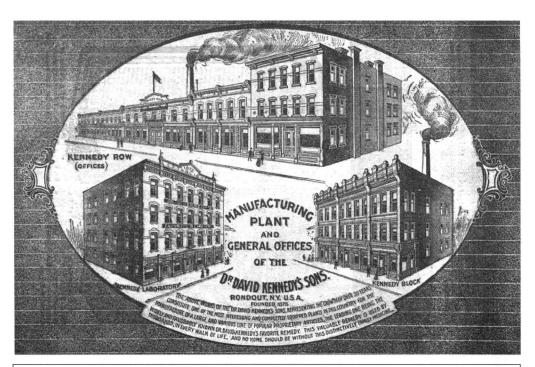

Factories belching smoke, ornate office buildings and sturdy laboratories, were offered as images of commercial success, on the covers of medicine almanacs and in other nostrum advertising.

One nostrum tycoon explained the secret of his success this way: "First, a man must be a born advertiser. He must have the nerve and the faith to put out his money freely in advertising—map out the plan and stick to it; second, he must have the patience to wait for a return."[7]

Some direct testimony in favor of expensive advertising was offered by the manager of Tarrant & Company (Tarrant's Seltzer Aperient, Hoff's Malt Extract). "If you would catch a trout you must put your heart on the hook," wrote Mr. William A. Hockemeyer. "A poor advertisement costs as much as a good one . . . One advertisement preserved is better than a thousand thrown away."[8] The task was not any easy one, said Mr. L. A. Sandlass, Manager of the Charles A. Vogeler Company. "There is a natural repugnance to the use of all medicines that must be overcome before people will buy. Prominence of position and boldness of appearance would seem to be the first essentials [in advertising copy]."[9]

One cynic, writing in 1891, put it this way:

> "Frankly speaking, nostrum vendors no longer rely on the curative powers of their drugs. They depend now on the power of advertising exclusively. They have a literary man to "write up" the remedy in ingenious fashion; an artist to show the patient "before and after" using the panacea; a poet to compose odes and lyrics; a liar who rivals Munchhausen; and a forger who signs all kinds of testimonials."[10]

To some extent the exigencies of advertising and merchandising may have shaped the product itself. George P. Rowell describes the "ideal" patent medicine, designed for maximum sales success.[11] It must be "clean," that is, no suggestive or objectionable words must be needed to advertise it. (A cure for syphilis could not be considered ideal.) It must address some malady existing both in cold and warm climates and at all times of the year. (This rules out remedies for the sniffles.) The mixture itself must withstand extremes of temperature without freezing or spoiling. It should be light in weight for delivery by mail, a dry powder if possible. There should be no need for a heavy container to avoid breakage or evaporation. The ingredients should be inexpensive. Alcohol is unacceptable as an ingredient on several of these grounds including expense, and the fact that it offended the temperance sentiment. Lastly, it should have a made-up name that could be easily copyrighted.

The willingness to invest heavily in the public print may of itself have enabled some proprietors to lift their products above the sea of competing nostrums, but there is no doubt that a number of these individ-

Laboratory of P. H. Drake & Co., New York.

Factory interiors also invited consumer attention. Above, a page from the almanac for Drake's Plantation Bitters. Note the commodious rum vault for storing a principal ingredient. *Collection William M. Helfand.* Below, the proprietors of Morse's Indian Root Pills apparently believed that the public interest extended to the individual machines.

Dr. MORSE'S INDIAN ROOT PILLS

FACTORY.

W. H. COMSTOCK, Sole Proprietor, MORRISTOWN, N. Y.

Dr. MORSE'S INDIAN ROOT PILLS

WORK SHOP.

W. H. COMSTOCK, Sole Proprietor, MORRISTOWN, N. Y.

"TONO-
BUNGAY"

BY
H. G. WELLS

THE EPIC OF A PATENT
MEDICINE BUSINESS

A leaflet advertising *Tono-Bungay*, not a medicine but the title of a novel by H. G. Wells (1886-1940) about the career of a patent medicine king. Wells was a sociologist and popular historian whose works addressed changes in society and moral beliefs.

uals possessed an instinctive gift for the commercial use of the picture and the written word. In the early days at least, the proprietor himself was likely to write the copy and the successful medicine entrepreneurs were as much advertising men as they were manufacturers. Their individual success stories make fascinating reading and a number have been well told by able historians.

Showmanship characterized the personal as well as the business pursuits of these aggressive entrepreneurs. Asa T. Soule of Rochester, who made a large fortune from Hop Bitters, gave lavishly to various causes and to temperance societies in particular. He also offered $100,000 to a nearby college if it would adopt the name Hop Bitters University. He sponsored boat races here and in England and sent out on tour a baseball team, which the local wits referred to as the Rumbleguts or the Liverpads. After a number of dubious contests, the team was also called the Gambler's Friend & Hope.

For the last seven years of his life, Soule put his money and energy into land promotion in Western Kansas. He financed a 96-mile irrigation canal and a 35-mile railroad in Gray County to put on the map the town of Soule, renamed Ingalls after a favorable U.S. Senator. Soule owned half the township. Land costing little more than a dollar an acre could be worth many hundreds of times that sum if a new prairie town could win the designation as county seat. Political bribery, voter intimidation and actual bloodshed was involved in some cases. Soule hired gunfighters from Dodge City, including the famous Bat Masterson and Bill Tilghman, in a shooting war between Ingalls (pop. 200) and Cimarron (pop. 1,500), which was six miles distant. Cimarron won in 1887, Ingalls prevailed in 1889, and Cimarron won again in 1893. By that time Soule had died and his prairie empire, financed by Hop Bitters, crumbled away.[12]

The homes of the patent medicine kings were often showplaces, featured on the almanac covers. G.G. Greene, proprietor of Greene's August Flower, lived in a Victorian monstrosity of heroic proportions set in a carefully landscaped park that also included his laboratory and general offices. A hardcover album was issued to the trade showing photographs of the interior of Mr. Greene's home, his gardens, stables and his private railway car.[13] Dr. David Jayne built a home with silver door knobs and had the likeness of his daughters' faces sculptured into the mantels. It required a twenty-five page will to dispose of the fortune he left upon his death.[14]

Apparently the abundant wealth of the medicine millionaires did not gain them acceptance in the highest social circles as it did with others of the new industrial rich. Even in these freewheeling days, educated people condemned the fraud and the exploitation of the ignorant that was all too apparent. Frank Presbrey tells of a young woman who has just discovered that the good friend she has made on shipboard is the daughter of a patent medicine king. What to do? "That's all right, dear," says her

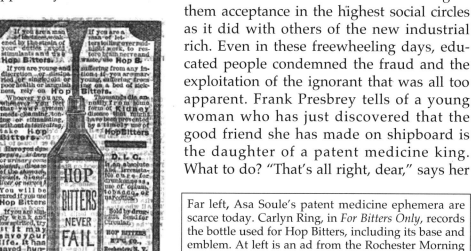

Far left, Asa Soule's patent medicine ephemera are scarce today. Carlyn Ring, in *For Bitters Only*, records the bottle used for Hop Bitters, including its base and emblem. At left is an ad from the Rochester Morning Herald of August 7, 1880.

THE LAKE.

CABINET MANTEL IN RESIDENCE.

DR. GREEN'S PRIVATE CAR.

The cover of *Green's Wit and Wisdom*, issued in 1890, gave an overview of the proprietor's property in Woodbury, N.J., which included his residence, laboratory and factory. The photographs are from a hardcover album of 66 pages issued by the G. G. Green company, that was entitled *Home of August Flower and German Syrup.*

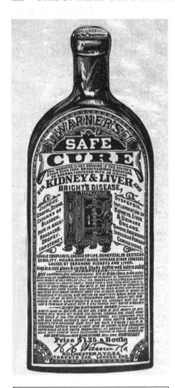

This slope-shouldered bottle of thick brown glass was heavily embossed with the outline of a banker's safe, the Warner trademark, here covered with a finely-printed label.

Warner's 1891 almanac emphasized the enormous world market he developed for his products, but within a few more years, H. H. Warner was bankrupt from various speculations unrelated to his medicine business.

mother. "We won't let your friend know that we know."[15]

Hulbert Harrington Warner furnishes another striking example of the rapid rise to wealth that was possible, the dubious financial manipulations practiced at the time, and the human drama played out to the full by one nostrum millionaire.[16] Worldwide, Warner's Safe Kidney and Liver Cure was one of the best known patent medicines of all time. The heavy slope-shouldered brown bottles are sought after by present day collectors. Incredibly, it took Mr. Warner only ten years to build his company and his fortune to its peak.

H.H. Warner was a farm boy from western New York State. Apprenticed to a tinsmith at age 15, he opened a hardware store in Michigan at 18, went bankrupt, and at age 28 became a dealer in Rochester for a predecessor of the present Mosler Safe Company. Warner conducted various enterprises within overlapping time periods. In 1879, at age 37, he founded his medicine company in Rochester, presumably with his earnings from selling safes. By 1884 H. H. Warner & Co. had offices in London, Toronto and Rangoon as well. At this point Warner sold his safe business although reportedly it employed 200 salesmen and grossed two million dollars a year. The medicine business was to gross about 1.3 million a year over seven years, but its profit for the period was a phenomenal 32 percent. In 1888, Warner was reputed to have the largest proprietary medicine business in the world.[17]

The Safe Kidney and Liver Cure catered to a widespread fear of Bright's Disease, a wasting kidney condition first described by an English doctor, which was popularly blamed for many forms of back and abdominal distress. Warner told the time-honored story of discovering the medicine through the cure of his own illness by a local doctor. Actually, Warner bought the formula from a group of investors in New York. The medicine itself contained a few herbs, glycerine, water, alcohol and potassium nitrate. The last two were the principal active ingredients and both are kidney irritants that would hasten the death of anyone suffering from Bright's Disease.[18] Safe Kidney and Liver Cure was accompanied by Safe Diabetes Cure, Safe Nervine, Safe Bitters (later called Tippecanoe) and in time by a Safe Asthma Cure and a Safe Rheumatic Cure (Plate 15). It is not known what difference there was, if any, in the composition of these various products.

In his advertising Warner used the herbal theme and the far-off lands theme (South America) but his real brilliance lay in the choice of a banker's safe as his trademark, an image that reflected the Victorian fondness for puns, but nevertheless conveyed assurance, protection and dignity at a glance. He concentrated heavily on this simple approach and it gained a national consciousness very quickly. Warner's success lay in the quantity of his advertising and his ability to keep in the public eye personally. At its peak, his company was said to issue 35 million mailing pieces a year.[19] It claimed to have advertising contracts with 5,000 of the nation's 8,000 newspapers and to maintain 15,000 square feet of space for its racks of current newspaper files.[20] One of Mr. Warner's best devices for getting himself in print was to build an observatory for a local hardware dealer named "Doctor" Lewis Swift, an amateur astonomer without academic credentials who had managed to discover several new comets. Warner offered $200 in gold for such discoveries which, critics alleged, seemed to appear with suspect abundance whenever public attention lagged. In ten years Swift detected a total of six new comets and 900

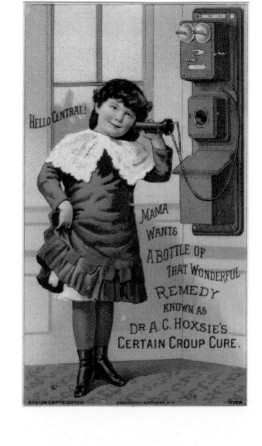

Plate 11. Steamships still carried sails when the advertisement above appeared for Bucha-Paiba, an herbal remedy for kidney and bladder problems. Note the early telephone used by the girl at right in the card for Hoxie's Croup Cure.

Plate 12. Two cards for Humphrey's Witch Hazel Oil show further turn-of-the-century wonders. A primitive biplane appears on the advertising postcard, below left. The open roadster, below right, was a very opulent vehicle for its time, pre-World War I.

Plate 13. Horseflesh was a natural interest of the farmer and the sportsman alike. Above, Hibbard's Rheumatic Syrup shows us a famous racehorse and, at right, Dr. Morse's Indian Root Pills gives us a trotter, with their best times shown in each case.

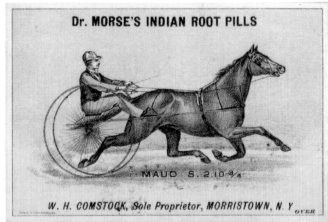

Plate. 14. Sports in the 1890s included the relatively new game of baseball, pictured at left on one of a series of comic stock cards used by Merchant's Gargling Oil. Lutted's Cough Drops gives us the striking image below of the more leisurely sport of tobogganing.

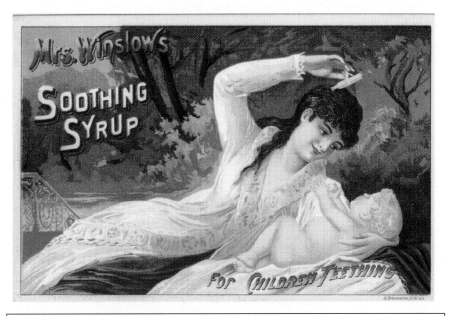

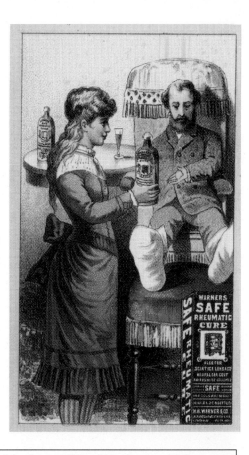

Plate 15. Mrs. Winslow's Soothing Syrup, above left, widely prescribed for babies, contained morphine. At right, H.H. Warner's line of Safe Cures did not contain narcotics but were laced with alcohol and harmful chemical ingredients.

Plate 16. Lash's Bitters, advertised in the small booklet shown at left, was a long-lived brand typical of this class of product for its high alcohol content and laxative properties. The logo on the label shows eorge slaying the dragon. The sarsaparillas were another very popular type of patent medicine that also contained alcohol in abundance and various herbs. The Ayer's Sarsaparilla card, below right, shows the Deacon and Liza, two characters from a play of the 1880s. This image was also furnished as a cardboard statuette 13 inches high for ten cents in stamps or coin.

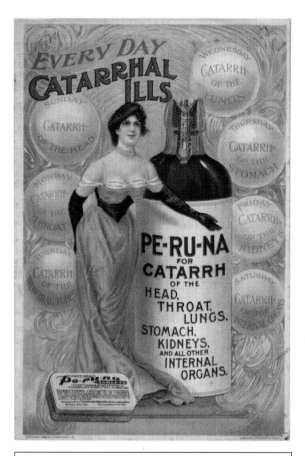

Plate 17. Dr. Hartman's Peruna was intended to cure many ills as this almanac cover illustrates. Almost every disease was, in his view, a type of catarrh.

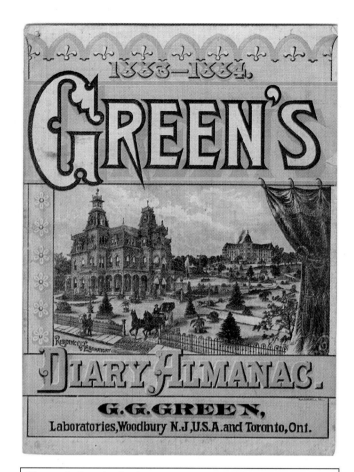

Plate 18. Dr. G. G. Green, proprietor of Green's August Flower, and several other products, lived and worked in this elaborate park in Woodbury, New Jersey which contained his residence, laboratory and manufacturing establishment.

Plate 19. Dr. R. V. Pierce sold some 23 patent medicines including Dr. Pierce's Golden Medical Discovery and Dr. Pierce's Favorite Prescription. He also operated the World's Dispensary Medical Association, Invalid's Hotel and Surgical Institute in Buffalo, New York, shown on this trade card.

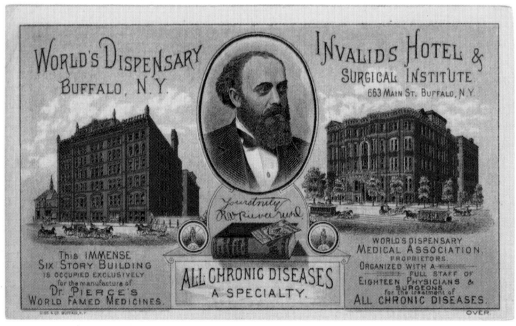

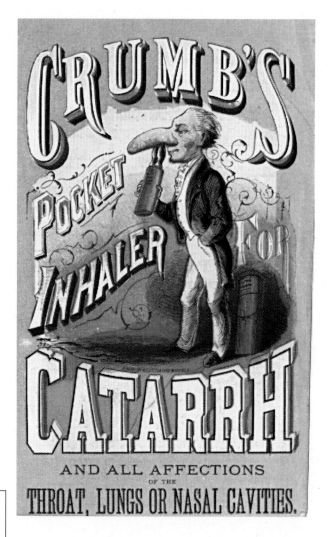

Plate 20. Coca Wine was typical of the preparations compounded from coca leaves and ordinary wine which included the famous Vin Mariani and Pemberton's French Wine Coca, the forerunner of Dr. Pemberton's Coca Cola compound.

Plate 21. Crumb's Catarrh Inhaler may or may not have contained cocaine or acetanilid, as did most of the catarrh "snuffs". Persistent inhalation of cocaine can produce the inflamed and sensitive nose shown in the caricature at right.

Plate 22. Fahrney's Panacea is an early medicine still using the Greek word for cure-all in its product name.

Plate 23. Brown's Panacea, top left, promised to cure a number of assorted ills listed at the bottom of the trade card. The other medicines shown here, for more specific use, were advertised with the word "cure".

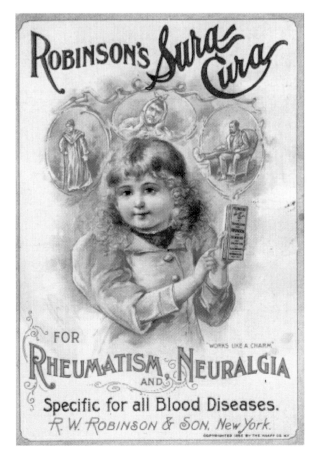

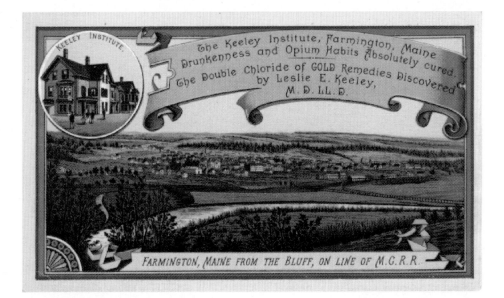

Plate 24. Habit cures addressed several addictions. The Keeley Institute, shown on the postcard above, promised to cure both alcohol and narcotic problems. Keeley's medicine, it is believed, contained a good deal of alcohol as well as a compound of gold. On the other hand, Perrine's Malt Whiskey, below left, was prescribed for several diseases without apology.

Plate 25. No-To-Bac, advertised in the booklet shown below, promised to cure a less dangerous habit. Its other slogan was "Makes Weak Men Strong".

Plate 26. Typical advertising for bitters. These patent medicines contained as much as 45% alcohol and they were often sold by the drink in the saloons of the 1880s, as well as in the country store and the drug store.

nebulae.[21] Warner also commissioned three large paintings at $30,000 each. Niagara Falls was his favorite subject and Indian life a close second. The Niagara pictures were used extensively on the Warner almanacs and reproductions were offered at a modest cost.

It was Warner's credo that every businessman should take part in public life. He arrived in Chicago at the Republican National Convention of 1884 with two Pullman cars full of local politicos and press as his well-entertained guests. Mr. Warner was one of two delegates who voted for Robert Todd Lincoln while James G. Blaine took the nomination from the incumbent President, Chester Alan Arthur. Warner attended two more presidential conventions in his usual style, but it became evident that his interest in national politics was sporadic and aimed principally at notoriety. He participated in organizing the Rochester Chamber of Commerce and in 1887 became its first President.

Warner's restless business energy led him early into various speculative business ventures which he conducted at the same time that he was building his enormously successful Warner's Safe Cure Co. In 1880 he made a major investment in the manufacture of glucose in Kansas City. In 1881 it was the Horseshoe Silver Mining Company near Denver; 1882, Warner launched the Seven Stars Mining Company, with interests in a North Carolina gold mine and timber in Mexico. All of these enterprises resulted in financial setbacks for Warner. In 1889 he used his medicine company for a gigantic stock

Other Warner's Safe products as shown in contemporary advertisements. Tippecanoe was first marketed as Warner's Safe Bitters, then as Warner's Safe Tonic Bitters. The bottle was intended to represent a log with a mushroom growing out of one end. Note the corkscrew attached to the neck.

manipulation in England. He sold his company to a syndicate of English brokers for almost four and a half million dollars, a huge sum in those days. In two weeks time he reacquired eighty per cent of the stock, through the use of options, and made several hundred thousand dollars in the process.

From this time on Warner regarded himself as a financier and began to neglect his medicine business. In truth, he became little more than a stock promoter. He even used the Safe Cure Almanacs to peddle his Warner's shares.[22] The common stock was stated to pay dividends of 17.5%. In fact it seems that the company was not in as good condition as this suggested, and the fabulous dividends were only paid on the shares in public hands. Mr. Warner paid out no dividends on the shares he owned himself. At this point the United States suffered a business recession. The Panic of 1893 gripped the stock market and dried up the credit on which Warner had been operating. His stock was the principal asset securing his debts. When he could not raise enough cash, he lost it all in bankruptcy.

If that were not enough, the English directors of the company pursued Warner for wrongs that they said he had committed as managing director. They eventually sold the American branch of the company to a Rochester distillery that made Duffy's Malt Whiskey and had supplied Warner with most of the alcohol for his products. In another fifteen years, the Pure Food and Drug Act sounded the death knell for the patent medicine industry as it once was. The Warner's Safe Cures became Warner's Safe Remedies and lost much of their alcohol. In this fashion the product managed to live on until 1946.

EXTRACTS
—FROM—
President H. H. Warner's Address.
FIRST PRESIDENT OF THE
Rochester Chamber of Commerce.

We have a beautiful and attractive city. Its surroundings are much more than ordinary, and strangers are attracted and animated by them. The beautiful drives, leading in many directions about the city, are seldom surpassed; within a half-hour's drive from our city line is the second Coney Island of America, and one of the most beautiful of lakes, forming the last link in the chain of lakes between the Mississippi and the Gulf of St. Lawrence.

Within twelve hours' ride by steamer is that beautiful summer resort, the Thousand Islands, having no equal on this continent for recreation and sport; and two hours' ride brings us to that great cataract, Niagara Falls, which many people travel thousands of miles to see. Our people are happy and prosperous, our mechanics are skilled, and in no other city in the United States can so many artizans and laborers point to comfortable

ROCHESTER WELCOMES ALL NEW COMERS.

Hulbert Harrington Warner died in 1923 at the age of 81. He spent the last thirty years of his life in poverty and obscurity, trying for a comeback in the medicine business or the advertising business. He must have thought often in those later days of his castle on East Avenue in Rochester, his private observatory, his hunting lodge in Michigan, his island in Canada, and his luxurious yacht *Siesta*. In his day he was saluted as one of the ten greatest names in proprietary medicine. In death he received about one column inch in the *New York Times*.[23]

Warner's charitable endeavors were an effective form of self-advertising. They included patronage of the arts, or the art that appealed to Mr. Warner, and an observatory directed by Lewis Swift. Swift-Tuttle, a comet he discovered in 1862, attracted great interest in 1992 when it crossed earth's orbit again at a relatively close distance.

INTERIOR WARNER OBSERVATORY ROCHESTER N.Y.

The Warner Observatory is of Lockport white sandstone, and, excluding the $13,000 Telescope, cost $60,000. It is the most noteworthy building in Rochester. The Telescope is 22 feet long, 16-inch aperture, and weighs with mountings two tons. It is the finest instrument in the United States. Dr. Lewis Swift, the famous comet finder, is the Director.

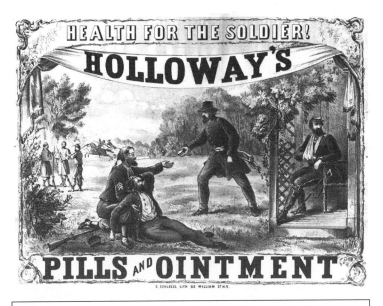

Health for the soldier! Holloway's Pills, Hostetter's Bitters, and other nostrums, promised to cure malaria, dysentery and various ills associated with the appalling sanitary conditions of the Civil War army camps. Concentrating on the military continued to pay off when the soldiers returned home. *Poster Courtesy the Library of Congress.*

5.   Boom and Decline

A number of factors in American life contributed to the success of patent medicines in the nineteenth century. One was the rapid expansion of our population and its dispersal over the continent, especially in the West after the Civil War. The war itself left a legacy of injury and disease and helped to draw national attention to health problems. At this point in our history, over seventy per cent of Americans lived on farms. Doctors were few and distant from the farm family and medical care was expensive. The country store was the most important point in the distribution of medicines. For some, the only remedies available were those sold over the tailgate of the pedlar's wagon. These sources catered to those ignorant of proper medical treatment. Self-dosage was practical and appealed to the self-reliant and the hypochondriac alike. Later, cheap postal rates facilitated doctoring by mail-order.

Over the decades of its development, the patent medicine business reflected most of the economic forces that produced what we call the industrial revolution. The itinerant pitchman, who mixed his own nostrum in the wagon and bottled it beside the stream just before he reached town, evolved into the factory owner who produced millions of bottles per year and shipped them great distances. The cheap machine-made bottle helped this process. So did the cheap transportation offered by the railroads and other improved forms of transportation. The extraordinary aggressiveness of the medicine proprietors made patent medicines among the first consumer products to achieve

Progress from pitchman to proprietor. A drawing from the Akers and Chrysler Collection illustrates the career of John F. True of Auburn, Maine from 1851 to 1900.

Certificate Of Purity.

DR. KILMER.   The Great Kidney and Bladder Specialist.   JONAS M. KILMER.

THIS IS TO CERTIFY that Dr. Kilmer's Swamp-Root, the Great Kidney Remedy, is PURELY VEGETABLE and does not contain any calomel, mercury, creosote, morphine, opium, strychnine, cocaine, nitrate potash (saltpeter), bromide potassium, narcotic alkaloid or any other poison or harmful drugs. Swamp-Root was discovered through scientific research and study by Dr. Kilmer, who graduated with honors and is now actively engaged in the practice of his profession, which calling he has successfully followed for many years.

State of New York, County of Broome,   )
City of Binghamton.   )   s.s.
)

Jonas M. Kilmer, senior member of the firm of Dr. Kilmer & Co., of the City of Binghamton, County of Broome, State of New York, being duly sworn deposes and says that the guarantee of purity of Swamp-Root, as described in the foregoing certificate, is in all respects true.

Subscribed and sworn to   )
before me April 26,1898.   )

Jerome B Hadsell Jr.,
Notary Public

Jonas M. Kilmer

This Certificate is an absolute guarantee of purity.

☞ All our Remedies are purely vegetable, most carefully and scientifically prepared, and are sold by all druggists. When writing always address, Dr. Kilmer & Co., Binghamton, N. Y.

> This "certificate", from an 1899 Almanac for Kilmer's Swamp Root, played to a public awakening of the dangers inherent in some patent medicines. Kilmer's was a strictly herbal concoction.

anything like a national market under a single brand name. Advertising was at the same time the creator and the servant of the nostrum phenomenon. The growth of the advertising industry stemmed in turn from the rapid expansion of all systems for dissemination of the written word.

In time the safety of the patent medicines used for self-dosage became a subject of popular concern. Advertising based on this theme was a good sign, pointing to some recognition of what these nostrums contained. Before 1906, the labels on the bottles themselves were of course no help. It took decades before social consciousness was general enough to result in the disclosure of ingredients and effective regulation of the medicine business. In the interim, some manufacturers found it profitable to assure the customer that their medicine, at least, was perfectly safe.

After 1906, advertisements for children's preparations hastened to deny harmful ingredients. Nostrums like Indian Blood Syrup began to claim that they were "guaranteed" under the Pure Food and Drug Act.

Children's remedies in particular began to stress in their advertising the absence of specific dangerous substances. Hand's Remedies for Children used the back of its trade cards to denounce the use of laudanum, probably with the thought that the public knew this form of opium was used generously in Mrs. Winslow's Soothing Syrup, a more widely known preparation (Plate 15).

The "muckrakers," journalists and scholars of many kinds, began a literature of exposure and protest in the later decades of the nineteenth century that started with general social and economic problems, and later focused on the evils of particular industries and firms. Popular magazines led the push in print for reform. The *Ladies Home Journal*, under Cyrus H.K. Curtis, rejected all medical advertising in 1892 and lost an estimated $3,000,000 in revenue the next year as a result.[1] It was not until 1896 that the *New York Times* under Adolph Ochs began to reject nostrum copy.

Doctor A. J. Read, of the Battle Creek Sanitarium, recently made for the periodical "The Life-Boat," of Hinsdale, Illinois, an interesting experiment for the purpose of testing the alcohol in patent medicines: He reports that he put in one can 4 drams (1 tablespoonful) of "Hostetter's Stomach Bitters"; in a second can the same amount (1 tablespoonful) of "Peruna"; in a third can a similar amount of "Lydia Pinkham's Vegetable Compound," and in a fourth can a tablespoonful of Beer. The cans were connected by rubber tubes to a gas burner and mantel, heat was applied, and the vapor gave bright illumination as follows:

Can No. 1: Hostetter's Bitters burned for . . . . 4 minutes
Can No. 2: Peruna burned for . . . . . 2 minutes 40 seconds
Can No. 3: Lydia Pinkham's Vegetable Compound burned for . . . . 2 minutes 35 seconds
Can No. 4: Beer burned for . . . . 20 seconds

The popular writers exposed not only the medical dangers presented by leading products on the market but also their shoddy advertising practices. The *Journal* castigated James T. Wetherall for writing copy that invited lonely and anxious women to confide in Lydia Pinkham twenty-two years after her death. Editor Edward Bok ran a picture of Lydia's tombstone and another showing a row of alcohol burners operating merrily on Lydia Pinkham's Tonic, Peruna and Hostetter's Bitters.[2] Bok was unkind enough to suggest that the letters of the suffering ladies were a source of ribald amusement in the proprietors' office, and others added that the names and addresses on them were sold at five cents each on "sucker lists" for further exploitation.[3]

The most famous series of articles on patent medicines, written by Samuel Hopkins Adams, ran in *Colliers Weekly* from October 1905 to February 1906. It was entitled *The Great American Fraud*, and it discussed the composition and effects of a wide variety of products on the market. The first article contained a cartoon of a skull entitled "Death's Laboratory." The American Medical Association, having at last turned a corner and shaken off its lethargy on the subject of proprietary medicines, began to reprint and distribute such articles. Later, the AMA compiled the basic text on dangerous and useless medicines and treatments, entitled *Nostrums and Quackery*, which was issued in 1911 and later expanded into three volumes.

The photographs, shown on this page with their original captions, are from *The Ladies Home Journal* for September 1905. At left are alcohol lamps fueled by three popular patent medicines.

.. cure the d. blame the woman. embarrassing to detail some ..ptoms of her suffering, even to ... .anily physician.
It was for this reason that years ago Mrs. Pinkham, at Lynn, Mass., determined to step in and help her sex. Having had considerable experience in treating female ills with her Vegetable Compound, she encouraged the women of America to write to her for advice in regard to their complaints, and being a woman, it was easy for her ailing sisters to pour into her ears every detail of their suffering. * * * * *
No physician in the world has had such a training, or has such an amount of information at hand to assist in the treatment of all kinds of female ills.
This, therefore, is the reason why Mrs. Pinkham, in her laboratory at Lynn, Mass., is able to do more for the ailing women of America than the fam'. physician. Any woman, therefore, is responsible for her own suffering who will not take the trouble to write to Mrs. Pinkham for advice.

This Advertisement of "Lydia Pinkham's Vegetable Compound" was Printed on June 27, 1905 (About Two Months Ago).

At right is a portion of a Lydia Pinkham advertisement that implied Lydia was still alive, 22 years after her death. At far right is her tombstone.

MRS. LYDIA E. PINKHAM'S MONUMENT
in Pine Grove Cemetery, Lynn, Massachusetts.
Mrs. Pinkham Died May 17, 1883 (22 Years Ago).

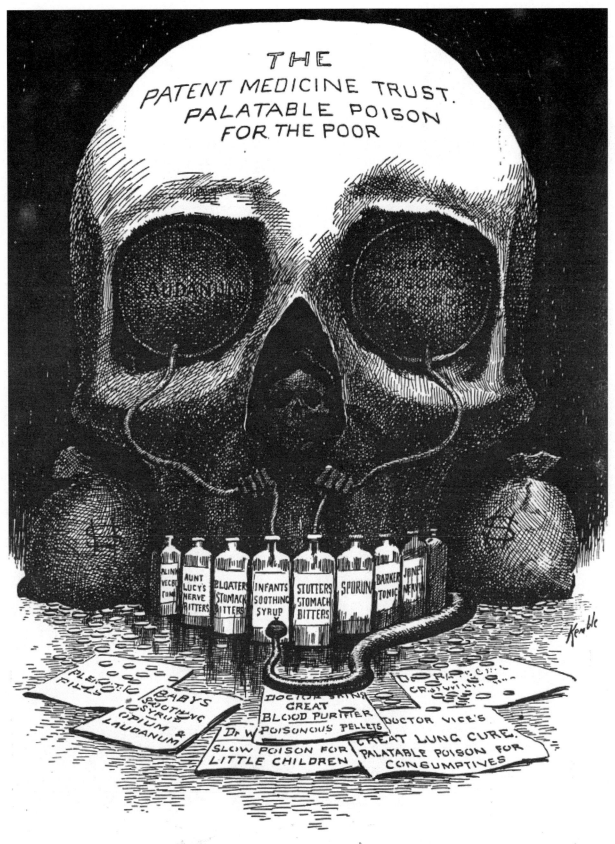

DEATH'S LABORATORY

The famous cartoon drawn by J. W. Kemble that ran in *Colliers* for October 7, 1905 with the first article in the series by Samuel Hopkins Adams entitled "The Great American Fraud".

Dr. Harvey Washington Wiley, Chief of the Bureau of Chemistry of the Department of Agriculture, who provided leadership for those seeking to regulate the medicine industry by means of the Pure Food and Drug Act. *Courtesy The New York Academy of Medicine Library.*

Between 1870 and 1905 more than one hundred and ninety measures were proposed in Congress for regulating commerce in food or drugs.[4] Most states had some food or drug laws on their books by 1905, but these had only an intrastate effect and formed a confusing and conflicting patchwork. On the federal scene, little headway was made until after the turn of the century against the influence and resources of the medicine manufacturers and their trade group, the Proprietary Association of America, which had played a prominent role for decades in defeating or sidetracking legislation affecting the industry.

The efforts of reformers working for the regulation of medicines became linked with those fighting adulterated food and liquor and unsanitary conditions in the food processing industry. They included the American Medical Association and the Women's Christian Temperance Union. They enlisted in their cause Dr. Harvey Washington Wiley, Chief of the Bureau of Chemistry of the Department of Agriculture. The prestige, talent and energy of this man advanced considerably the movement for an effective national law.[5] Food was actually the primary concern of most of those working for the new federal act and the recently elected progressive President, Theodore Roosevelt, barely referred to drugs in his brief endorsement of it to Congress. The pure food issue was clearer and subject to less counter-lobbying. Upton Sinclair, then an unknown

President Theodore Roosevelt in 1906. His support for the new law was based largely on a desire to regulate the "Beef Trust" and to mandate pure food. *Courtesy Chicago Historical Society.*

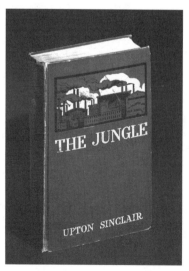

The first edition of *The Jungle* by Upton Sinclair, initially serialized in a Socialist weekly magazine. It added significantly to the furor that resulted in the Pure Food and Drug Act. By the end of 1906 more than 100,000 copies of the novel were sold. *Photo courtesy The Chicago Historical Society.*

Upton Sinclair who was an obscure writer in 1906 when, at age 28, he met the President of the United States. Roosevelt was impressed by his graphic true-to-life story of the horrifying conditions in the packing plants of Chicago. *Courtesy of The Lilly Library, Indiana University, Bloomington, Indiana.*

socialist writer, dramatized the shocking conditions in the meat packing industry with his novel, *The Jungle*. The public furor generated by this book had a very real negative effect on meat sales, and carried over to the pending legislation.

The Pure Food and Drug Act was signed into law on June 30, 1906.[6] The Act was not a final death sentence for the quack nostrum but it proved to be a monumental watershed for the medicine industry. The law required the manufacturer to state on every label the quantity of alcohol, opium, cocaine and certain other specified substances if they were present. The proprietor could be silent about substances not on the list, but he could not make his label lie. If he mentioned a drug it must be there in the strength and purity asserted, or the medicine would be considered "adulterated." If the label stated, for example, that no opium was used–which many proprietors hastened to make clear–then this statement must also be true.

There was a prohibition against unclear and misleading statements on the label which, after clarification by the Sherley Amendment in 1912, stopped positive claims like "sure cure." Many familiar product names were altered. "Piso's Cure for Consumption" became "A Medicine for Coughs, Colds, etc." Lydia Pinkham's "Sure Cure for Falling of the Womb" became "Recommended for the treatment of non-surgical cases of weakness and disorders of the female generative organs." "Castor Oil Pills," which contained no castor oil at all, maintained approximate euphony as "Casca Royal Pills." "Japanese Oil" became simply "En-ar-co Oil," taking the initials of the proprietor, National Remedy Company. "Radam's Microbe Killer" was itself finally slain in 1915.

Medicines change their slogans, packaging, and even their names. McElree's Wine of Cardui switches from "a certain cure" to "recommend for...". Japanese Oil communicates its name change on the side of a self-addressed envelope. Piso's Cure becomes Piso's Remedy. The images at bottom are postcards, a little-used form of patent medicine advertising.

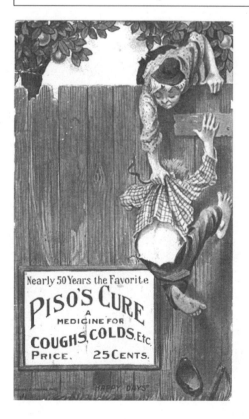

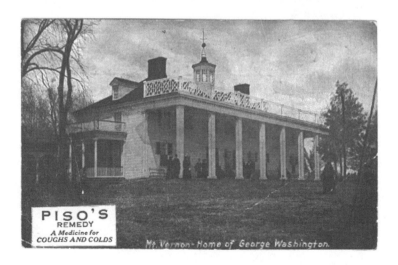

Underlying the legislation was a broad change in social and legal attitudes. The demise of the fabulously successful Hartman's Peruna illustrates the public's awareness of the true role of alcohol in patent medicines.[7] Some authorities claim that Peruna contained as much as 40% alcohol (it was increased in winter to be sure the customer's bottle would not freeze.) Over the years, Hartman's nostrum sustained attacks of many kinds. The alcohol level of his product earned him the backhanded compliment of competitors who offered their products as "cures for the Peruna habit." In 1906 Hartman was sued on the grounds he was using a medical formula that belonged to someone else. Reflecting the new climate of opinion, a New York court held that there was no imitation, because Peruna was not a medicine at all! The herbs cubeb, stone root and collinsonia canadensis were found present but in such small quantities that they could be disregarded. Next the Treasury ruled that Peruna had to show more medical effect or be subject to a liquor tax. Peruna scaled down its alcohol content to about 12% and the proprietors added blackthorn bark, a harsh laxative. A marked decline in sales began at this point.

The other popular "boozers" suffered in a similar manner. After many public attacks, Lydia Pinkham's Compound changed its composition and never regained its popularity. Medicines like Warner's Safe Cure (renamed Warner's Safe Remedy) dropped their alcohol entirely and substituted glycerin to make them more palatable. Paine's Celery Compound disappeared completely after 1906. Only a few survivors remained like Hostetter's Bitters which, it is interesting to note, was manufactured until 1957.

The death knell sounded for the patent medicine leviathans. Paine's Celery Tonic died first and Warner's Safe Cure later, after a change both in name and ingredients. Peruna lasted into the radio age.

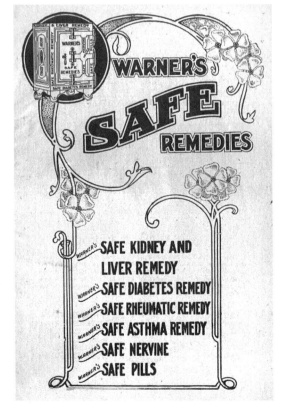

PATSY MONTANA and LITTLE BEVERLY

COWBOY SLIM RINEHART

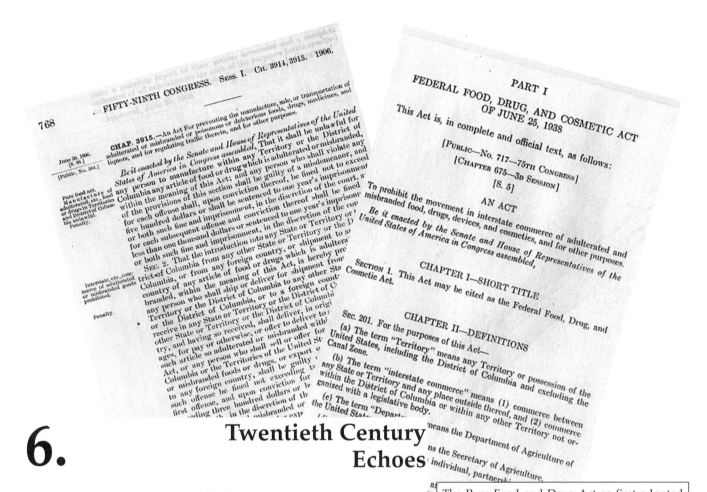

6. Twentieth Century Echoes

The free-wheeling days of the old nostrum vendors ended in 1906 with the passage of "Dr. Wiley's Law," but it soon became evident that much more was needed to insure the safety and quality of the medicines used by millions of Americans and to see that they were advertised in a truthful manner.

The Sherley Amendment of 1912 improved labelling. The Harrison Anti-Narcotics Act in 1914 subjected those substances to far greater control. Other loopholes in the 1906 law were closed by the Federal Food, Drug and Cosmetic Act, adopted in 1938 under Franklin Roosevelt's New Deal. The Durham-Humphrey Act of 1951 increased the control of dangerous drugs by prescription and reduced self-dosage in this area. The regulation of medicines and their advertising was greatly strengthened by the Kefauver-Harris Amendment in 1962. The law finally placed the promotion of new drugs under the supervision of the Food and Drug Administration and required manufacturers to prove that each new drug was efficacious as well as safe.[1]

This abbreviated list of legislative measures barely hints at the complexity of the regulatory problems in the twentieth century and speaks not at all to the political struggles that have attended the development of the present pattern of government controls. The tales of two more recent "patent medicines," Hadacol and Laetrile, illustrate how the nostrum vendors have fared in modern times.

The modern logo of the Food and Drug Administration which is currently staffed by about 8,500 employees. The advertising of prescription drugs is regulated by this federal agency. The advertising of non-prescription ("over the counter") remedies, which represents the vast majority of medicine advertising, is regulated by the Federal Trade Commission.

1951 HADACOL ALMANAC

Presented by

SEN. DUDLEY J. LeBLANC

To prove that the old advertising formulas can still be effective one need only look at the astounding career of Dudley J. LeBlanc.[2] "Cousin Dudley," a small-time Louisiana politician, created Hadacol in the late 1940s. He had a jugular instinct for back-country merchandising and breathtaking effrontery. He plowed his gross sales back into advertising as fast as they rolled in, with a pyramid effect that, incidentally, made no provision for taxes or creditors. At one point his advertising budget reached a million dollars a month and covered as many as five thousand radio spots and ads in forty-five hundred weekly papers. He gave away Hadacol "T" shirts that glowed in the dark, Hadacol comic books and gold replicas of the twelve millionth bottle. He advertised for a parrot that would say "Polly wants Hadacol." He authored "The Hadacol Boogie" and "Everybody Loves That Hadacol." His updated version of the medicine show was a caravan of white trailers, bringing to the home folks winsome young ladies and such performers as Mickey Rooney, Carmen Miranda, Chico Marx, George Burns and Gracie Allen.

The first *Hadacol Almanac*, published in 1951. At right, the Millionth Bottle of Hadacol on a parade float. Below, some of the 100 blue and white Hadacol trucks that went on tour. *Courtesy of* Look Magazine.

Hadacol was sold for $1.25 per bottle. It cost 21 cents to make and was composed of vitamins, minerals and alcohol. One eight-ounce bottle was equivalent to two highballs. The twelve-week suggested trial cost the sufferer $26.25. Dudley LeBlanc was asked what Hadacol was good for. His famous reply was, "Well, it was good for five and a half million dollars last year."[3]

A much more complicated problem is illustrated by the purported cancer cure, Laetrile. This patent medicine managed to make an end run around most of the federal regulatory structure that had been erected for the protection of the public during the preceding half century. Its appeal to the afflicted succeeded so well

Gathering testimonials in the 1950's. Above is the top of a sheet, tucked into an almanac, that solicited statements from happy Hadacol users.

that it lifted Laetrile promotion to the level of politics, where the public interest in honest advertising approached a conflict with the principle of freedom of speech.

At its peak of public support in 1977, the legislatures of seventeen states had made it legal to prescribe Laetrile, despite the fact that it was banned from interstate commerce under federal law. A federal judge had ruled that Laetrile could be legally imported from a foreign country by any terminally ill person who had a doctor's affidavit.[4] At this late remove, The Food and Drug Administration found itself holding hearings on the merits of a substance that it had declared medically useless years before. The nation's leading medical authorities all testified that there was no scientific evidence whatsoever to indicate that Laetrile could be effective against cancer.[5] The head of the National Institute of Health and the FDA Commissioner in charge of cancer drugs were supported by the American Medical Association, the American Cancer Society, and Sloan-Kettering Cancer Center. What then was responsible for the Laetrile phenomenon?

Laetrile was the commercial name for a substance found in the pits of certain fruits including apricots, prunes, cherries and bitter almonds. Its pharmaceutical name was amygdalin and its molecular composition included cyanide, which was released from the compound by an enzyme found in

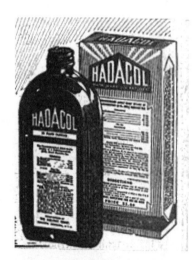

Hadacol, tonic and bracer, the liquor with vitamins, was a lineal descendant of the bitters nostrums that were sold in the nineteenth century.

various parts of the body. A California doctor named Ernst Krebs claimed in 1926 that it was effective against cancer in mice, but more of his mice died than were helped. His son, Ernst Krebs, Jr., developed a purified extract from apricot pits and obtained a British patent upon it in 1949. Krebs, Jr. was not a doctor but he attracted others who supplied several useful pseudo-medical rationales to support a sales campaign.[6]

At first it was claimed that Laetrile released its cyanide selectively to kill cancer cells and spare healthy cells. Later it was claimed that Laetrile caused the liver to manufacture an anti-cancer agent. Finally it was claimed that Laetrile cured cancer in conjunction with special dietary factors and certain enzymes. Krebs began to call his drug Vitamin B17 as part of this nutritional, metabolic approach. From the point of view of the quack promoters this was doubly advantageous. Health foods and dietary supplements were not subject to the same rigorous provisions of law as regular medicines. Laetrile became available in pill form by this time, as well as by injection, and the pills could be sold to the fearful as a cancer preventative as well as a cure.

For a long time Laetrile was distributed to doctors "for investigational purposes" and only promoted as

A sign near the U.S. border at Tijuana, Mexico, where the "drug" made from peach pits was sold at a highway restaurant. *Photo by C. Grant LaFarge, M.D.*

The Food and Drug Administration declared that Laetrile was medically useless, but the Commissioner's decision was drowned out by the hysteria of Laetrile's proponents.

a cancer cure by word of mouth, making it difficult for the FDA to act. The Laetrile operators were also very cognizant of the territorial limits of the United States law. When Laetrile operations were closed down in this country, manufacture moved to Canada and then to Mexico. Quack operators would approach cancer patients or members of their families, especially in California and the Midwest, and suggest that they cross the border for treatment. A large Laetrile clinic opened in Tijuana, Mexico and there was another one in West Germany. Sometimes Laetrile was smuggled into the U.S. by the operators and sometimes by patients. Then the obliging federal judge in Oklahoma made importation a simple matter of getting an affidavit, and the operators had only to supply a little paperwork.

Laetrile fitted perfectly the profile for a successful patent medicine. It was directed to a life-threatening disease, the second largest cause of death in the U.S., after heart disease. Cancer is often painful. Radiation and chemotherapy, which may accompany or substitute for cancer surgery, can be painful or have undesirable side effects. The fear and pain of cancer have been the primary source of power wielded by cancer quacks down through the decades. The cost of conventional cancer therapy can be a heavy burden for cancer victims. It was about $20,000 a year on the average in 1977 when Laetrile was offered at $10 per injection and $1 per capsule.[7] The Laetrile operators argued that the drug industry and the medical profession opposed them because of a threatened loss of profits and prestige. This challenge to the medical establishment coincided with a renewed public interest in many food fads and a generally naturalistic approach to health. Testimonials from cancer sufferers were the major proofs of efficacy offered by the proponents of Laetrile. Thus the classic themes of the nineteenth century patent medicine era were strongly recurrent in the matter of Laetrile.

The quacks welcomed public argument because it made their apricot extract better known. Once the Laetrile controversy, aided by considerable media attention, reached a certain size, its supporters were ready for political action, something that had never been undertaken before on behalf of a patent medicine. The Laetrile operators used mass meetings, write-in campaigns, and organized audiences at legislative hearings.[8] They authored pamphlets and films, and distributed paperback books, of which there were a surprising number on the subject. It is one thing for the FDA to regulate labels, product brochures supplied with the product, and radio or video salesmanship, but no one was ready to let a federal agency take books out of book stores. Similarly, authors of bona fide articles in newspapers and magazines have always been able to make health claims that could be made nowhere else.

The FDA has never been a popular agency. At the time, it

Two lapel buttons with different viewpoints are shown superimposed upon a few of the thousands of press clippings generated by the Laetrile controversy.

Cancer
Quackery

Laetrile

American
Cancer Society

The publications of two professional societies that worked to bring some sanity to the furor about Laetrile, the patent medicine that became a political cause.

Reprinted from:

Politics, Science, and Cancer: The Laetrile Phenomenon

Edited by Gerald E. Markle
and James C. Petersen

Copyright © 1980 by the American Association for the Advancement of Science
Published by Westview Press, Boulder, Colorado 80301

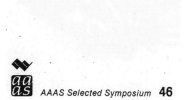

AAAS Selected Symposium 46

was laboring under freshly revived criticism of some merit that its bureaucratic procedures for testing new drugs were unduly protracted and conservative. The quacks were quick to point out new drugs developed in Europe that proved their worth in wide use long before they were legally available here. The FDA had also recently banned saccharin, an ill-advised move that it soon reversed. In 1977 the states' rights philosophy was widely and strongly held. Its adherents could join hands with civil libertarians in making a case for individual freedom in health matters. It was easy for confused local politicians of any stripe to take the position that if people wanted Laetrile, and it was not harmful, they should have it, especially if they were terminally ill. The primary Laetrile campaign organization was named The Committee for Freedom of Choice in Cancer Therapy. The sad truth was that most Laetrile users were not making an informed choice, and that by allowing them to be victimized, cancer sufferers lost their chance of being saved by other treatments that had been proven effective.

The Laetrile controversy was not resolved by the FDA hearings in 1977 or those held by a Congressional subcommittee chaired by Senator Edward Kennedy. The promoters of Laetrile appeared to have won the impasse that they sought. They were not interested in proving either the efficacy or the safety of Laetrile in properly designed, tightly controlled, clinical trials, as required for every new drug since 1965. They preferred to rest on their testimonials and their "state's rights."

An extraordinary situation produced an extraordinary solution. The National Cancer Institute itself began to test Laetrile. It first attempted to study physicians' records of cancer patients alleged to have benefitted from Laetrile. After appealing to 400,000 doctors for records, only 91 cases were received and only 22 of these were fit for evaluation. Animal testing of Laetrile had already proved negative and was inconclusive on the question of pain.[9]

Ultimately and very reluctantly the medical authorities proceeded to test the worthless apricot extract in humans, despite grave ethical reservations. Strict clinical trials were conducted by four large medical centers of undisputed integrity, upon a total of 178 terminal patients suffering from one of the major forms of cancer. In 1981 the findings were released. At the end of eight months of treatment, using the full metabolic regime of Laetrile, enzymes and diet, only one-fifth of the cancer patients were still alive. The results were comparable to these 178 people receiving *no treatment* at all.[10]

Laetrile finally dropped out of the news. This may have dealt it the worst blow of all.[11] The evidence has mounted that cancer is not a single disease but rather the product of multiple factors, environmental and possibly genetic. Science may never find a single magic bullet able to end this dread affliction in all its manifestations. Cancer research marches on with renewed vigor and resources, but quackery in medicine has not been abolished. The virus feeds too readily on the fears and the gullibility of the public for permanent eradication. It is tolerated too easily in its attenuated form, the harmless but near-useless product. The legal weapons of the regulators are too cumbersome to be brought to bear quickly in each case. The spirit of the old patent medicine pitchman is still at work.

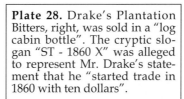

Plate 27. The word "cordial" in the name of this bitters implies a benefit to the heart. In later usage, a cordial can mean any after-dinner drink taken neat.

Plate 28. Drake's Plantation Bitters, right, was sold in a "log cabin bottle". The cryptic slogan "ST - 1860 X" was alleged to represent Mr. Drake's statement that he "started trade in 1860 with ten dollars".

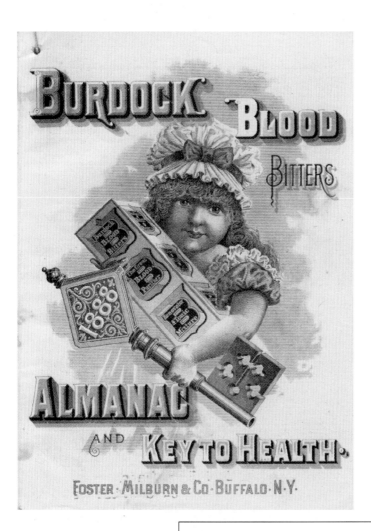

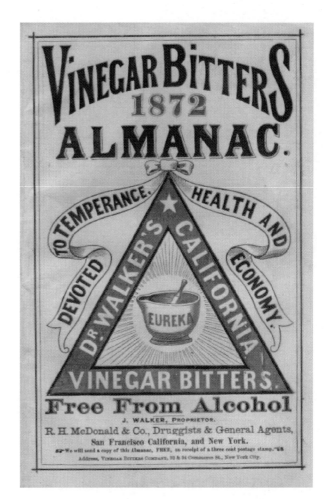

Plate 29. Two almanacs for prominent brands of bitters are shown above.

Plate 30. The full name of the product advertised at left, Scovill's Sarsaparilla or Blood & Liver Syrup, emphasizes the historic claim made for the herb sarsaparilla. "Cleansing the blood" had a secondary meaning that suggested the medicine could act as an anti-syphilitic.

Plate 31. The very well known trade card top right, for Ayer's Sarsaparilla, was reprinted many times and differences crept into the renderings on successive lithographic stones. In one version the wine glass on the table has been replaced by a spoon.

Plate 32. Warner's Log Cabin Sarsaparilla (package illustrated at lower left) was one of the fourteen products of the H. H. Warner Company. Graefenberg's Sarsaparilla, lower right, was one of the ten Graefenberg Family remedies. Most of the large patent medicine firms had a sarsaparilla in their line.

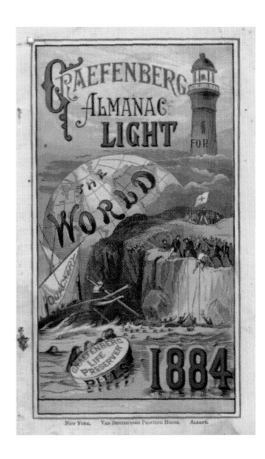

DR. KILMER'S FEMALE REMEDY.

Plate 33. Dr. Andral S. Kilmer, proprietor of the Female Remedy advertised in this High Victorian scene, left no doubt as to the gender of this product. The two products offered in the almanac at bottom right, printed by The Chattanooga Medicine Company, were not intended solely for women but were heavily pitched in that direction. There was also a Black Draught Stock and Poultry Medicine.

Plate 34. Lydia Pinkham's determined face was one of the most ubiquitous images in nineteenth century advertising. The charming picture of Lydia's grandchildren, below, made from a painting in 1889, shows a warmer, more colorful approach. Despite Lydia's success, it was uncommon to find a woman as the suggested source of a preparation. The early card at right, for Aunt Betsy's Green Ointment, shows another one of the few proprietor images in this category.

AUNT BETSY'S GREEN OINTMENT.

LYDIA E. PINKHAM'S Grandchildren.

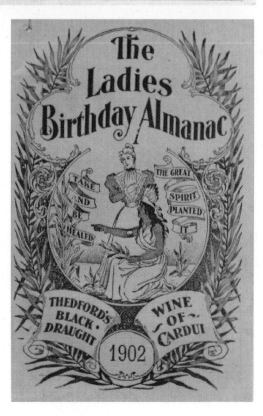

The Ladies Birthday Almanac

TAKE AND BE HEALED

THE GREAT SPIRIT PLANTED IT

THEDFORD'S BLACK DRAUGHT

WINE OF CARDUI

1902

Plate 35. The Pinkham Medicine Company published more than a hundred booklets on various subjects which were distributed at the point of sale and also by mail. These four are a typical sampling.

Plate 36. Remedies for the loss of manhood were discreetly advertised by several proprietors. At upper left is an almanac of the Van Graef Trochee Company and at upper right is a trade card for Mormon Elder's Damiana Wafers. A trochee or "trokey" is a small lozenge.

Plate 37. Veterinary medicine was big business in the nineteenth century. Barker's Komic Picture Souvenir advertised several products in this field with 48 pages of thigh-slapping cartoons like that shown on the cover.

Plate 38. A number of veterinary products were sold for use (at different dosage levels) by both man and beast. Two preparations that made this claim were Sapanule and Merchant's Gargling Oil. It has never been satisfactorily explained how a horse can gargle.

Plate 39. None of the products referred to in the three trade cards shown above had any connection with electricity or magnetism. These words were used in the product names to capitalize on the public interest in these developing fields of science.

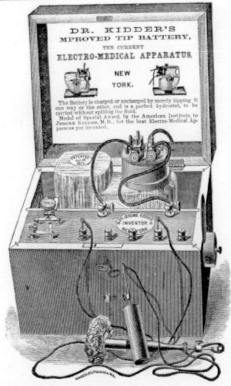

Fig. 5282.—Kidder's Improved Tip Battery..........$27 00

Plate 40. Kidder's Electro-Medical Apparatus, shown in the catalogue illustration at left, delivered a satisfying shock from the genuine electric current produced in the battery jar to the rear. Fleming's device at right was a much more expensive cabinet model for the doctor's office.

ELECTRIC BATTERIES AND APPARATUS.

Flemming's Batteries Discount 20 per cent.

5272

Fig. 5272.—Flemming's Cabinet Battery..........$300 00

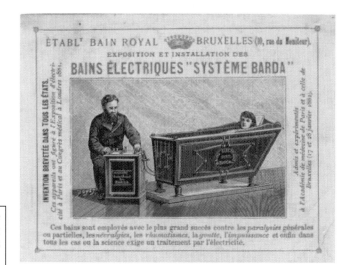

Plate 41. For people who were really into electricity, there was an electric bath, produced by a Belgian firm and named "Systeme Barda".

Plate 42. Two second-generation electric devices are the Calumet, at left, which irradiated with mild ultra-violet rays, and the more powerful Campbell Model E Coil, shown below, which produced X-rays from the naked generating tube shown projecting from the left of the box.

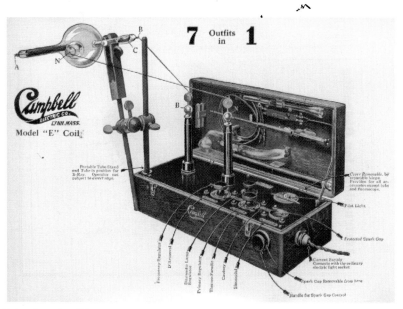

PART TWO

The Products

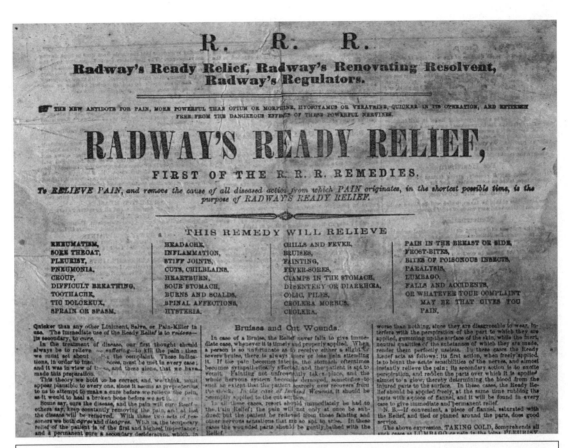

The tattered old broadside above contains testimonials dated 1854. It was typical of the panaceas, offering to cure such diverse ills as cholera, frost-bite and hysteria.

7.

The Cures

A look at the whole drugstore shelf will give an idea of the range of nostrums and other products of the patent medicine proprietors that lent themselves to special kinds of huckstering.

In colonial days, medicines claimed to cure a long list of diseases, and some claimed to cure every disease. The early proprietors used the Greek word "panacea," meaning all healing, in the names or descriptions of their products (Plates 22 and 23). Another Greek word for cure-all was "catholicon," meaning universal in application. In time these unlimited claims became less credible and the ancient words lost favor. They were supplanted in medicine advertising by the word "cure" (Plate 23).

Almost every nineteenth century medicine promised a positive cure of something. Before the turn of the century there were no restraints on the happy advertiser except the limits of his imagination and a shrewd appraisal of the public's gullibility. Even the advertisements of some of the most reputable ethical specialties made these positive assertions, supported no doubt by evidence that some patients had been cured by their use, but couched in terms that in later days would be proscribed by legislation as overly broad.

"Catholicon" also means "cure-all." Dr. Marchisi used the name on this 1892 almanac but product claims were limited to female complaints.

41

Definite cures were promised, not only by lesser-known proprietors like Dake, but also by firms that are with us today, like Carter's Little Liver Pills (renamed Carter's Pills in recent years) and by proprietors who, then as now, were primarily manufacturers of ethical specialties.

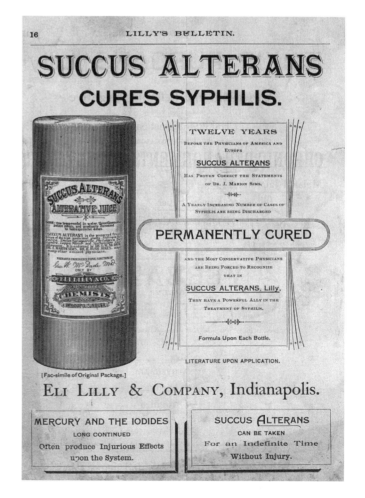

Those who collect bottles define a "cure" as a medicine that actually used this word as part of its name. This is a convenient demarcation for the advertising of a very large category of nostrums. The word "cure" fell into eclipse after the enactment of the Pure Food and Drug Act in 1906 and finally became an illegal misrepresentation with the passage of the Sherley Amendment in 1912. At this point many cures became "remedies" and patent medicine advertising underwent substantial revision.

Early nostrums used the word "cure" in a general, unspecified way —Warner's Safe Cure, Sura-Cura, the A-1 Cure, Dewitt's Electric Cure, Bennett's Magic Cure. Most later Victorian cures limited their claims to one sort of malady. There were throat cures, rheumatism cures, fever cures, abscess cures, asthma cures, ague cures and consumption cures, to name a few. The larger proprietors, like Dr. Kilmer, covered more than one base. Kilmer had his Female Remedy, Indian Cough Cure, Meadow Plant Ointment, Ocean-Weed Heart Remedy and Prompt Parilla Pills in addition to his famous Swamp Root Kidney, Liver and Bladder Cure.

The promise of a cure was refined (clockwise) from the general and vague assurances of Vincent's, to the time-specific statements of Dr. Thomas, to the ultimate, Dr. Shoop's waiver of payment for failing to cure.

The drunkard's time-table was repeated countless times on the inside covers of the Walker's Vinegar Bitters almanacs. Walker's claimed to be "the only temperance bitters".

There is one group of cures that is particularly interesting from a marketing standpoint, because some of them claimed to cure the effects of other cures. The theme of their advertising might be expressed, "Kick the Habit."

The presence of considerable alcohol in many patent remedies was recognized with delight by a number of users and with concern by another faction in the body politic, the Temperance element. A good many products appealed to the morality of the teetotalers with the chaste reference in their advertising, "contains no alcohol." Walker's Vinegar Bitters went the whole way (Plate 29). It announced itself as "the only temperance bitters." Its almanac contained an elaborate illustrated time table for the Grand Trunk Railway, showing the drunkard's journey from Sobriety to Guttersburg.

This of course was the practice of preventative medicine. There were also remedies that got at the vile disease of alcoholism directly. One obscure and expensive chemical, bichloride of gold, was offered by several sources as a cure for inebriety. The most famous purveyor was Leslie E. Keeley, a railroad surgeon who in 1879 founded a drying-out hospital in Dwight, Illinois that did not close its doors until 1966. He established a similar institution near Farmington, Maine (Plate 24) and several others operated under his general supervision. He also did a respectable mail order business.[1]

It is suspected that in the beginning, Keeley's Gold Cure for Drunkenness itself used considerable alcohol. Evidently an

effort was made at the Keeley Institute to compound progressively weaker mixtures for individual patients and to practice in secret a simple weaning process. Of course the mail order side of the business did not lend itself to tapering off and only offered the habitual drunkard a little more "hair of the dog."

Dr. Keeley used a variety of distinctive embossed bottles for his remedy that were to be returned when empty, or destroyed. All are desirable collector's items today. There was a "final" bottle presented to "graduates" upon leaving the Keeley Institute and there were "companion" bottles, each half-round with one flat side. It was explained that this made it convenient to ship these bottles in pairs. It also made them convenient to carry as hip flasks.

By 1904, an analysis of the Keeley mixture revealed no more than salicin (extracted from willow bark), chinchona, gentian and columbo. An independent commentator asserted that this compound would "antagonize and eliminate alcohol from the system and restore the brain to its natural condition," but he conceded that the patient must feel an earnest desire to be cured in order for the remedy to be effective.[2]

Keeley had imitators in the gold chloride game and also competitors whose treatment proceeded along different lines. Anxious wives were encouraged to slip a little White Star Secret Liquor Cure into their husband's evening coffee to destroy his craving for strong drink. The preparation was

Two bottles of Keeley's Gold Cure, one for the alcohol habit and one for the tobacco habit.

tasteless and odorless and could be ordered from Sears Roebuck.[3] "Secret" liquor cures had a special way of keeping their promise. Hubby usually went peacefully to sleep on the parlor sofa rather than off to the saloon. The potion was, of course, a heavy sleeping draught.

The nostrum peddler also addressed himself to the tobacco and the narcotic habits. No-to-bac and Baco-Curo made their pitch mostly on the theme that ladies do not like men who smell of nicotine (Plate 25). The drug cures are suspected of a more insidious approach. It appears that most of this small group of nostrums were consciously designed to make a permanent customer of the addict by supplying him with morphine in a less recognizable form. There was considerable pharmacological ignorance about some narcotics. Upon occasion, heroin was prescribed as a cure for the morphine habit. This cure undoubtedly worked. In place of the morphine habit you got the heroin habit.

Drug addiction was not widely recognized in the Victorian era, and at first was not regarded as a serious vice. Conan Doyle's early stories find Dr. Watson giving only a mild reproof to the respectable Sherlock Holmes when he took to the cocaine needle for relief from boredom.[4] The widespread use of the coca leaf, source of the alkaloid cocaine, illustrates how little that particular substance was understood. As is well known today, during the period 1885 to 1903, coca leaves were an important ingredient in Coca-Cola. The story of this preparation is instructive in several ways.

Coca-Cola began life as a medicinal tonic, advertised as a cure for sick headache, neuralgia, hysteria and melancholy. Reference to the latter two conditions, and use of the slogan "the intellectual beverage," evidences some recognition of its effect on the emotional perception of the user.[5] The tonic was invented in 1885 by an Atlanta chemist named John Stith Pemberton, who was already the proprietor of two local products named Flower Cough Syrup and Triplex Liver Pills. His new product, Pemberton's French Wine Coca, was an admitted adaptation of the popular import, Vin Mariani, a compound of coca leaves in wine. Pemberton added kola nut, another herbal substance which was then enjoying substantial vogue. It contained caffeine. He dropped the wine in 1886 under the pressure of a local prohibition ordinance, and substituted sugar syrup. The resulting mixture, renamed Coca-Cola, could be charged with carbonated water and sold at ordinary food and drink emporiums as a temperance tonic or "Sunday soda."[6]

An advertisement for a liquor cure that worked. It put the sufferer to sleep before he could sneak out to the corner saloon.

A page from a booklet published by Antikamnia, an analgesic for mild pain and fever containing acetanilid. It is noteworthy for its ringing endorsement of heroin as a remedy for chest ailments demonstrating once again that the dangers of narcotics were very little appreciated.

WHITE STAR SECRET LIQUOR CURE.

Regular retail price............................$2.50
Our price, complete, box of thirty treatments.........94

THIS EXCEEDINGLY SUCCESSFUL LIQUOR CURE is designated as a Secret Liquor Cure because it can be administered secretly without the knowledge of the drinker and can be given in tea, coffee or food, without the consent of the unfortunate victim of the drink habit.

OUR PRICE, ONLY 94c

Regular Retail Price, $2.50

THE WHITE STAR SECRET LIQUOR CURE contains the following ingredients in correct proportion: Gold Chloride, Ammonium Muriate, Scutellaria, Erythroxylon Coca, Ext. Cayenne, Ext. American Valerian, Cephalis Ipecac, Ext. Bleeding Heart, Saccharaum Lactis.

THIS REPRESENTS an odorless and tasteless preparation in powdered form, which, given to the drinker in tea, coffee or food will not upset the patient, but by its action on the system and the tonic stimulating effect upon the nerves, it often removes that desire, that craving for intoxicating liquor, in a comparatively short time.

IT IS NOT CLAIMED that there is a liquor cure, secret or otherwise, that is absolutely infallible in all cases, but so many have been entirely cured and stayed cured, so many have been reclaimed for months or years before they suffered a relapse that it would really seem a neglect of duty not to make the attempt to help them, even save them against their will, especially when you can undertake this treatment without the slightest risk, so far as expense is concerned, without any risk whatever of harming the patient.

THE WHITE STAR SECRET LIQUOR CURE will do no harm in any case. It will always improve the general condition of the drinker to a marked degree. It is considered one of the best prescriptions to be employed secretly in the treatment of the liquor habit. Neither you nor we ourselves can tell, however, beforehand, what it can and will accomplish for the patient whose treatment you contemplate, nor do we wish you to be disappointed in the results and we therefore make you the following liberal offer.

SEND FOR A BOX of the White Star Secret Liquor Cure, which contains thirty treatments, give it according to directions, a small powder in tea or coffee. After you have made a fair trial according to instructions, if there is no benefit derived, write us. State that this is the first box that you have tried and we will promptly refund your money.

REMEMBER, the price is only 94 cents per box of thirty complete treatments.

Full directions sent with each box. Medicine sent in a plain sealed package. No. 8F151 Price, 3 boxes for, $2.50; per box......................94c

If by mail, postage extra, per box, 12 cents.

MEMBRANOUS COMPLICATIONS
(Throat, Bronchi and Lungs)
......BY......
WALTER M. FLEMING, A.M., M.D.,
NEW YORK CITY
Member State and County Medical Societies, Medico-Legal Society, Qualified Examiner in Lunacy, Superior Court, New York.

The experimental stage of observation of the action of heroin on the human system has passed, and its use has very largely extended. The medical profession now recognizes the merit and offices of that drug as almost a specific in the treatment of winter coughs, colds, bronchitis, incipient pneumonia, oedema of lungs, and the multitude of complications characteristic of congestive membranous troubles. Even whooping cough, universally regarded as incurable and so intractable and obstinate as to preclude the hope or probability of yielding to abortive measures, certainly yields kindly and gracefully in its incubating stage, so far as its violent paroxysms are concerned, to the persuasive eloquence of hydrochloride of heroin, particularly in its combination with the well-known analgesic, and antipyretic — its "running mate," antikamnia.

With all the experience of more than a quarter of a century, in the treatment of winter cough, and all its complications of

This 1893 poster recommends Coca-Cola for its therapeutic effects. Later advertising took up the theme of refreshment. The coca leaves, still used for flavoring in 1903, were stripped of their potency after that date. *Courtesy the Coca-Cola Company.*

The rights to Coca-Cola were purchased in 1888 by Asa G. Chandler, also of Atlanta, who exploited its true commercial possibilities and made it one of the greatest consumer product successes in the history of American business. He eliminated the medicinal references in Coca-Cola advertising and described it simply as "refreshing" and "exhilarating." The formula for Coca-Cola is a very closely held trade secret and one of the most valuable in use today. The original compounding, however, persisted in the folk memory of small Southern towns, where as late as the 1930s, a Coca-Cola was referred to as a "dope."

According to the American Medical Association, writing in 1912, a number of Coca-Cola imitations were still using raw coca at that time, sometimes with and sometimes without the kola.[7] Some of them were: Cafe Coca, Celery Cola, Coca-Bolo, Coca Calisaya, Dr. Don's Kola, Koca-Nola, Kola-Ade, Kola-Coca, Kola Cordial, Kos-Kola, Rococola, Vani-Kola and Wiseola.

Coca leaves were used as a flavoring ingredient of Coca-Cola until 1903, when this drew the attention of reformers who were pressing for the legislation that became known as the Pure Food and Drug Act. From this time on, the cocaine alkaloid was extracted from the leaves before their use in the flavoring process, and until 1969 the company was required to demonstrate this fact to the federal government.

In the story of Coca-Cola we see a medicinal preparation, whose habit forming tendencies were not fully understood, and a radical product change leaving unaffected the product name, which had achieved great value. We see, further, a great business success stemming from a new way of using the product and the skillful use of advertising.

Vino-Kolafra, made in Brunswick, New Jersey, might be suspected as a Coca-Cola look-alike but it was advertised for relief from the effects of alcohol, opium and cocaine.

8.

The Bitters

A second large category of nostrum advertising promoted the sale of products that were styled as "bitters" (Plates 26-29).

Bitters were generally composed of water, alcohol, and a bad tasting herb to give a medicinal flavor. The alcohol was frequently provided by very bad whiskey. The herb or herbs often had laxative properties. The traditional taste of medicine bitters can be experienced to a degree in some products sold today as "digestives." One of these, Angostura Bitters, is used principally as a flavoring in certain cocktails. Others, such as Fernet Branca and Campari, are sold as aperitifs to stimulate the appetite before meals, or as cordials, to follow the meal. A wider selection of these modern bitters may be found in Europe than in the United States. The term "cordial" derives, of course, from the Latin word for "heart," and in earlier days referred, not to an alcoholic beverage, but to a potion with reviving or invigorating properties.

It should be noted in passing that whiskey itself was seriously regarded as a medicinal stimulant in the nineteenth century. An 1884 almanac proclaimed that "Duffy's Malt Whiskey is good for the tired clergyman . . . the professional worker . . . the

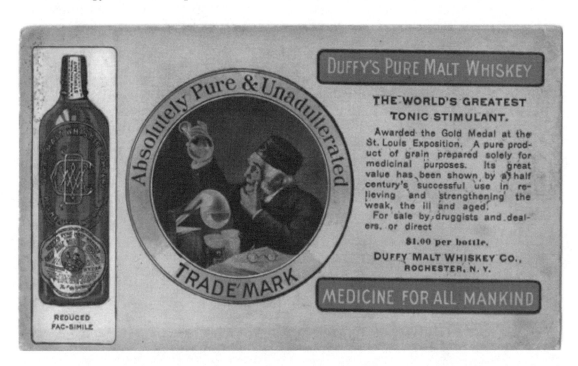

A blotter advertising whiskey for medicinal purposes, long before this became a popular way to circumvent the Volstead Act during Prohibition.

nursing mother." More specifically, it was "a cure and positive cure for consumption." The scientific reason propounded was that it "supplies the system with more carbon than the disease can exhaust." Duffy's said "The formula was specially prepared for us by the great German scientist Dr. von Vonders." One wonders indeed how this could be received with a straight face.

Even in the 1920s during Prohibition, liquor could be obtained legally upon prescription. Duffy's Pure Malt Whiskey and Perrine's Pure Barley Malt (Plate 24) used a therapeutic argument in much of their advertising at the turn of the century, and the names of some patent medicines reflected in a very frank manner their liquor base, among them Boneset Bourbon Tonic, Dr. C.V. Giraud's Ginger Brandy and TLS Gin Bitters.

The opportunities and the problems of those who sold bitters, derived from the fact that their alcohol content was easily appreciated by those who chose to recognize it. Bitters were treated like a special brand of liquor by many patrons. They were sold over the bar in the saloons of the Old West and were still to be found in civilized watering places many decades later.

The early bitters were sold in bottles that suggested the barrels in which whiskey was shipped. They were elongated cylinders with flat shoulders and short neck like a spout, often decorated with raised bands resembling barrel hoops. Another early form was the "cabin bottle" (Plate 28). That used by the distiller, E.C. Booz, was the approximation of a log house, embossed with doors and windows. Mr. Booz, incidentally, did not give rise to the informal name for alcoholic refreshment. It is thought that "booze" developed much earlier from the Middle English "bousen," meaning to tipple.

Most "cabins" were more stylized. They had log patterns on the shoulders and sometimes at the bases. The

Duffy's Malt Whiskey consistently favored mothers and babies on the covers of its almanacs, above. Sager's TLS Gin Bitters, below, attempts to do the same thing with another spiritous liquor.

The barroom nature of bitters sales is captured well in this turn of the century drawing for the famous brand of Lash's.

A variety of brands and bottle shapes. The bitters were sold in the most distinctive and elaborate bottles as well as some of the simplest and most utilitarian.

standard bitters bottle of later years was square, with angled (but not rounded) shoulders and a strong neck.[1] Barrels and cabins are regarded as the aristocrats of patent medicine bottles by collectors, who routinely pay hundreds of dollars today for rare examples. In any event, the patent medicine proprietors achieved a clearly defined market image with these containers.

The exact composition of particular nostrums, including bitters, was always arguable. For one thing, the ingredients were changed from time to time. It was not until 1906 that the manufacturer was required to state the percentage of alcohol on the label. Often the presence of alcohol was explained as "just enough to act as a preservative" or "just enough to keep the mixture from freezing."

One authority reports that the Hostetter's Bitters sold in North Dakota in wintertime reached 43% alcohol. The major medicinal ingredient of this product was quinine. It would have taken 20 ounces of Hostetter's to get the proper daily dosage of quinine to ward off malaria— if that was the problem in North Dakota—and at that rate many sufferers would have been perpetually inebriated. The effects of Hartman's Peruna beame so well known as to create the phrase, "a Peruna drunk."

There were a number of other patent medicines containing alcohol in an abundance that would delight any secret drinker. In the female remedies and certain "vegetable mixtures," this was much better disguised from an advertising standpoint. They managed to avoid the liquor image of the bitters for many years and enabled grandma to enjoy the benefits of a cocktail (and move her bowels) without troubling her temperance views. Even knowing there was alcohol present, the user could take umbrage in the notion that it was simply a question of how much one took before one was abusing the medicine. A more general term came to be used by the reform groups to include Lydia Pinkham's Vegetable Compound,

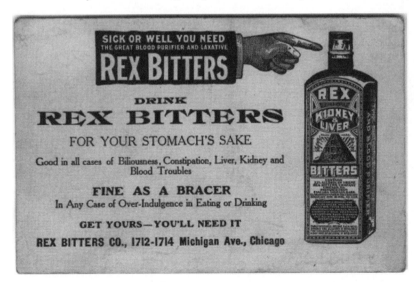

Paine's Celery Compound, despite criticism from its many detractors, stuck to the homey image of a vegetable preparation for the infirmed and aged. It disappeared soon after it was forced to disclose its alcohol ontent.

Clayton & Russell's Bitters were sold after 1906 with the fact, disclosed on the label in accordance with the Pure Food and Drug Act, that they contained 37% alcohol. It was not a widely known brand.

Paine's Celery Compound, Hood's Sarsaparilla and other alcoholic medicines with a similar posture of innocence. They called them "bracers" or "boozers."

Analyses published in the *Ladies' Home Journal* in 1904 showed the following alcoholic content of other popular preparations at that time.[2] Editor Edward Bok also published a picture of a row of spirit lamps burning brightly with the use of some of these products as a fuel.

Ayer's Sarsaparilla	26.2%
Baxter's Mandrake Bitters	16.5%
Brown's Iron Bitters	19.5%
Burdock Blood Bitters	25.2%
Dana's Sarsaparilla	13.5%
Faith Baldwin's Nerve Bitters	21.5%
Greene's Nervura	17.2%
Hartman's Peruna	28.5%
Hartshorn's Bitters	22.2%
Hood's Sarsaparilla	18.2%
Hoofland's German Tonic	29.3%
Hop Bitters	44.3%
Kaufman's Sulfur Bitters	20.5%
Lydia Pinkham Compound	20.6%
Paine's Celery Compound	21.0%
Parker's Ginger Tonic	41.6%
Schenck's Seaweed Tonic	19.5%
Warner's Safe Tonic	35.7%

In time, the temperance activists and public awareness caught up with the bitters and the bracers. Most disappeared but a few lowered their alcoholic content to avoid classification as beverages and were able to hang on for many years with reduced sales. The tendency to self-delusion in this area remains strong. Consider the men, women and children happily dosed, in the aggregate, with over twelve million bottles of Hadacol in the 1950s. Each bottle was equivalent to two high-balls. Essentially a liquor with vitamins, Hadadcol was a twentieth century version of the bitters, and it met with considerable success.

Hostetters's Bitters trademarked its famous logo in 1859 and used it for 98 years. The covers of its almanacs remained essentially the same throughout the life of the product although the ingredients were changed markedly after 1906.

A sarsaparilla almanac, spotted with age, emphasizes the venerability of this remedy which, if not sold at King Solomon's Temple, as pictured, goes back at least to the 1500s.

9.

The Sarsaparillas

Today we have a carbonated soft drink called "sarsaparilla." The same beverage is also known as "root beer" or "birch beer." Sarsaparilla has a time-honored place on the American scene and an association with natural ingredients and country life (Plates 30-32).

The name "sarsaparilla" applied originally to a class of patent medicines flavored with a widely recognized aromatic. In yester-year's sarsaparilla, this was sassafrass root or the extract of some other plant in the Smilax family. The similar flavoring in today's root beer is birch oil. It appears that sarsaparilla was never sold alone as a remedy and that the medicinal sarsaparillas always had many other ingredients. Most frequently they included potassium iodide, a chemical that is dangerous unless properly prescribed, and alcohol in abundance.

The medicine called sarsaparilla was prescribed as a specific for syphilis as early as the sixteenth century. After a period in eclipse, it experienced a renaissance in the nineteenth century to "eliminate poison from the blood," a polite expression that did nothing to discourage the belief that it was helpful with venereal problems and with the unsightly swellings and skin eruptions collectively referred to as "scrofula."

The other medicine of choice for syphilis during this period was mercury, in various compounds.

Two trade cards for highly popular sarsaparillas, Ayers's and Hood's, both made in Massachusetts. The Ayer's card, with slightly biblical overtones, makes the point that sarsaparilla was known to many peoples and tongues.

Above, an explanation by the C. I. Hood Company of its label, discussing some of the many ingredients of sarsaparilla. At right, trade cards for two lesser-known brands, Bristol's and Gold Medal.

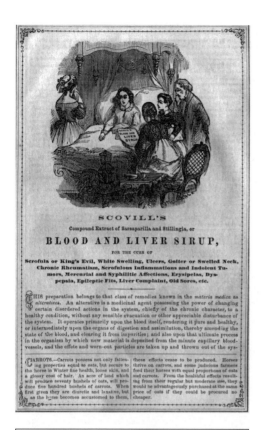

Greenville Sarsaparilla is the only one, as far as it is known, to claim that these herbs increased the user's mental powers.

Part of a page from *Scovill's Farmers and Mechanics Almanac* for 1868, mentioning a few of the symptoms that sarsaparilla was alleged to cure.

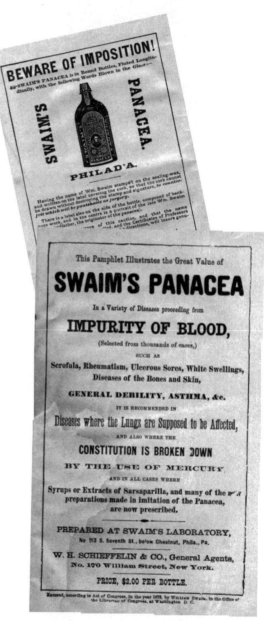

Properly administered by a doctor it could be of some help, but even in those days, it was recognized that indiscriminate self-dosing with mercury could lead to a particularly unpleasant type of poisoning.

The popular belief in sarsaparilla produced a shocking result in the hands of William Swaim, who started his career as a bookbinder in New York. In the 1820s, Swaim produced a sarsaparilla compound that he had improved with the flavor of wintergreen, and marketed it as a cure for a great variety of diseases. Swaim's Panacea promised to cure blood diseases "without mercury" and its proprietor collected impressive testimonials from reputable doctors that this result was achieved in some cases. At length, however, an investigation by the Philadelphia Medical Society disclosed that corrosive sublimate of mercury was in fact a secret ingredient of this mixture. One might imagine that the ensuing outcry would have destroyed Mr. Swaim. Not at all! This was 1827. Public inattention, confusion and cupidity were such that forty years later Swaim's Panacea was still selling well and Mr. Swaim died a wealthy man.

Today we know that the herb sarsaparilla is medically useless but patent sarsaparillas were among the most well-known nostrums of their day. There were probably as many sarsaparillas as there were bitters.[1] Hood's Sarsaparilla, an inventive and prolific advertiser, was a large factor in the market for patent medicines for over fifty years. Sarsaparilla also appeared as a

You might be better off with the imitation! The front cover (lower image) of this 1887 pamphlet suggests that Mr. Swaim's compound will repair the ravages of mercury. It fails to say that mercury was one of the prime ingredients of Swaim's Panacea.

Sarsaparilla in two other forms. Mrs. Dinsmore, at left, makes a virtue out of necessity. It is not possible to produce an alcoholic *wafer*. Kilmer's Prompt Parilla Pills, above, attempt to shorten the name that no one can spell anyway.

solid, in Mrs. Dinsmore's Sarsaparilla Wafers and in Dr. Kilmer's Prompt Parilla Pills, although the shortened form of the name did not enjoy much of a vogue.

In later years most Americans probably regarded sarsaparilla as a "spring tonic" for cleaning the whole system, something like a sophisticated version of the traditional sulphur and molasses. It is one old-fashioned name that has weathered the decades and the dubious associations, and achieved fondness in the regard of the public.

In Bell's trade card from the 1880's we see the "spring tonic" notion fighting hard with the "wonder cure" theme.

Gilbert's product, advertised on this comic stock card, attempts a combination of the two best selling types of patent medicine, the sarsaparillas and the bitters.

Plate 43. Health and invalid foods held a tidy niche in the market. Imperium Granum, above left, was a cereal that finally won a patent in 1881 as a medicinal product. Ridge's Food, at right, was a milk substitute. Prima Tonic and its associated beverages, below left, were malt-based. Kumysgen, below right, was a milk product.

Plate 44. The advertisement for Buckingham's Dye, above, is a metamorphic trade card that can change its appearance. The same card is shown below with the flap folded down, illustrating the difference that the product could make in the gentleman's beard.

Plate 45. Barry's Tricopherous, above right, promises to grow hair on bald heads. Hall's Vegetable Sicilian Hair Renewer, below right, makes the more modest claim that it will prevent gray or falling hair.

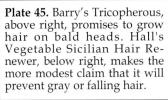

Plate 46. A number of the patent medicine manufacturers were also in the fragrance market. The trade card for Austen's Forest Flowers Cologne, above left, was printed on a small blotter, impregnated with the scent being offered. Murray & Lanham's Florida Water, above right, is still sold by a successor company.

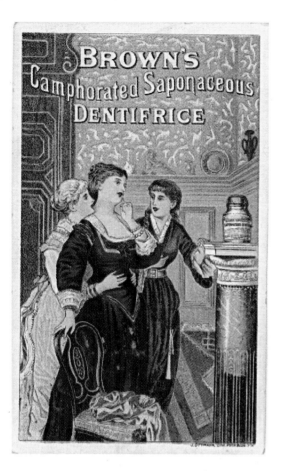

Plate 47. Brown's Dentrifrice, top left, contained camphor and soap, if we can believe the name. Rubifoam, bottom left, produced a red froth in the mouth.

Plate 48. Two skin creams with charming advertisements. Hagan's, bottom right, is no longer in the market but Hinds, top right, is still going strong.

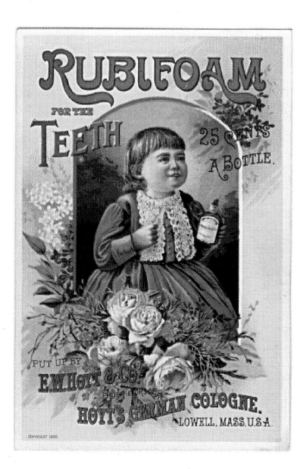

Plate 49. Fear advertising, in the early days, featured Death with his scythe, seen hovering in the clouds on the poster for Parr's English Pad, at left. *Courtesy The New-York Historical Society, N.Y.C.* The logo at right for Hunt's Remedy, a man fighting a skeleton, was an image used by several patent medicines.

Plate 50. The scene at right was published by Antikamnia, a headache remedy that contained acetanilid. The Greek name means "opposed to pain". This calendar was distributed to doctors only. The trade card below, Mason & Pollard's Anti-Malarial Pills, shows less fearsome evil spirits and was characteristic of the waning phase of fear advertising.

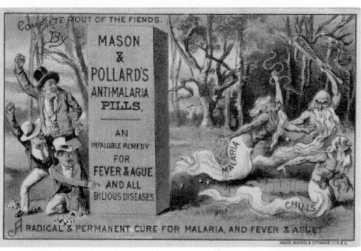

THE FAMILY
DOCTOR

"Choose a doctor as you
choose a friend"

Plate 51. The doctor was used, in the three adjacent examples, as an image of respectability by the patent medicine proprietor who wished to associate himself and his product with the medical establishment. The hard-working physician was frequently a family friend and mentor who might actually prescribe some patent medicines.

Plate 52. The greedy or uncaring doctor, who cost far more than over-the-counter medicine, was an opposing image that some nostrum proprietors sought to exploit. The message on the cover of the almanac shown at right reads "No need of you, Doctor, now that we have Tutt's Liver Pills". The doctor on the trade card below for Wright's Indian Vegetable Pills says, "Why bless me, but you are taking the wrong pills", to which his happy patient replies, "Not at all, doctor. I'm taking the Wright Pills".

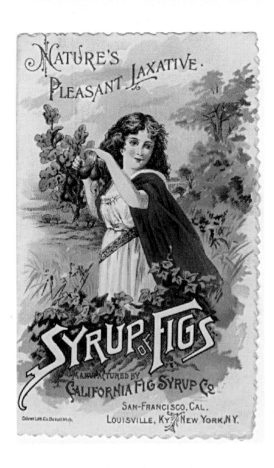

Plate 53. "Back to nature" advertising offered nostrums associated with familiar fruits or vegetables. Natural remedies were presumably less harsh and more reassuring. Alas, the popular Syrup of Figs, shown on the booklet cover at upper left, gained its laxative effect from senna, a natural substance but a very powerful one.

Plate 54. Himalaya was not a kola compound, as the almanac indicates. It contained potassium iodide, peppermint and licorice, as well as a heavy dose of jungle mystique.

Plate 55. Taylor's Sweet Gum and Mullein contained morphine, according to a 1909 report of the American Medical Association.

Plate 56. The spurious herbal advertising of some patent medicines should not let us forget that many common plants, both well-known and obscure, were valued for supposed benefits by serious doctors. They were sold in compressed form by almost all of the reputable drug houses, for compounding in regular prescriptions.

Lydia E. Pinkham (1819-1883) had the most famous face in medicine advertising and one of the most potent and durable images in the battle of product identities. It is said that her son, Dan, originated the idea of using his mother's portrait as a trademark.

10. Women's Medicines

What sold the concoctions of Mrs. Lydia Pinkham was her boldly feminist approach. The success of the Pinkham advertising evidences the nineteenth century stirrings of what we now call Women's Liberation, that found early political expression in the Suffragette Movement. Her medicinal preparation was first advertised as a general tonic. Promoting it as a women's specific was the mark of true genius. Lydia played this tune for all it was worth (Plate 34).

The "Age of the Womb," as one scholar calls it, was drawing to a close.[1] The prevailing view of a woman's proper role in life no longer centered as heavily upon her reproductive function. A wider recognition of women's capabilities and prerogatives was ready to find a counterpart in the attitude of commercial advertisers. As for the medical profession, the inadequacies of conventional practice in the area of gynecology was becoming more apparent. These factors created Mrs. Pinkham's opportunity .

Lydia Pinkham's Compound was not a feminine hygiene product. It was taken by mouth in a large spoonful, tasted appropriately dreadful, and contained, over the years, a motley assortment of herbs and a generous percentage of alcohol. The original formula included false unicorn root, true unicorn foot, life root, black

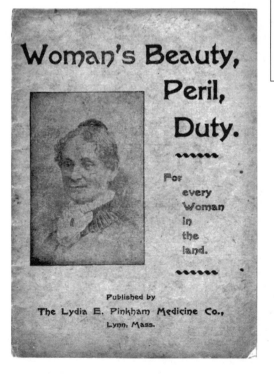

Two Pinkham booklets emphasizing a new responsibility and a more positive role for women. An 1893 edition at left, 1903 at right.

SONG OF LYDIA E. PINKHAM
(Sung to a hymn tune entitled "Our Redeemer")

CHORUS
****

Oh! we'll sing of Lydia Pinkham
And her love for the human race
How she sells her Vegetable Compound
And the papers they publish her face.

****

There's a face that haunts me ever.
There are eyes mine always meet,
As I read the morning paper,
As I walk the crowded street.

May her fame be spread more widely
And the papers get more space
For her testimonial women
And her dear old motherly face

We will sing of a famous lady
And her wondrous healing powers.
May her name be spared to bless us
In this hectic world of ours.

Oh! She knows not how I suffer;
Hers is now a world wide fame.
But 'til death that face shall greet me;
Lydia Pinkham is her name.

Tell us, Lydia, of your secret
And the wonders you perform;
How you take the sick and ailing
And restore them to the norm.

Ninety-eight of every hundred
Of their sex go smiling through.
Some are married, some are single;
Let us tell you what it'll do.

Lizzie Smith had tired feelings,
Awful pains reduced her weight.
She began to take the Compound;
Now she weighs six hundred and eight.

Mrs. Jones from Walla Walla,
Mrs. Smith from Kanka Kee,
Mrs. Cohen, Mrs. Murphy,
Sing her praises lustily.

Mary Jane was married 10 years
And no children did appear.
Then she took your Vegetable Compound;
Twins now come three times a year.

"There's a baby in every bottle",
Thus the old quotation ran.
So be sure you get the right one
For it might be black and tan.

A few of the many verses from Lydia Pinkham's favorite song.

cohash, pleurisy root and fenugreek seed.[2] The claims made for this nostrum varied over the years. At times there was a heavy suggestion that it increased fertility. "A baby in every bottle" went one line of the old Lydia Pinkham song. Always present was the assurance that cramps would be relieved and the spirit brightened. The alcohol component took care of that.

Lydia Pinkham advertising featured the proprietor herself. It was direct and personal. Her signature appeared on her trade cards over the words, "faithfully yours." Through all of her material ran a just-us-girls tone. "Men don't understand" was one slogan. Women were invited to confide in Lydia about their troubles, medical and non-medical. In time her mail organization became huge. Women were still writing to Lydia many years after her death and Lydia was still answering.

"No harmful drugs or narcotics" was the message here. The alcohol content was ignored. Inside were Lydia's directions for preparing simple infusions from 15 different herbs for various specific purposes.

A very effective attack on Lydia Pinkham's Compound was made by Edwards Bok's article in the *Ladies Home Journal* in 1904, entitled "How Private Confidences of Women are Laughed At."[3] Clerks opened the letters, he said, and they are never seen by a doctor. The names and addresses are sold later to other medicine houses for up to five cents each. Lydia's name was not mentioned by Bok in his article but his readers knew whom he had in mind. Earlier, Bok had published a picture of Mrs. Pinkham's tombstone to persuade the doubtful that she really was dead.

After the turn of the century, and well into the 1930s, The Pinkham Company addressed a variety of subjects with a less medical and more social appeal, in a flood of booklets translated into several languages (Plate 35). They dealt with family, children, home and kitchen in a manner that was not exactly intellectual but essentially sound. Before the ultimate eclipse of the Lydia Pinkham products, America had entered the radio age, and the company sponsored short talks (also available in loose leaf form) on dating, marital happiness and other subjects considered bold at the time, but handled in a suitably abstract fashion.

At right, two of the foreign-language booklets among the many issued by The Lydia E. Pinkham Medicine Company.

Lydia communicated with her faithful by letter in 1884 when the booklet above was issued. By 1932 she used the "Voice of Experience" radio talks. A few scripts are shown at right.

Two trade cards for nineteenth century patent medicines that appealed solely to female consumers.

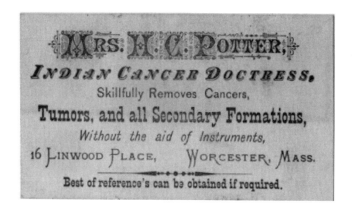

INVALID LADIES !

THIS IS FOR YOU.

THERE are thousands of females in America who suffer untold miseries from chronic diseases common to their sex. This is due largely to the peculiar habits of life and fashion, and the improper training of girlhood. Then, too, the physical changes that mark the three eras of womanhood (the maiden, the wife, and the mother), have much to do with their sufferings, most of which is endured in silence, unknown by even the family physician and most intimate friends. To all such whose hollow cheeks, pale faces, sunken eyes and feeble footsteps indicate nervous and general debility bordering on consumption, we would earnestly recommend that grand system-renovating tonic,

BURDOCK BLOOD BITTERS.

It makes pure, healthy blood, and regulates all the organs to a proper action, cures constipation, liver and kidney complaint, female weakness, nervous and general debility, and all the distressing miseries from which two-thirds of the women of America are suffering. All Invalid Ladies should send for our Special Circular addressed to Ladies Only, which treats on a subject of vital importance.

Address FOSTER, MILBURN & CO., Buffalo, N. Y.

Presented By

P. V. HEPBURN,

Druggist, Bookseller & Stationer,

COLTON, N. Y

The back of a trade card for Burdock Blood Bitters. At right, an advertisement for an early female practitioner in the cancer cure business.

It must not be supposed that Lydia's was the only nostrum of this kind on the market. It was simply the one that has enjoyed the most lasting fame. There were many other products designed to appeal specially to women: Dr. Kilmer's Female Remedy, Mrs. Sarah J. VanBuren's Ladies' Tonic, Mrs. Freemen's Female Restorative Cordial, and Femina, to name a few (Plate 33). Other nostrums made a play for the ladies without confining themselves exclusively to the gentler sex. "Invalid Ladies . . ." was the caption of many advertisements for Burdock Blood Bitters, but it promised to strengthen anyone. McElree's Wine of Cardui and Thedford's Black Draught, both made by the same Chattanooga manufacturer, were tonics with a similar appeal that did very well on the Southern market (Plate 33).

A few medicines employed the maternal image in fields unrelated to female weakness. In this category we find Mrs. Dinsmore's Great English Cough and Croup Balsam, Faith Whitcomb's Liniment, Aunt Betsy's Green Ointment (Plate 34) and Mrs. Potter, the Indian Cancer Doctress, who obviously believed in adding one mystique to another.

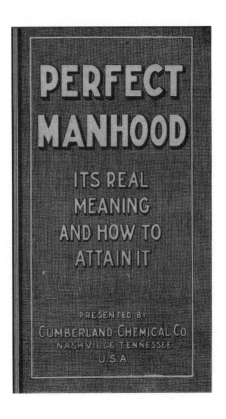

11.

Virility Aids

It was not easy for advertisers in the Victorian era to discuss sexual problems of any sort in print, but nevertheless they managed to sustain a lively interest and a good market for products that offered assurance against "loss of manhood."

One clever nostrum merchant found it possible to hide behind a reference, semi-religious in tone, that was perfectly clear to his readers. He called his product "Mormon Elder's Damiana Wafers." The allusion was of course to the plural wives and numerous children per family for which this sect was famous in the 1800s. One trade card for this product showed a soberly dressed gentleman well past his middle years, engaged in pinching the maid when his angry wife enters the room (Plate 36). Helmicker's Damiana Wafers went a bit further in a scene showing a dandy with handlebar moustaches leering at a well-endowed lady in her underwear.

"DO YOU KNOW THEY SAY WE ARE LOOKING SO WELL. DARLING SHALL I TELL THEM WE ARE TAKING DR. HELMICKER'S DAMIANA PILLS."
Depot, 106 Eighth Avenue. Price, $1.00 per Box.
[OVER.]

Helmicker's Pills, advertised on the trade card above, contained the herb damiana, an alleged aphrodisiac no longer regarded as having any medical effect.

Ko-Kol had no hesitation in asking personal questions of potential purchasers.

Damiana, a vegetable substance since dropped from the pharmacopeia, was long thought to be an aphrodisiac. Cantharidies, popularly known as "Spanish Fly" because it is extracted from a species of small flying beetle, was another common component of virility potions. This substance is essentially a blistering agent and was used as such in chest plasters. When taken internally it causes engorgement of the penis through irritation of the urinary tract. It is truly dangerous unless the dosage is carefully controlled.

A good many virility products leaned heavily towards mail order. Some of the order blanks, like that for Ko-kol, were unblushingly detailed. One gets the impression, from references to self-abuse, that some early advertising psychologists in the virility product area were playing strongly to Victorian guilt.

"Electrical" apparatus that was sold to restore manhood. The Supreme Electric Belt cost $25.00, a large price for 1901 when the almanac was issued. The curative power was applied by the three electrodes shown bristling with regenerative force. Pulvermacher's device, illustrated below, had one electrode at the spine and numerous "gold" threads sewn into the suspensory pouch.

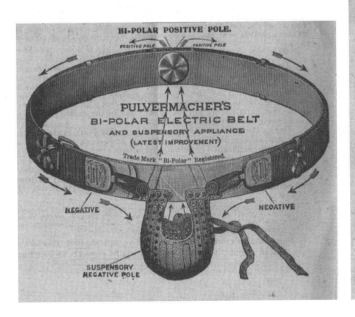

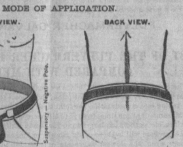

The purveyors of medical electricity were heavily into the manhood game. The standard item was a belt studded with "galvanic" discs, sewed to felt that was impregnated with a mildly irritating substance. The products of Dr. Von Graef and of Mr. Pulvermacher were of this sort. The presence of such a device with its "electric" flashes of discomfort undoubtedly lent very effective reassurance in cases that were essentially in the mind of the wearer.

Other treatments, like Dr. Rudolphe's, were more complicated. In fact there were private sanatoria that specialized in restoring virility. Information could be had in these cases through booklets that not only were mailed in a plain wrapper but also had no identification whatever on their plain white covers.

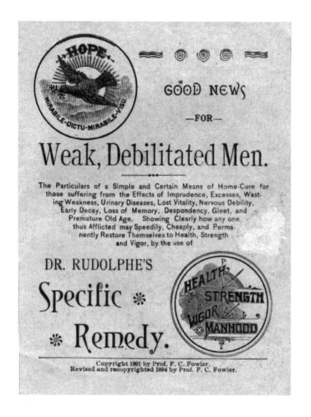

Dr. Rudolphe's Specific Remedy was a medicine which he solemnly agreed never to patent. It came in packages that cost $3.00 and Dr. Rudolphe said that one package could effect a cure in an ordinary case. The Von Graef Medical Company sold troches, or lozenges. They cost $3.00, $5.00 or $7.00 per package, according to strength.

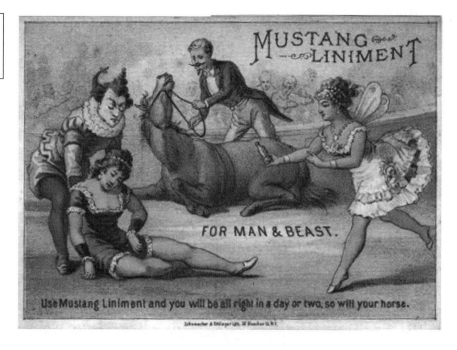

12. Veterinary Medicines

To the farmer in largely rural nineteenth century America, a medicine was a medicine. It either cured disease or it did not. If it did, it ought to cure disease in his numerous farm animals as well as in his numerous children. The only question was the proper dosage. "One for a man, two for horse" was the common maxim in medicine advertising.

Minard's Liniment was advertised with a resplendent image of Chancellor Bismark on horseback, as "the great internal and external remedy for man or beast." It contained ammonium chloride, turpentine, camphor and soap. This remedy was later styled as "The King of Pain," a slogan that may have had a special meaning for anyone who swallowed more than a spoonful.

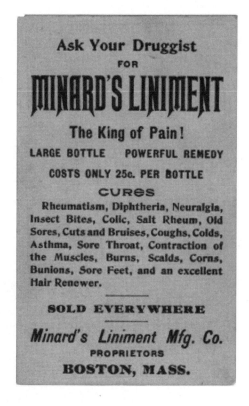

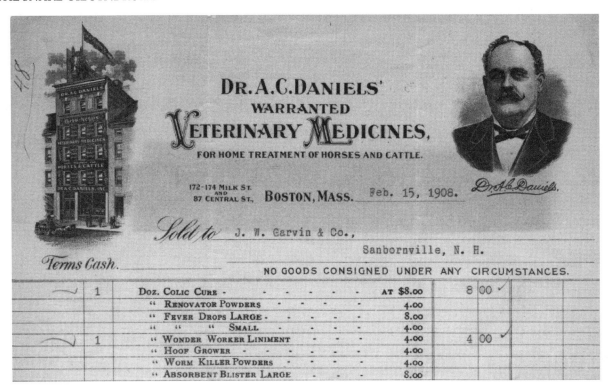

Dr. A. C. Daniels and Professor Flint stuck to animals. The partial billhead, above, shows a few of the many items that a line of veterinary products might contain.

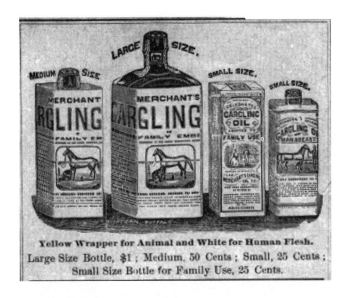

Yellow Wrapper for Animal and White for Human Flesh.
Large Size Bottle, $1 ; Medium, 50 Cents ; Small, 25 Cents ;
Small Size Bottle for Family Use, 25 Cents.

The advertising of Merchant's Gargling Oil has won a special affection among collectors. The companion horseshoe pieces, below, illustrate the dual use of the medicine in an understated manner, as did the different color wrappings for the same medicine when packaged for man and, in larger sizes, for the horse.

Dual appeals were not limited to a few local nostrums sold in rustic communities. Merchant's Gargling Oil was packaged in white for humans and in yellow for animals. (Can a horse gargle?) It employed a famous but rather ambiguous scene as its trademark, showing a fine Arabian stallion, attended by an Arab, outside a colorful tent that could have been pitched without embarrassment at Camelot (Plate 38). Merchant's also used images of girls framed by horseshoes, and horses chattering over the watering trough.

The line of sophisticated Dr. Warner's Safe Remedies was aimed at a variety of specific human diseases, but it included one bottle, embossed with the usual banker's safe, that was two and a half times the regular size. Collectors have argued whether or not Mr. Warner intended his products to be used for animals, and whether this rare container held the "animal cure." The answer is found in an obscure paragraph in Mr. Warner's almanac for 1893. His medical benefits were offered to all living creatures, but quietly.

FIRST INTRODUCED 1833.
MERCHANT'S GARGLING OIL is the standard Liniment of
the United States, and is good for Burns, Scalds, Rheumatism,
FleshWounds, Sprains, Bruises, Lame Back, Hemorrhoids or Piles,
Toothache, Sore Throat, Chilblains, Chapped Hands, and many
other diseases incident to man and beast.—Yellow wrapper for
animal and white for human flesh.
Manufactured at Lockport, N. Y., by M. G. O. Co., and sold by
all druggists. JOHN HODGE, Sec'y.

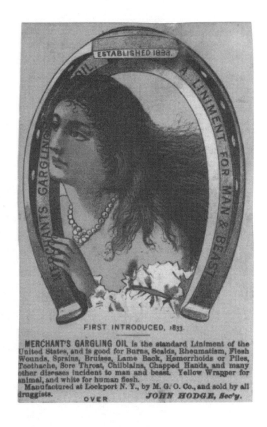

FIRST INTRODUCED, 1833.
MERCHANT'S GARGLING OIL is the standard Liniment of the
United States, and is good for Burns, Scalds, Rheumatism, Flesh
Wounds, Sprains, Bruises, Lame Back, Hemorrhoids or Piles,
Toothache, Sore Throat, Chilblains, Chapped Hands, and many
other diseases incident to man and beast. Yellow Wrapper for
animal, and white for human flesh.
Manufactured at Lockport N. Y., by M. G. O. Co., and sold by all
druggists. OVER JOHN HODGE, Sec'y.

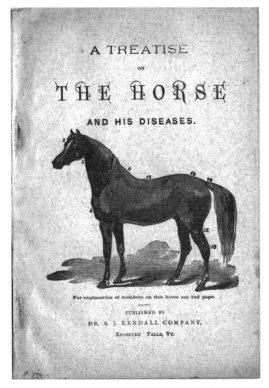

Almanacs, trade cards and posters were also devoted to products intended for animals only (Plates 37 and 38). There was an impressive array of nostrums for the horse, Gordon's Hoof Ointment, Gombault's Caustic Balsam, Cole's Veterinary Carbolisalve, Kendall's Spavin Cure, and Ulmer's Heave Powders, to name a few. Dr. Daniels had a full line of horse medicines and authored a heavy booklet entitled "The Horse." He also had a thinner one entitled "The Cat," which is seen less often.

Dr. Haas produced a "Horse & Cattle Remedy" and a "Hog & Poultry Remedy." Barker's did the whole job with one Horse, Cattle and Poultry Powder. Uncle Sam's Condition Powders were an earlier version of the same thing. What, specifically, were they good for? They put the critters in a better condition, of course.

Three learned treatises from the proprietors of medicines for animals. Clockwise, 96 pages from Dr. B. J. Kendall, manufacturer of a spavin cure; 64 pages from Dr. Frederick Humphreys about his homeopathic specialties for animals; and a mere 32 pages from Clay Glover, V. S., on how to feed the dog.

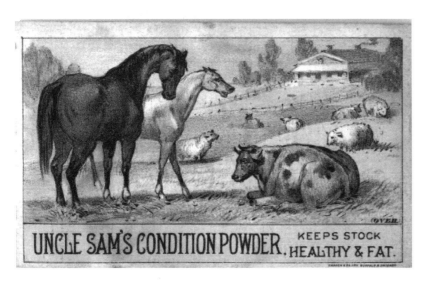

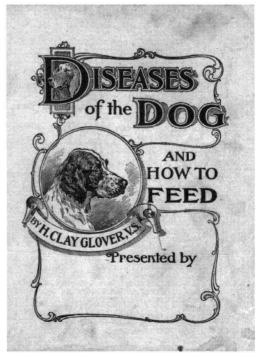

THE ELECTRIC TRINITY COMPLETE.

DR. CRAM'S
FLUID LIGHTNING!

Is a CERTAIN and almost INSTANTANEOUS cure for Head-ache, Neuralgia, Tic Doloureux, Tooth-ache, Ear-ache, and all other pains and suffering having their origin in a derangement of the nervous system. It leaves no scars! It leaves no stain! It is cleanly and easily applied! It is compact and portable. It is always ready for use, and is the cheapest medicine extant; from two to five drops are sufficient.

Images that associated medicine with electricity. Above, Alessandro Volta is shown on a trade card for Steifel's Boracic Soap. At left, Benjamin Franklin and his kite are appropriated by Cram's Fluid Lightning.

13.

Medical Electricity

A strong commitment to science fiction and a vast reservoir of credibility were the principal selling aids for devices predicated upon the medical benefits of electricity. As usual, there was a grain or two of scientific fact somewhere in the picture but this hardly amounted to a new system of health.

An Italian scientist named Luigi Galvani published his theory of "animal electricity" in 1791, based on experiments with the legs of a frog. He was able to show that muscle contraction produced a tiny current. Conversely, when two strips of dissimilar metal were joined, and the free ends were stuck into a pair of freshly dissected frog's legs, the legs jumped once or twice without the benefit of the rest of the frog. The two metal strips plus the juices of the frog do produce a tiny flow of electricity which causes the leg muscles to contract. The conclusion was irresistible that electricity must be a life-giving force.

Galvani's friend, Alessandro Volta, eliminated the frog in 1800 and instead used discs of dissimilar metal separated by pads soaked in salt water. His stack of discs, called a "voltaic pile," was the first crude battery. This simple arrangement lent itself easily to the construction of devices that could be applied to

Two almanacs that sold electric medicines, Dr. Christie's Magnetic Fluid and Trask's Magnetic Ointment. "Electric" was used interchangeably with "galvanic" and simply referred to a life-giving force.

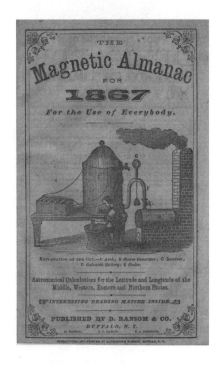

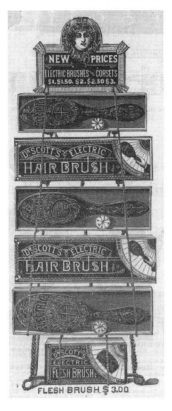

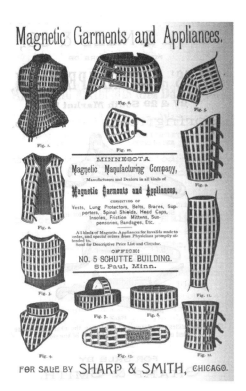

Dr. Scott's electric brushes are shown top left. Above, magnetic, or galvanic, articles worn beneath the clothing, as sold by Sharp & Smith, a large manufacturer of surgical instruments. At right, an electric belt studded with electrodes that provided a chemical tingle at least.

Diagram from The West Electric Cure Company of Chicago, illustrating what one proprietor called "the strengthening, life-giving, vitalizing influence of Galvanism" in his medicine.

the human form. There were many on the market during the patent medicine era that purported to generate and apply electricity of the right kind in the right place. They ranged from magical finger rings to bracelets, belts, corsets and even more elaborate devices. Some were intended to be worn under the clothes and others were made for administering treatment in the privacy of the bedroom.

The belts and some of the corsets and bracelets employed discs of copper and zinc sewn on flannel. There was a possibility of generating "galvanic" electricity here, using the moisture of the body and the chemicals in the flannel, but it seems that most scientific benefactors wanted to be sure the customer felt something. They impregnated the cloth with capiscum (extract of red pepper) or some other irritant that gave the wearer comfort of mind.

The electric theory also extended to such devices as Electric Hair Pins, Electric Hair Brushes and an Electric Nerve Pencil (Plate 39). These were not self-grooming aids driven by electric motors. They were passive devices that simply possessed and conveyed the life force. Following the same sound scientific theory were products for internal consumption like Electric Bitters, Electric Ointment, Electric Plaster, Cram's Fluid Lighting, Dalley's Galvanic Horse Salve, and Magnetized Food. Thomas' Eclectric Oil no doubt derived some benefit from phonetic confusion with these products without necessarily subscribing to the electric theory.

For those who sought health in a real jolt of electricity there appeared in the late 1880s a number of small well-made wooden boxes for the self-administration of appreciable amperage. They all contained batteries and a small transformer coil. The sufferer held onto one electrode with each hand, or he strapped one to his forehead and perhaps one to his leg. The shocks were mild enough but extremely satisfying. (Plate 40).

After the turn of the century, more kindly boxes appeared, covered with black imitation leather and lined with purple plush. Typically the lid held a half a dozen hollow glass instruments with electrodes visible within them. These could be fitted into a handle connected to a coil and a battery in the bottom of the box. When the apparatus was turned on, the tubes glowed with a faint ultraviolet light. The shapes of these curious glass tools defy description, except the one for irradiating the scalp, which was clearly designed as a rake (Plate 42).

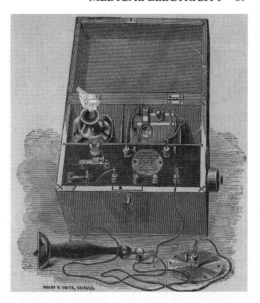

Two instruments that employed real electricity. The illustration above shows a bottle of acid for the adjacent wet cell battery in the rear of the box. The coil and vibrator are beneath the panel at the front. Displayed below with another battery box is a selection of electrodes that were applied to the patient.

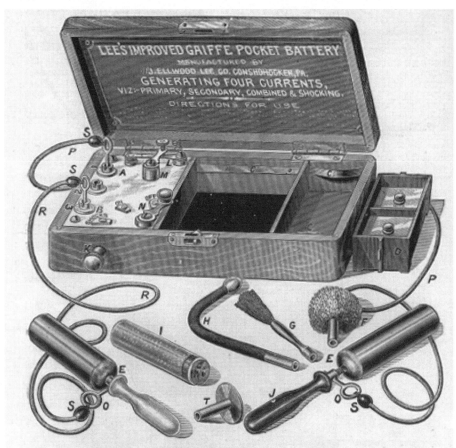

Explanation of Electrodes and Accessories which go with this Battery.

A. Positive Pole.   B. Negative Pole.   C. Springs to hold Cell.   D. Gaiffe Cell.
E. Nickeled Cylinder Handles.   F. Sponge Electrode.   G. Tinsel Brush Electrode.
H. Olive Pointed Electrode.   I. Bottle Bisulphate Mercury.   J. Universal Handles.
K. Current Regulator.   L. Rheotome.   M. Rheotome Regulator.   N. Current Switch.
O. Cord Tips.   P. and R. Doubly Insulated Silk Cord.   S. Insulators for Tips.
T. Circular Exciter Electrode.

4205. Price Complete with all Electrodes, $8.00.

OXYPATHOR DIRECTION BOOK   127

Showing Method of Treating for Tonsilitis

such a proceeding are extremely rare. The tonsils were created for some good purpose, supposedly to aid digestion and to guard the body against infection. Do not have them cut out or mutilated if they are troublesome, but use the Oxypathor instead and you will be delighted with the result.

Typhoid Fever—Typhus Fever and Other Fevers Without General Eruption.

Typhoid Fever.—Three-quarters of typhoid fever cases (there are approximately 250,000 in the United States annually) are attributed to the use of foul water; the rest to foul milk, food contaminated by flies or floating particles of filth, or to the inhalation

The Oxypathor, a typical "gaspipe", is shown in detail at right. Above is a page from the book of instructions with some of the claims made for this device.

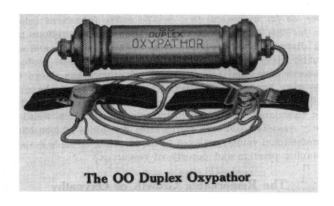

The OO Duplex Oxypathor

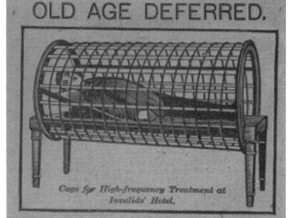

OLD AGE DEFERRED.

Cage for High-frequency Treatment at Invalids' Hotel.

The High-frequency treatment, if persisted in, gives relief and gradually overcomes the tendency to decay of the vital forces. Patients of seventy years of age, after a course of treatment, express themselves as feeling from ten to twenty years younger than when they began the treatment, and their general appearance certainly bears out the truth of their statements. The languid lose their apathy and feel able and active; the bilious obtain relief; the sluggish liver and bowels take on their normal activity and the result is improved vigor and general tone.

Even more impressive cabinet models of these machines were sold for use in doctors' offices. Once again there was a grain of medical benefit lurking among the quackery. Ultraviolet rays, in sufficient strength, can kill germs and also stimulate the skin to produce sun tan and a little Vitamin D. Deep radiant heat is now applied to sore muscles by electronic diathermy machines. The ultimate electrical developments, diagnostic and therapeutic X-rays and the CAT scan, have been such a revolutionary benefit to medicine that perhaps we can excuse electrical doctoring for feeling its way.

There was one class of medical devices that did not bother with the simulation of electric current. This sort of instrument, later referred to as a "gaspipe," operated strictly on the power of suggestion. Most of them consist-

ed of a short section of nickel tubing with a cap at each end, connected with a cloth-covered wire to a metal electrode. The user placed the metal capsule in a bowl of water, strapped the electrode on the offending part of his anatomy, and relaxed on his bed of pain. The life-giving force flowed out of the charcoal and sawdust or whatever had been stuffed into the gaspipe. Hercule Sanche made a fortune with his Oxydonor, which was modeled along these lines. His success stimulated imitations, produced by others, named the Oxypathor, Oxygenor, Oxygenator, Oxytonor, and the Oxybon.

More direct descendants of the irritating belt and the mysterious gaspipe are the rings and bracelets of special metals worn today by some arthritis sufferers. If they alleviate pain, why should we care whether it is overcome in the wrist by a force not yet understood, or overcome in the mind by the force of belief.

An advertisement from the 1917 edition of *Dr. Pierce's Memorandum Book Designed for Farmers, Mechanics and All People*. This high-frequency treatment was presumably available, even at this late date, at Dr. Pierce's Invalid's Hotel and Surgical Institute in Buffalo.

Plate 57. The American Indian was the source to which many nostrum manufacturers attributed their "natural" remedies, and this subject matter furnished a great many advertising images.

Plate 58. The Kickapoo Almanac, left, was issued by Healy & Bigelow, a Connecticut firm that was famous for its Indian medicine shows. Below, the improbable contest of Indian and bear on the cover of Dr. Morse's almanac was actually the logo of that proprietor. It recalls the image of St. George slaying the dragon, which graced every bottle of Lash's Bitters.

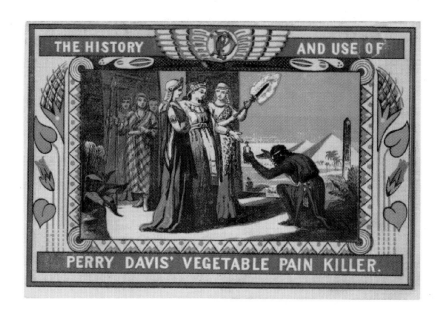

Plate 59. The mystique of foreign lands was evoked often in patent medicine advertising. A "returned missionary" was sometimes alleged to be the source of a remedy with an exotic name.

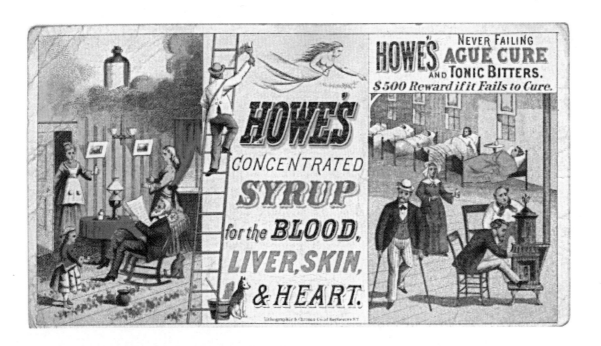

Plate 60. Patent medicines lent themselves readily to the before-and-after message, an advertising technique that they made into a visual cliche. Athlophoros, at bottom right, managed to convey the thought in a single image.

HIS MAJESTY *on the Esplanade at* WEYMOUTH

Graciously accepting a Box of Ching's Patent Worm Lozenges which was presented to him as a Valuable Medicine.

THE GENUINE
JOHANN HOFF'S
MALT EXTRACT

The Old Standby

Plate 61. An early testimonial, in the product endorsement category, is the English print above showing King George III accepting a box of Ching's Patent Worm Lozenges. *Courtesy of The British Museum*. At right, in a much later trade card, Hoff's Malt seeks to imply the patronage of Chancelor Bismark of Germany.

Plate 62. Lily Langtry, the actress, appears on the trade card below for Brown's Iron Bitters. It is doubtful that the nostrum proprietors secured the permission of the many stage celebrities they portrayed but they were furnishing free publicity. At bottom right is the ultimate in product endorsement, a testimonial from God! This French poster for Gaston Monier's Cod Liver Oil was published about 1900. It reads: "Take it! God orders it!" *Courtesy of The Philadelphia Museum of Art, William H. Helfand Collection.*

BROWN'S IRON BITTERS
THE BEST TONIC

MRS. LANGTRY
THE JERSEY LILY

Prenez-en !..
HUILE DE FOIE DE MORUE ··· ··· GASTON MONIER
BORDEAUX
Dieu l'ordonne

Plate 63. Public issues and current events were the subject of comic advertisements during the patent medicine era. At left above, a suffragette patiently urges the vote for women. At top right, is an allusion to Darwin's new theory of evolution, the descent of man from the ape. The trade card below left spoofs the Gilbert and Sullivan operetta, "Trial by Jury." At right we see Nellie Bly, the pioneering lady reporter, preparing for her famous trip around the world in emulation of the Jules Verne novel "Around the World in Eighty Days."

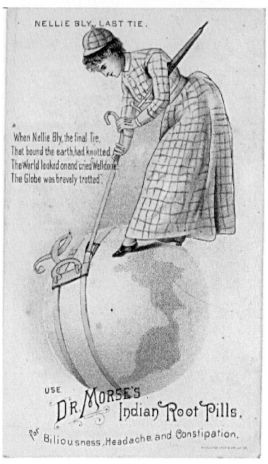

Plate 64. The rather crude cartoon, above, appeared on a stock card that could be used by any advertiser, who overprinted his name on the fence shown behind the racehorse. The lithograph below was on the back cover of an advertising pamphlet published by Sulphur Bitters about 1880. Was this an appeal to prejudice or a comment on changing social attitudes in the wake of Reconstruction? It shows Abolitionist leader Frederick Douglass and his white wife. The caption ends "...Golly he is going to take de Sulphur Bitters for his complexion."

Plate 65. Ethnic satire was not directed at the blacks alone. It lampooned all of the major immigrant groups in nineteenth century America: the Irish, the Germans and the Chinese. The pesticide Rough on Rats, produced by nostrum proprietor Wells Richardson & Co., chose to illustrate the persistent slur that Chinese ate rats.

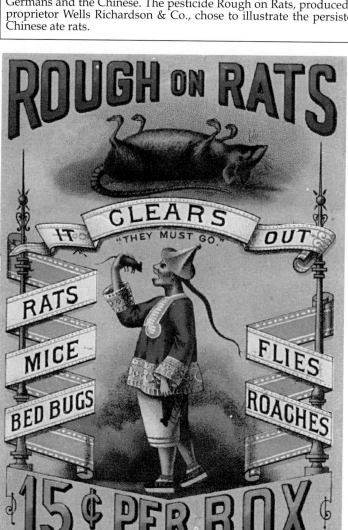

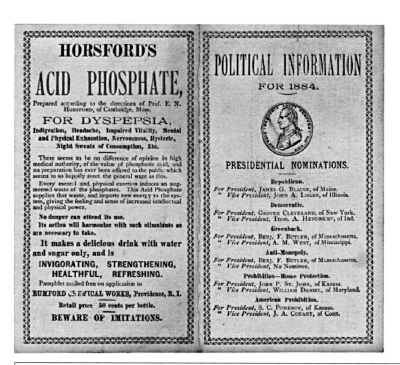

Plate 66. The use of political figures in their advertising made some of the patent medicine proprietors appear to take sides. Shown here are three trade cards from the bitter and often scurrilous campaign of 1884, won by Grover Cleveland, the Democratic candidate. The portrait of Jefferson Davis at bottom right, was distributed by Harter's Iron Tonic in 1888, apparently to suggest that the leaders of the Old South were not to be forgotten.

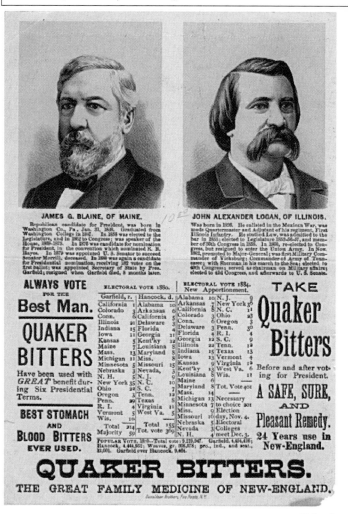

14. Health Foods

On the edge of the medicine category, but nonetheless popular shelf items worthy of note, were products that promised to supply physical strength through nutrition (Plate 43).

Some of these, like Wheat Bitters and Duffy's Malt, must be classified with the bracers. Others undoubtedly bore a close relationship to the maltous beverages. Malt Tonic, Maltine, Malt Nutrine, Hoff's Malt, Hop Tonic and Hops and Malt all appear to follow this line. Best Tonic was in fact a medicinal product of the famous beer makers, the Anheuser Busch Brewing Company.

The vinous beverages must not be thought lacking in nutrition. In this category are Vin Malt, Vinol, Vino Kolafra and Beef Wine and Iron.

Honest to goodness solid cereals recommended themselves to invalids and children. Imperium Granum was packaged in a large yellow box and advertised by trade cards featuring an abundance of babies (Plate 43). This product, patented in 1860 by one Edward Heaton, struggled for official recognition as a medicine, which it won in 1881. Mellin's Food, Ridge's Food and Eskay's Food also made a pitch for the infant market.

Lastly there were products with a milk base: Carnrick's Soluble Food, Well's & Richardson's Lactated Food, Lactart, Bovinine and Kumysgen. Most of these managed to get a cow into their advertising.

Health foods were advertised primarily with children in mind and, as you would expect, children's images predominated.

Malt extracts were a major contender in this class. Nicholson's Liquid Bread had a high nutritive value but a substantial alcoholic content. The Hoff's trade card shows an exhibit at the World Columbian Exposition of 1893, looking rather like Berlin's Brandenberg Gate. Pabst's Malt was a great favorite, well advertised. Bovinine was a meat extract.

15.

Cosmetics and Perfumes

By the end of the century many of the medicine proprietors sold a line of products that included cosmetics, perfumes and various aids for personal grooming. The medicine salesman, while still affectionately called a "drummer," no longer spent his days making a pitch to the consuming public on the sidewalk. The product was retailed over the counter in response to the demand created by advertising. On his visits to the drugstore the salesman could conveniently offer a plurality of wares.

These additional products did not necessarily bear the same name as the medicine that gave his company its start. It is likely that several were developed by another proprietor and acquired along the way during the series of corporate successions and acquisitions that characterized the medicine industry during its later decades. At one time, the famous Charles N. Crittendon manufactured Dean's Rheumatic Pills, German Corn Cure, Glenn's Sulphur Soap, Dr. Graves' Heart Regulator, Hale's Honey of Horehound and Tar, Hill's Instantaneous Whisker Dye, Japanese Corn File, Dr. Eli Osborne's Golden Liniment, Morse's Revivum Hair Restorer and Knowles' Insect Powder. The all-important assets traded through the years were, of course, the well-known names and product images built up by diligent advertising.

Ladies' fashions of the last half of the nineteenth century favored very long hair. In the days before there were numerous beauty parlors that catered to the average woman, she spent considerable time taking care of her own tresses. Many products offered to help her. There were hair conditioners, hair strengtheners, hair restorers and hair dyes. Usually the hair product suggested that it could fulfill several of these functions. Hair products for gentlemen were largely baldness cures or whisker dyes.

The most famous preparation for the hair was a smelly concoction promoted by the Seven Sutherland Sisters, no great beauties but possessed of enough hair between them to make the mythological Rapunzel green with envy. Each of these ladies' tresses reached almost to the floor and there was no doubt of them being genuine. The sisters came from Lockport, New York, an area that gave the world several renowned patent medicines and perhaps that is what inspired the family. The seven ladies travelled extensively to promote their Hair Grower and were highly successful. Later life

Products for the hair were an important part of the personal care market. Hall's and Ayer's preparations were among the most widely sold.

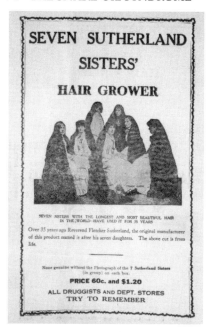

found the sisters still in Lockport, eccentric spinsters living together in an elaborate mansion reflecting considerable wealth.

Hall's Vegetable Sicilian Hair Renewer was manufactured in Nashua, New Hampshire by Reuben P. Hall who allegedly obtained the formula from a destitute Italian sailor. It was composed chiefly of lead acetate and sulfur to which, in later days, was added glycerin, capsicum and bay rum. J.C. Ayer & Co. of Boston bought out the product in 1895, after about 15 years of business, probably to eliminate it as a competitor to Ayer's Hair Vigor. Another prominent hair preparation was Barry's Tricopherous for the Skin and Hair, a concoction of castor oil, alkanet root, oil of bergamot and, at some point, cantharides. Neither the composition nor the jaw-breaking name appeared to hinder its popularity (Plate 45).

Certain products emphasized their ability to grow hair where it no longer appeared. Hair Revivum offered pictures of infants suddenly become hirsute far beyond their years. Parker's Hair Balsam showed a queen surrounded by bald courtiers, probably a reference to Elizabeth I of England whom historians have long suspected was subject to this distressing condition.

Men had a hair dressing problem in the Victorian era that time has largely solved. This problem was the promotion and care of the luxuriant beards decreed by fashion. A dark black beard was the most envied. Hill's Whisker Dye and Buckingham's Whisker Dye were two aids to the perfection of this kind of adornment. Buckingham's distributed fine metamorphic trade cards that substituted a black beard for the white one with a flick of the finger, erasing with one stroke half the years of the family patriarch (Plate 44).

Macassar Oil, another preparation for males, added lustre to the hair. This vegetable product was extracted from a bean grown in the area of the Macassar Straits, between Borneo and Celebes. It smelled strongly and left a stain, giving the name "antimacassars" to the white doilies that were placed on the high backs of Victorian arm-chairs.

Cocoaine was another hair oil, extracted from the pod of the cocoa plant that also produces chocolate. The product was made by the Joseph Burnett Company in Boston. Nowadays the

A spectrum of hair growers and conditioners, including the renowned Seven Sutherland Sisters concoction *(William H. Helfand Collection)* and the product with the confusing name, Cocoaine.

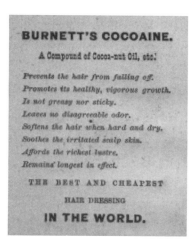

Clockwise, a die-cut trade card for Oriental Toothpaste, which seemed to owe little to the Far East, and a trade card for Phenol Dentrifice, which must have tasted a bit like Lysol disinfectanct. Trix was a breath purifier and Deodoriferouspedes was a foot powder. The modern type of personal deodorant was not a market factor during the patent medicine era.

brand name is frequently misspelled and you see Burnett's "cocaine" listed as a Victorian pain killer.

Oral hygiene was not unknown during the great patent medicine era but its advertising was nothing to compare with that of the toothpaste and mouthwash industry today. A few quaint Victorian items of this nature appear: Oriental Toothpaste, Geer's Phenol Dentrifice and Ivory Polish for the Teeth. The best advertised dentifrice was Hoyt's Rubifoam, a pink powder that caused the user to froth at the mouth like a mad dog (Plate 47).

Bad breath was attacked forthrightly in post-Civil War days by Aromatic Breath Cartridges whose trade card displayed a fine picture of a Zoave in full dress uniform (Plate 68). There was also Trix Breath Perfume, which advertised with great brevity for its day. At the other end of the anatomy stood Deodoriferouspedes which, despite its semi-Latin name, was a humble preparation for rendering hot tired feet more attractive.

The line between medical aid and cosmetic beautifier has never been an easy one to draw. The effect of a number of the druggists' products was admittedly only skin deep. Among them were Dr. Hebra's Viola Creme, Cuticura Soap, Pozzoni's Complexion Powder, Frekleine, Mrs. Soule's Eradicator, Laird's Bloom of Youth, Hagan's Balm, and Hind's Honey and Almond Cream (Plate 47). Also in this general category we must put the corn cures, corn files and medicated gloves for the hands at night.

Perfume advertising during the patent medicine era is worthy of a volume in itself. The subjects of illustration tended to be pretty girls, pastoral scenes and children, but they included some examples of great beauty (Plate 46).

The trade cards for Murray & Lanham's Florida Water, showing birds and flowers, must be accorded a

Skin care products of the nineteenth century included Dr. Hebra's, named for a prominent dermatologist, and two products that are still on the market today, Cuticura Soap and Williams Shaving Stick.

The Ricksecker's trade card was distributed at the New Orleans Exposition of 1885. The Hoyt's card was die cut and the bottle image would punch out to form a hinge. It could be slipped over the top of the page to act as a bookmark. At bottom are four mini-almanacs issued when Colgate & Co. was primarily a perfumer.

place among the most striking lithography of their day. Hoyt's German Cologne issued a charming series of "ladies' calendars" that were actually large trade cards showing girls and children. It also distributed die-cut bookmarks that stand up, bearing children's faces.

The perfumes advertised on trade cards were the popular-priced brands: Austen's Forest Flower Cologne, Belgravia Cologne, Lazell's, Reid's, Solon Palmer's, Eastman's Fraxinella, Armant's and others. A few names like Colgate & Co. and Caswell & Massey are still familiar to us today. Colgate's issued a few mini-almanacs with richly decorated covers.

Some trade cards for these perfumes were produced on absorbent stock, rather like stiff blotting paper, impregnated with the scent that was being advertised. This paper did nothing for the quality of the lithography and its softness has caused most specimens to show considerable wear, particularly at the corners. However, if you are lucky, you may still be able to catch an authentic whiff from the bygone days when these bright bits of advertising were on the drugstore counter.

PURITY

The above picture is a miniature reproduction of Rowan's celebrated painting, entitled "PURITY." A copy of the artist proof edition, size 19 x 26, without any advertisement, may be secured through your Druggist by purchasing a package of PURITY. Perfume (retail price $2.00) ; sending the coupon attached to the bottle and 25 cents for express charges to

FRENCH, CAVE & CO., 435 Arch Street, Philadelphia, Pa.

(SEE OTHER SIDE)

Four trade cards used to sell popular-priced perfumes in the patent medicine era.

PART THREE

The Message

16.   Fear

There are a number of ways to persuade a man that he is sick and needs to buy a medicine, as one turn-of-the-century writer has pointed out. "You may wheedle him, cajole him, intoxicate him with promises, tickle his fancy or frighten him out of his boots."[1] This Part will examine the principal advertising themes that were used to sell patent medicine.

In the early 1800s, as we might expect, the instruments of persuasion aimed at the sick and suffering were rather simple and direct. We have already seen examples of one such approach—unreserved assurance that the medicine was a positive cure for whatever was amiss. A few nostrum advertisers chose to play on the opposite emotion—the fear of illness and death—in an explicit fashion whose terror has faded to a quaint charm. The Parr

The dangling spider with swords for legs is marked *La Grippe*. The chess players are Constipation, in military uniform, and Consumption, with a Chinaman's pigtail. In the background, left, is Biliousness wearing a crown. This cartoon, full of threatening symbols, advertised Oxien Tablets, a cure for influenza composed of sugar, starch, and the oils of sassafrass and wintergreen.

English Pad showed the cloaked figure of Death, with a scythe, hovering over the pitiful sufferer (Plate 49). Radam's Microbe Killer offered the image of a man fighting off a skeleton with the aid of a large club. This logo was copied, without apology, by Hunt's Remedy.

The most macabre advertising was probably that issued in the late 1890s by Antikamnia on several calendars that were sent to members of the medical profession. They showed remarkably faithful death's-heads in a variety of everyday scenes to remind the doctor, if he needed reminding, that the grim reaper was staring him in the face at every turn (Plate 50).

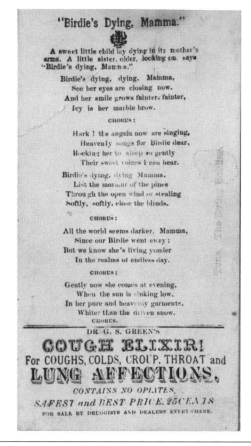

Dr. G. S. Green has given us several of the many verses of the unabashed tear-jerker, "Birdie's Dying, Mama", which painted an all-too-true picture of a child dying from tuberculosis in the nineties.

The demons that cause pain. There is nothing funny about the travails of this sufferer who is chasing away his ills, described as "a cough", with German Syrup.

Several proprietors used spooks, with a greater or lesser degree of ghostliness, among them Mason & Pollard's Anti-Malarial Pills (Plate 50). In time, these spirits were reduced by Parker's Tonic and Myer's Girondin to the level of impudent demons, the kind with little pitchforks that cause horrible stomach cramps or splitting headaches.

At length, we see comic mourners, a corpse sitting up in a casket and finally death reduced to a pun by Wood's Cough Drops ("Stop your Coffin").

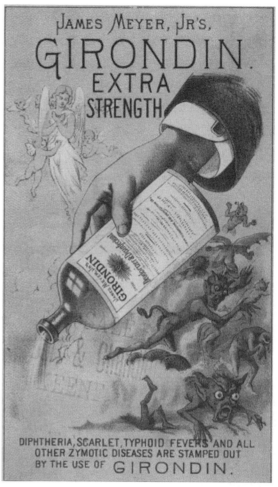

The weight of fear has lightened a bit in these somewhat later images. Fitzgerald's Invigorator shows us a talking corpse who wishes the medicine had been invented a bit earlier. Meyer's Girondin is scattering the imps of disease, and Wood's is making the whole thing a simple joke.

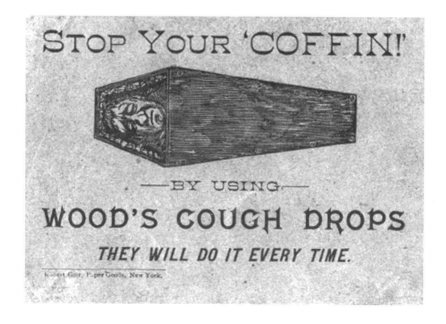

Some of the almanacs and booklets of pseudo-medical advice used highly unpleasant drawings of diseased organs in an advanced state of disrepair. Two particularly unattractive examples are found in Scovill's Almanac for 1863 and a booklet advertising Cancer Plant Remedy.

For downright realism, however, there was nothing to beat an actual tapeworm. This creature was a truly frightening symbol in an age when these intestinal parasites were an all too frequent danger to health. Specimens were exhibited in jars by sidewalk pitchman and at medicine shows. These were usually worms of abnormal size, several feet in length, which most commonly occurred in cattle and were usually purchased by the medicine peddler at the local slaughterhouse.

JOHN G. M'DONALD, Esq.
Cured by Swaim's Panacea.

Two examples of the realism school of scare advertising from an 1883 pamphlet of Dr. Swaim, who was not known for his tenderness with the public.

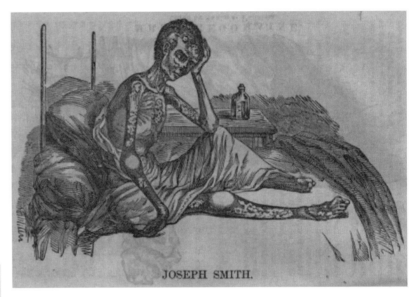

JOSEPH SMITH.

At right, two clinical pictures from a pamphlet selling Fluid Extract of Cancer-Plant. It seems that the medicine was aimed chiefly at ulcers and skin eruptions more typical of secondary syphilis, than of cancer.

Left, is the inside cover of *The Kickapoo Oracle* (1894). The tapeworm was a common disease in the days before proper inspection and refrigeration of meat.

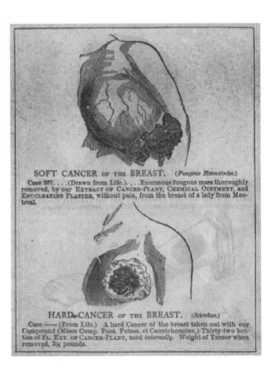

SOFT CANCER of the BREAST. (*Fungous Hæmatodes.*)
Case 287....(Drawn from Life.)....Enormous fungous mass thoroughly removed, by our EXTRACT OF CANCER-PLANT, CHEMICAL OINTMENT, and ENUCLEATING PLASTER, without pain, from the breast of a lady from Montreal.

HARD CANCER of the BREAST. (*Scirrhus.*)
Case ——— (From Life.) A hard Cancer of the breast taken out with our Compound (Misce Comp. Fuss. Potass. et Caontchoucine,) Thirty-two bottles of FL. EXT. OF CANCER-PLANT, used *internally*. Weight of Tumor when removed, 8½ pounds.

17. Doctors and Druggists

From the standpoint of marketing, the patent nostrum grew up independent of the normal established channels of medicine sales. Its merchandising descended, at least in spirit, from the wandering pedlar with his wagon. In the nineteenth century, the doctor dispensed pills and often mixed and sold other medicines. The pharmacist was in business to compound medicines himself, rather than to distribute medicines produced by others. It was only later, when patent medicine advertising boosted the popular demand for particular products, that they began to appear on the shelves of the pharmacy.

After the itinerant pitchman, the other classic source of patent medicine sales was the country store. America was predominantly rural in the 1800s, its population further dispersed after the Civil War with the pacifying of the Indians and the opening of vast new lands in the West. Small clusters of farms might not support a pharmacy but any country store could carry such medical achievements as Hostetter's Stomach Bitters, Smith's Bile Beans or Paine's Celebrated Green Mountain Balm of Gilead. Later, the medicine manufacturer would also counsel and sell his customers directly, by mail.

In all, the patent medicine proprietor was ideally suited to attack the doctors, the druggists and medicine in general, at the same time that he was selling it. Nineteenth century doctors were frequently criticized, even within their own profession, for over-prescribing harsh chemicals. The nostrum manufacturer was able to use this issue. The prescription written by the doctor was, after all, the chief competitor of the pre-bottled nostrum, and the patent medicine proprietor was likely to benefit from distrust of the medical profession. It is not surprising to find the doctor portrayed in patent medicine advertising as pompous and elegant, therefore priced out of the reach of the average American.

Consider two striking examples of "bad doctor" advertising (Plate 52). "No need for you, Doctor, now that we have Tutt's Pills," says the lady on the face of the Tutt's almanac. "Not at all Doctor . . . I'm taking the (W)Right Pills," says the patient in his easy chair, pictured on the Wright's trade card.

While some nostrum proprietors sold their potions by inveighing against the medical profession, the chemicals

The Doctor Image. Dignifed, wise, reassuring, the portrait of an established physician was a powerful sales tool. The anti-doctor argument was also used to sell some patent medicines.

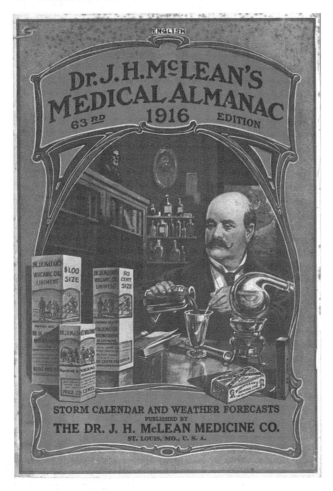

they prescribed and the fees they charged, others were equally successful with advertising built upon the image of the "good doctor" (Plate 51). Certainly in less sophisticated communities the doctor had a respected position in society and undoubtedly deserved it, for the long hours of poorly compensated efforts that were the lot of most medical men. Yet deeper than this, the mystique of the doctor is as old as the tribal chaman, and reassurance in a personal form has always been especially effective in matters of health.

In the 1800s, more than a few ambitious and business-minded practitioners became nostrum proprietors after witnessing the success of something they had first mixed themselves. Other proprietors of nostrums became instant doctors for advertising purposes. For those who drew up short of an outright deception on this score, there was at least the possibility of claiming that their remedy was discovered by a doctor and for that reason bore a doctor's name.

The products that featured a doctor frequently characterized him as a benefactor willing to share the fruits of his expertise with the suffering at low cost. This approach was undertaken without restraint by

The druggist also came in for some attention. Dr. McLean, above, invoked the mystery of the laboratory. When the drugstore itself advertised, it was frequently on a color postcard. At right is a 1903 view of a famous old drugstore in Kansas City, known for the distinctive bottles of its proprietary medicines. The style is more that of the European apothecary shop than the corner drugstore typical of this country.

285.   Owl Drug Store, Kansas City, Mo.

Plate 67. The Hop Bitters Company had no hesitation in advertising its product across the face of the American flag. A number of other patent medicines were similarly advertised. Tippecanoe (trade card immediately above) was a bitters sold by the H.H. Warner Company in a bottle designed to look like a log. "Tippecanoe" was also the nickname that helped elect William Henry Harrison to the Presidency in 1840, recalling his most notable battle against the Indians.

Plate 68. The "Zoave" on the trade card for Aromatic Breath Cartridges, above, wears the uniform of a Union regiment in the Civil War. The cover of Doan's 1908 Almanac reflected the new naval strength of the United States and the intense patriotism engendered by the Spanish-American War fought ten years earlier. Uncle Sam is shown as the object of the envy of various foreign powers in the cartoon that graces the cover of Green's Almanac for 1911.

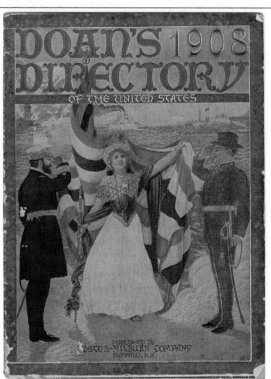

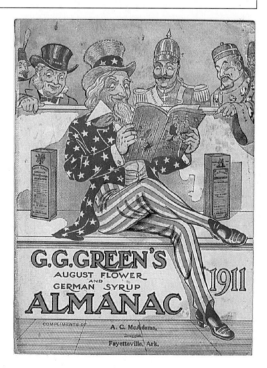

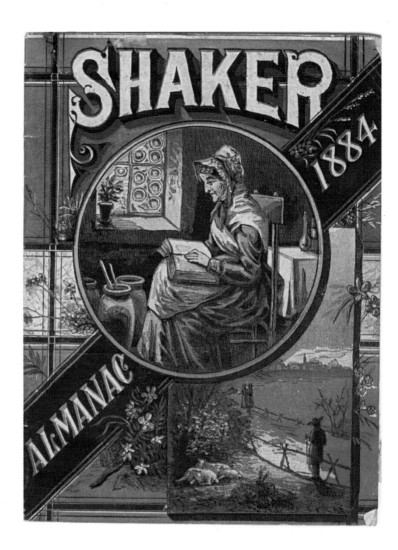

Plate 69. Religious themes were common in medicine advertising. At top right is the cover of a Shaker Almanac, advertising Mother Seigel's Syrup and other herbal remedies allegedly compounded by this sect, an offshoot of the Quakers. At left and below are two biblical scenes without advertising that were distributed by Jayne's Carminative Balsam. At left is "Rebecca at the Well," and at right is "Words of Comfort."

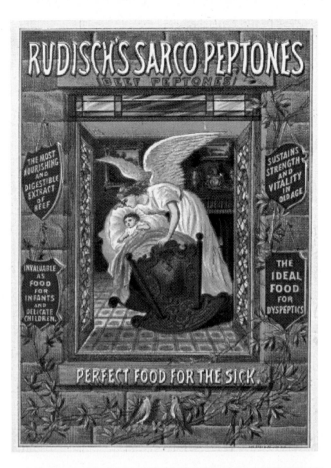

Plate 70. The image of an angel is found on early trade cards for patent medicines, like that above for Tolu Rock and Rye, and also on much later cards like that for Sarco-Peptones, right. The angel had a comfortable nondenominational association and also gently reminded the purchaser of human mortality.

Plate 71. Antikamnia, a headache remedy, issued a series of large calendar cards that included three or four of nuns in their habits. The 1904 calendar entitled "Confidence" is at left. The 1909 calendar, entitled "Purity" has a somewhat different appeal.

Plate 72. There were very few medicine advertisements that could be considered risque and even partial nudity was rare. The two examples here are intended to be allegorical figures.

Plate 73. When illuminated from behind, the hold-to-light card shown below allowed an image on the back to join the picture on the face. In this manner, the partly-clad lady at right appears in the space between the young man and the farmer gesticulating at left, courtesy of Lash's Bitters.

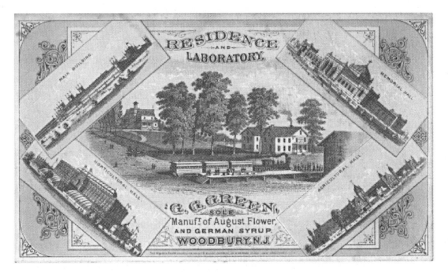

Plate 74. The Centennial Exposition of 1876, held in Philadelphia, helped the trade card to achieve prominence as an advertising medium. Views of four Exposition buildings are shown on the card above distributed for the occasion by the G.G. Green Company. Below is a mechanical card with a rotating disc held to the back of the image by a grommet, permitting the calendar page and the girl's face to be changed each month.

Plate 75. Immediately above and below is a metamorphic trade card advertising Scovill's Sarsaparilla, shown at top closed and at bottom open.

Plate 76. A rare side-opening metamorphic, advertising Hood's Sarsaparilla, is shown above, closed at the left and open at right. In the trade card immediately left, the stars spell out "Hood's Pills" when the card is held to the light and all of them become visible.

Plate 77. At right is a pop-up card, the rarest of the mechanical type of metamorphic trade card. As the card is opened, the little girl raises the toothbrush to her mouth.

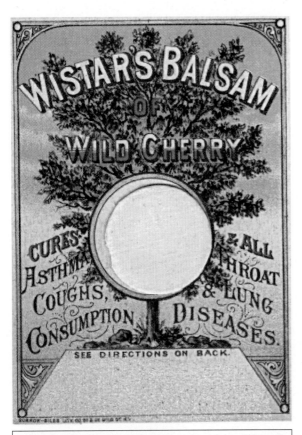

Plate 78. The trade card above, advertising Wistar's Balsam of Wild Cherry, has a disc at its center that glows faintly in the dark and an abrasive area at the bottom for striking matches.

Plate 79. The Lawson's Curative card above, was impregnated with cobalt chloride. When moist, the figures are pink and when dry they are blue, giving some indication of the humidity.

Plate 80. This charming advertisement for Krause's Headache Capsules, shown three-quarters of actual size, was die-cut from light cardboard but too fragile for extended use.

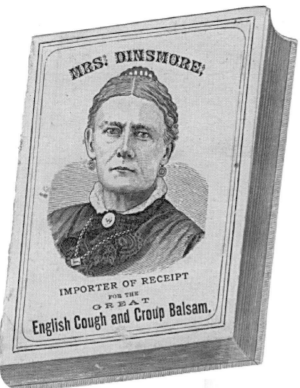

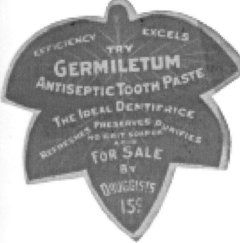

Plate 81. A selection of die-cut trade cards in fanciful shapes. The card that advertises Laird's Bloom of Youth, bottom right, is a miniature easel that can stand up against its paper back rest.

Dr. Pierce's Favorite Prescription, Dr. King's Wonderful Discovery and Dr. Radcliffe's Golden Wonder. Others were able to combine the doctor image with some of the "natural remedies" appeal used by the anti-doctors. The Dr.'s Kilmer, father and son, sold Kilmer's Swamp Root to succeeding generations of sufferers by blending medical professionalism with honest herbalism.

The doctor with his own medical breakthrough! Three nostrums that claimed a physician with a medical achievement of great magnitude.

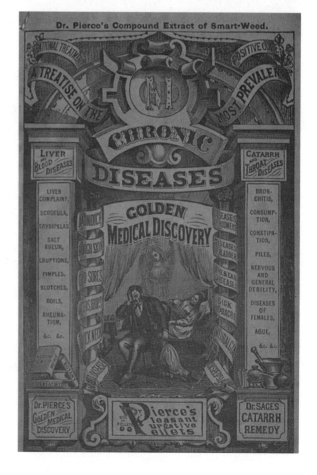

The Little Doctor. Children dressed as adults were a familiar contrivance with useful overtones. The child is emulating a role model and at the same time suggesting that the product has become a part of the family.

18. Nature's Remedies

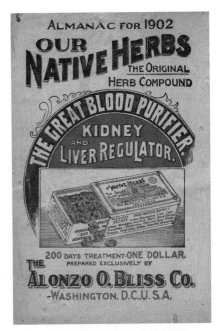

One response to the fear of harsh medicines and the antipathy to doctors was the "back to nature" advertising, embraced to the point of suffocation by the herbalist and Indian remedy people. In addition to the arguments that "natural remedies" were safer and more effective, there were philosophical overtones that enhanced this appeal and the patent medicine vendors exploited them fully.

The back-to-nature theme had many variations. It drew support from respectable medical opinion which had begun to suggest the dangers inherent in the unlimited use of compounds containing mercury, antimony, lead, arsenic and other chemical substances. Reliance on the leaves and roots of field and forest, and upon the folkways of earlier times, had a simple reassuring quality. The notion that plant substances were ordained to support and relieve living creatures offered a sort of philosophical harmony. Avoiding the expense of formal doctoring and drugstore prescriptions appealed to the practical and self-reliant.

To start with, there were patent nostrums based upon the alleged medicinal value of familiar fruits and vegetables. This approach has continued to be successful down through the years. California Syrup of Figs, Ficus Carica and a number of other fig products capitalized on the well recognized efficacy of this fruit as a laxative, a characteristic that it undoubtedly shared with many other "natural" products (Plate 53). Sad to relate, the well-known California Syrup, whose advertising featured clusters of ripe figs, was an elixir of senna. Other familiar garden products that inspired medicines were Brown's Sarsaparilla and Tomato Bitters, Smith's Pineapple and Buttermilk Pills, and the famous Paine's Celery Compound.

Certain herbs have served man well for centuries. Chinchona bark furnished quinine, which was the principal medicine for malaria until World War II gave an impetus to the development of the synthetic substitute, atabrin, among others. Digitalis for the heart came from the foxglove plant; the coca leaf produced cocaine, and the opium poppy, morphine. But before it was through, the patent medicine industry carried the herbal bit to extremes, presenting as scientific fact every whisper of folklore that ascribed a benefit to one of the common plants of the field. Medicines were based on prickly ash, buchu, dogwood, chickweed, liverwort, stargrass, boneset, male-fern, hollyhock, pipsissewa, snake-root, water pepper and pumpkin seed. Only a few of these botanicals are considered today to have any therapeutic value. Not only did the nostrum vendor tout these substances. Most of them were solemnly offered as pressed herbs or fluid extracts, for compounding prescriptions, by the reputable drug houses like Parke Davis, S.W. Gould, S.B. Penick, Allaire Woodward, and Cheny & Myrick (Plate 56).

The Bliss almanac, at top, advertises a compound of unspecified herbs, simply relying on the generic appeal of nature remedies. Smith's Pineapple and Butternut Pills, center, offer familiar vegetable substances. At bottom we see the exotic Sweetser's Iceland Moss Troches.

Indian medicines were, presumably, all natural. Here are three images of the squaw. At left, in informal dress, in an early poster courtesy the Library of Congress. At right, in what closely resembles a harem costume. Below, the lady gathering herbs. The golden secret of the Oswego turns out to be Austen's Swa-geh Remedy.

Some nostrums cited twenty or thirty herbal constituents, one of which could presumably offer the customer some prospect of help. Others, like Taylor's Sweet Gum and Mullein or Pierce's Smart Weed, used the name of the harmless plant and employed as the active ingredient morphine or opium (Plate 55).

Many of the herbal medicines sought to involve in their advertising an association with the primitive and foreign peoples who were said to cherish such remedies. Foremost among those was of course the American Indian, who, if all the proprietors can be believed, had a pharmacological use for everything that grew (Plate 57).

In the 1880s the disappearance of the frontier was very recent and the Wild West was only just tamed. The Indian as a symbol had a certain duality. In the East, the Indian was on his way to becoming a noble savage, betrayed by the advance of civilization. In the West, where there were still people with first-hand experience, the Indian was honored largely as the subject of the thrilling exploits of men like Wild Bill Hickock and General George Custer. Given the rudimentary state of national communications, each region was free to enjoy its own preferred image.

The American Indian was probably the most widely ascribed source of mysterious medical remedies. He suggested strength, independence and native sagacity. We have some of the same flavor today in the last-of-the-cowboys advertising represented by the Marlboro Man. The earlier advertising was more prone to depict

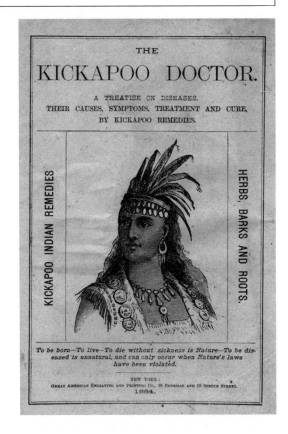

Yes, there really was a Kickapoo tribe and, in 1889, a Kickapoo Indian Agency that purported to supply Kickapoo braves for medicine shows.

incipient violence while the later pitches concentrated upon tranquility among the wigwams. The Indian maiden came in for a certain amount of attention. She was the one who gathered the herbs and tended the sick, so her portrayal was justified despite her sometimes scanty clothing.

The earlier medicines associated themselves with the Indian in the abstract. Indian Oil, Indian Sagwah and Indian Wine Bitters (Plate 26) are examples. Their advertising booklets recounted the "Secrets of Indian Life," usually derived from the enterprising trapper who rescued the chief's son from a bear and received the formula for the special potion in return.

In time, the medicine vendor sought added credibility by identifying a more particular Indian source. Nostrums were thrust upon unsuspecting tribes of alleged medical skill with colorful names, like the Kickapoos. A hundred years later, Al Capp can use a reference to Kickapoo Joy Juice, in his cartoon strip "Li'l Abner," with the certainty that it will

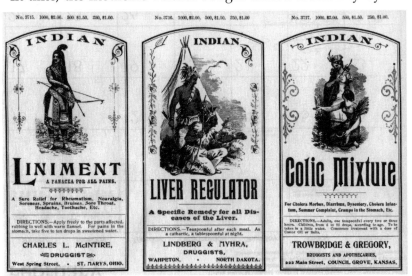

If it has an Indian on it, it will sell! Stock labels from the 1893 sample book of The Merchant's Publishing Company, as supplied to local druggists for their own mixtures.

Other exotic settings for the proprietor's patent medicine wares. At left, Anker has in mind Arabia, perhaps. Below, Royal Remedies has clearly identified India. Ayer's appears to show Ottoman Turks, although the back of this card has a text in Greek, which would seem to be a major public relations error.

not only entertain but ring true in the American folk memory. The extensive line of Kickapoo products was advertised well on a series of trade cards depicting Indian life and by a number of almanacs and booklets including "Life and Scenes Among the Kickapoo Indians," "The Kickapoo Indian Doctor," and "The Kickapoo Indian Dream Book" (Plate 58).

For those who might be less impressed by the American Indian, the mystique of foreign lands and exotic cultures was frequently invoked as an aid in selling patent medicines. Egypt was a distinct favorite. Pharaohs and lotus columns adorned advertising for Perry Davis' Pain Killer (Plate 59). Ayer's produced a "sealed" booklet entitled "A Night with Ramses II."

Arab medical skill was the message of Anker's Pain Expeller. Hayne's Arabian Balsam noted that its principal ingredient, pinetree gum, had been used by the Arabian people since biblical times. Turkish Cough Cure (Plate 59) and Persian Balm (Plate 97) added to the Near East parade.

The Far East was also well represented. There was Hindoo Kidney Cordial, Himalaya Compound and Kennedy's East India Bitters. Sapanule, an ordinary glycerin syrup for chest problems, pursued a Chinese theme on a number of trade cards despite the lack of any readily ascertainable link to the Orient (Plate 59).

A typical two-panel visual testimonial. The home before and after the benificent influence of Colton's Nervine Strengthening Bitters.

19.

Testimonials

The testimonial is designed, of course, to win faith in the product by presenting confirmation of the manufacturer's claims. A simple technique, used for many decades by the nostrum proprietors, was "before and after" advertising. It gave the reader a visual deomonstration of the difference that the particular remedy could make, usually in a two-panel sequence, and invited him to put his trust in the product. See? It works.

Parker's Ginger Tonic showed a fat laughing tonic user at the same table with a cadaverous sufferer from dyspepsia who obviously had not gotten the word (Plate 60). Hop Pills showed two friends meeting on the street after following radically different medical advice.

Colton's Nervine Tonic gave a view of the whole family before and after using that superlative remedy. Dr. Kline showed us a man on a bridge contemplating suicide and later, fortified with Elixir Vitae, strutting with the self-assurance of a dashing boulevadier. Howe's Concentrated Syrup for the blood contrasted a hospital scene with a happy family reunion (Plate 60). Athlophorus got it all into one picture—a man who dropped his crutches for this wonderful remedy (Plate 60).

The before-and-after device was even imitated by purveyors of veterinary products. Continental Hoof Ointment shows a before-and-after horse! Pond's gives us a dog with a hangover and one whose day had been brightened with a dose of Vegetable Pain Destroyer.

A single-panel visual. The happy man who has taken Hop Pills is discussing it with his friend who was not so forehanded.

Animals could testify to the efficacy of veterinary products, as these two pages from a leaflet point out.

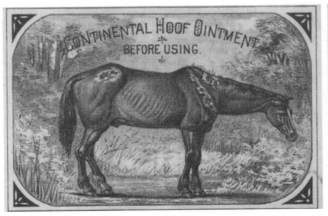

93

TESTIMONIAL SHEET.

(SUPPLEMENT TO "GUIDE TO HEALTH".)

EVERY TESTIMONIAL PUBLISHED BY DR. KILMER & CO. IS ABSOLUTELY TRUE.
The most searching inquiry is invited. The original letters will be sent on application.

FOR ALL KIDNEY, LIVER & BLADDER TROUBLES USE

DR. KILMER'S   SWAMP-ROOT,   THE BEST IN THE WORLD.

GIVEN UP TO DIE!

ANOTHER SWORN STATEMENT.

Cincinnati, Ohio. Jan. 12th, 1890.
My Dear and Noble Benefactor;-
                               It is
utterly impossible for me to express
to you in this letter how thankful I
feel for all your Swamp-Root, Kidney,
Liver and Bladder Cure, has done for
me, and therefore hope and pray
that before long I may be able to
tell you personally how greatly you
have benefited me, and how you have
brought **brightness** and **happiness again** to a noble young wife.
I am home here **perfectly** cured
and will stay for a few weeks in
order to recreate, and in the mean-
time will try and get another situation. I would be happy to travel
for your esteemed establishment, for
then an opportunity would be given
to show you plainly how anxious I
am both for your sake and for the
sake of all suffering humanity, to
introduce your remedies in localities
where they are not yet know.

Now to another subject. I have
stated above that **I am perfectly
cured** and I now authorize you to
use my **sworn testimonial** in
any form or shape that you see fit, and
hope it may be the means of **saving
many lives.** I remain with life
long obligation,
Your Ever Thankful Patient,
                T. G. Everhard,
        Cor. Court and Race Sts.

HIS WIFE ALSO WRITES.

Esteemed Sir;-
              I feel called upon to ex-
press to you my heartfelt thanks for
the great interest you have taken in
my dear husband's case, although an
entire stranger to you. He had spent
so much for doctors and medicine
that we had **given up all hope**
of ever seeing him perfectly well
again, and was amazed when he
came and told me all that had been
accomplished by your **Wonderful Swamp-Root.** We therefore owe you the greatest debt of
gratitude and how can we ever repay
you? Once more please accept our
thanks, in which my dear husband
heartly joines me. May Heaven bless
you with health and contentment,
and may your life be long and prosperous is the sincere wish of your

ever grateful,
                Mrs. T. G. Everhard.
P. S. Your dear picture and kindly
features will always have a *sacred
place* in our Album and in our Hearts.

---:o:---

A Quaker's Testimony.
She was an Invalid for Three Years.

Malvern P. O. Pa Aug. 20th, 1890.
On looking over some of your testimonials, I also have been encouraged to state the wonderful improv-
ment in my own health since I have
taken Swamp-Root. I had **been
an invalid for three years**
and had taken medicine **prescribed by five different
doctors,** but daily grew worse.
A friend asked me to try Dr. Kilmer's
Swamp-Root. On his strong rec-
ommendation, I got a bottle, which
alone did me so much good that
I felt safe in recommending it to
others. I am now using the fifth
bottle and am a **new woman.**
I can recommend your medicines in
most exalted terms.
            Thankfully Yours,
            MRS. A. M. STORM.

---:o:---

SAVED FROM THE GRAVE!
HEALTH AS A NEW YEARS GIFT.

Kenwood, N. Y. July 29th, 1890.
Dr. Kilmer,
              Dear Physician;- It is
now about one year since I wrote
you giving a description of my case.
I had at that **given up all hope**
of ever being able to do another day's
work or of ever living to see another
New Year. But thanks to God,
with the help of your Swamp-Root,
am now able to do as much work as
any one, and I can say with truth
that I **feel better to-day** than
I have **felt for five years.**
You told me to take your Swamp-
Root and I have taken five bottles
which cost me five dollars and to-day
I feel like a new being- my disease
was enlargement of the liver and
spinal, and kidney difficulties.
Thanking God for the wonderful cure
brought about through the agency
of your Swamp-Root, I remain,
      With Everlasting Respect,
            Mrs. James Jacobs.

A Dozen Doctors Prescribed For Him.
He took two Bottles and is now Well.

Hinsdale, Du Page Co , Ill. Aug. 10th; '90.
Dr Kilmer, Binghamton, N. Y.

Dear Doctor;- **God bless you.** Your
Swamp-Root has done wonders for me. I
had been troubled with Bladder Disease,
Enlarged and Sore Postate and had tried
everything without the slightest benefit. I
am in the Drug Sundry business and deal
with **Doctors** and about a **dozen had
prescribed** for me, all to no effect. I
began to think the painful urination had
come to stay, when a druggist in Aurora,
a friend of mine suggested your medicine,
Swamp-Root. I got a bottle of it, but
did not suppose it would amount to anything, but I concluded to try it. I was
greatly surprised to find in a very few days
that the pain had left me, and I began to
urinate without any irritation whatever.
After I had taken **two bottles** the discharge of pus from the uretha stopped and
I am now well. I will bear testimony
in favor of your Swamp-Root every time.
          Fraternally Yours,
              R. M. Banghart.

---:o:---

Troubled with Bad Blood for Ten Years.

          Eldorado. Ohio. Nov. 9th, 1888.
DEAR DOCTOR:—
      We have great need of your Swamp-Root,
Kidney, Liver and Bladder Cure here.

My Wife was troubled with kidney and liver
complaint, and *bad blood for ten years.* Her face
was covered with pimples and unsightly blood
humors. She was confined to her bed for two
months. We heard of your medicine, and got
two bottles of the *Swamp-Root and it cured
her.*
          Yours Truly,
            D. W. SLIFER.

---:o:---

HIS DAUGHTER CURED BY ITS USE.

          Wolf, Ohio. July 15th, 1890.
Dr Kilmer;
          Dear Sir - My Daughter says
your Swamp-Root has done her more good
than all the medicine she has ever taken,
and she has taken hundreds of dollars worth.
It has been of great benefit to myself in
Kidney and Urinary troubles.
              Jonathan Norris.

The written testimonial was a more sophisticated, personalized, version of the "before and after" pitch. Its basic requirements were readability and a ring of sincerity. While the medicine proprietors did not invent this advertising device, they made it a classic and ultimately ran it into the ground. Some medicine almanacs and newsheets consisted almost entirely of testimonials. They appeared on trade cards and even on labels.

Testimonials are greeted with a good deal of cynicism these days, and some patent medicine proprietors furnished ample basis for suspicion. Ripan's Tabules offered an onyx mantel clock with the name of the product on the face, to any customer who attested to the cure of his afflictions and supplied a picture of himself.[1] There was a "testimonial bureau" in Washington that could provide a letter from a Congressman for $40.00 or from a Senator for $75.00. Hartman is said to have paid $1,000 for the statement of Admiral Schley, the hero of Santiago Bay in 1904.[2]

The vast majority of testimonials offered by ordinary citizens were probably genuine and unsolicited, although undoubtedly edited in many cases.[3] There were always enough gullible citizens available who were pleased to see their names in print. One newspaper editor is said to have advised: "If your brains won't get you into the papers, sign a patent medicine testimonial. Maybe your kidneys will."[4]

The proprietors could even use the givers of testimonials, with a little additional persuasion, for individual confirmations. Members of the public actually wrote to those whose names and addresses were printed. Peruna and Lydia Pinkham offered the givers of their testimonials twenty-five cents for a copy of each inquiry together with the reply.[5] There was another bit of financial fallout from those who wrote to the medicine companies that invited them to describe their ills. The letters of the suffering could then be sold wholesale to other proprietors as prospects for mail advertising. One broker offered 55,000 female complaint letters, 44,000 for bust developers, 7,000 about paralysis, 9,000 on narcotic problems, and 3,000 about cancer. Only half a cent each![6]

Premiums like Reed's may have been rewards for celebrity endorsements, or for leading retailers. This clock measured 18 inches high.

Two pages of testimonials from the clergy, from an 1890's pamphlet that sold Mettaur's Pills.

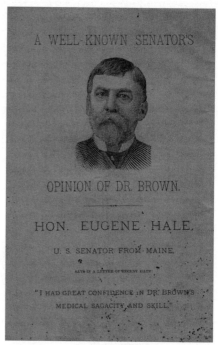
The back cover of a pamphlet used to sell Brown's Sarsaparilla and Brown's Laxative Pills in 1886. It is unclear whether we are looking at the good Dr. Brown or the good Senator from Maine.

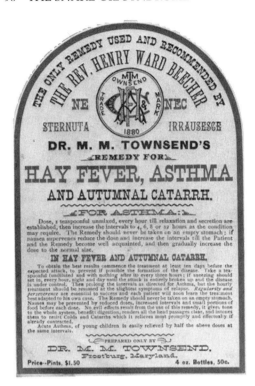

The Rev. Henry Ward Beecher was an influential Congregational preacher in the 1880's. His endorsement appeared on the label of Dr. Townsend's Remedy . His sister, Harriet Beecher Stowe, wrote *Uncle Tom's Cabin*.

It seems likely that the many actors and actresses who appeared on trade cards were compensated simply by the publicity. Henry Irving was an English actor and theater manager, knighted by Queen Victoria in 1895. Burdock Blood Bitters enjoys his reflected glory.

Certain products specialized in testimonials from a particular sector of society. Hartman's Peruna ran heavily to congressmen and military figures, which reflected Peruna's considerable lobbying power in government circles. Hostetter's Stomach Bitters favored doctors. Dr. Jayne's products found favor with officials of the American Bible Society, who must have liked the Old Testament scenes on the Jayne's cards (Plate 69). Duffy's Malt, sometimes and in some places advertised as Duffy's Pure Malt Whiskey, sought and found clergymen who were willing to disregard its high alcoholic content and focus solely on its invigorating effect.

The testimonial of a prominent or glamorous person was, of course, of greater interest than the testimonial of the nieghbors down the road. Statements by the famous tended to be brief and to omit the description of all those embarrassing symptoms. They are better described by the word "endorsement." It is this type of testimonial with which we are most familiar today. Who has not seen a baseball player recommending a breakfast cereal or possibly a bank, or an actress praising some cosmetic or perfume.

There was speculation, even at the time, as to how many, and in what manner, celebrities were compensated for their patent medicine endorsements. The American Statistical Association noted in a 1900 publication that "testimonials are much sought from prominent people and easily obtained, generally for a consideration. Men holding political positions and the holders of professional titles are not adverse to turning an honest penny in this way."[7]

Printer's Ink, the long-lived trade magazine of the advertising industry, approached the subject of celebrities' testimonials more pompously: "Many persons not acquainted with the principles of advertising imagine that they are bought." The writer of the 1899 article then went on to suggest how such statements were best secured. "Put together a liberal but not a vulgarly lavish offering of your wares . . . in a case of Russia leather lined with exquisite satin . . . Engrave a heavy coin-silver plate for the outside with a tribute to his or her beauty, genius, etc...."[8]

Some public figures were likely to derive a benefit simply from the publicity their endorsement provided. This applies most clearly to people in the entertainment business and to politicians. Trade cards were regularly used to advertise theatrical productions and in some cases advertised patent medicines on the back. It seems unlikely that the hundreds of actors and actresses whose pictures were used on trade cards were ever paid for this privilege. All of the major theatrical figures of the day can be found on trade cards for one product or another, including Washington Irving, Edwin Booth and Sarah Bernhardt. Lillian Russell appeared in a low-cut costume on a handsome colored card for Carboline (Plate 9). Lily Lantry's picture advertised Brown's Iron Bitters and several other medicines (Plate 62). Celebrities in other fields allowed their names

President Garfield and his signed letter appear on a sample envelope of Garfield Tea. The letter speaks of beneficial results from the product (a laxative).

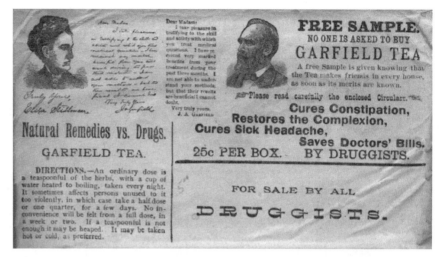

to be used. The Rev. Henry Ward Beecher endorsed Brown's Bronchial Troches and Townsend's Remedy for Catarrh. His name even appeared on the Townsend's label.

In 1856, Ayers secured the endorsement of the President of Mexico and in lieu of the President of the United States, Franklin Pierce, obtained a testimonial from his brother. Garfield's Tea made it with a testimonial from President Garfield himself, presumably obtained while he was an unsuspecting Senator. Even this could not match the splendor of an early trade card issued by Ching's Patent Worm Lozenges in 1805, showing his Majesty George III of England graciously accepting a box of the product on the street in Weymouth (Plate 61).

These achievements were topped by two French medicine proprietors. The product Vin Mariani was endorsed by Popes Leo XII, Pius X and Benedict XV. Gaston Monier, in a French poster, claimed the ultimate endorsement for his Cod Liver Oil. His advertisement showed the Almighty gesturing at a bottle, with the caption: "Take it! God orders it" (Plate 62).

Vin Mariani was developed by a Parisian pharmacist named Angelo Mariani, who brought the art of the endorsement to a level that reflected an obsession. It would appear that he wrote to most of the important people in Europe of his day, and many of the unimportant. Each flattering letter requested a picture, a signature, and a few lines handwritten by the subject. It was usually accompanied by a case of Vin Mariani. Recipients often expressed appreciation for the gesture rather than for the product, but the portion of their comments reproduced by Mariani in his ads did not always make this clear.

Mariani published more than a thousand endorsements of his product.

Angelo Mariani, whose coca wine inspired an extraordinary number of glowing endorsements from prominent Europeans in various fields of endeavor.

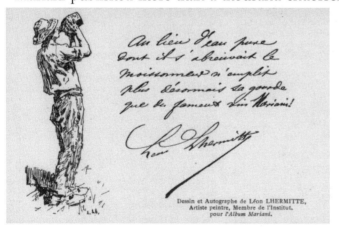

Two French postcards commissioned by Mariani. The painter L'Hermite was the artist at left, and the sculptor Lemaire, at right

They were from artists, actors, musicians, soldiers, politicians, clergymen and scientists, including of course medical men. In addition to the three popes, there were sixteen temporal rulers among them, including the monarchs of Spain, Greece, Sweden and Rumania.[9]

The endorsements appeared singly in newspapers and grouped in pamphlets. They also were collected in thirteen hardcover volumes issued between 1891 and 1913. Postcards were made of the illustrations furnished to Mariani by noted artists. Mariani paid for these in what he considered his role as patron of the arts.

The product at the focus of all this approbation was a modest wine in which coca leaves had been steeped. It was advertised unblushingly as a general tonic. The usual dose was a wine glass, two or three times a day. At this rate a bottle disappeared rather quickly. Mariani spoke freely of its stimulating effect on the nervous system, but he steadfastly denied that Vin Mariani had ever produced Cocainism, as the addiction to its active ingredient came to be called.[10]

A page from the Illustrated London News of 1892, above, listing some of the dramatic performers that Mariani made a part of his sales pitch. Below, a partial page from a Mariani newspaper supplement featuring Pius X, the Queen of Saxony, and the Crown Prince of Bulgaria.

20. Public Issues

Modern advertising tends to avoid public issues and controversies in order not to alienate any part of the consumer public. Not so the patent medicine proprietors, who in their exuberance or perhaps their naivete, commented freely in their advertising upon matters of social and political interest.

Most of the comments were offered in a humorous vein (Plate 63). Merchant's Gargling Oil lampooned Charles Darwin's theory of evolution with several monkey cards. Swayne's Liniment showed the journalist Henry Morton Stanley, who was in Africa looking for Dr. Livingston, lying in a hammock (Plate 9). Nellie Blye, a newspaperwoman who went around the world in the style of Jules Verne's story, was the subject of a series of caricatures on the trade cards of Morse's Indian Root Pills. The new Gilbert and Sullivan operetta, "Trial by Jury," was the obvious reference of a court of animals shown on a rare trade card for Dr. Kilmer's Swamp Root. Pleis' Fit Cure showed a vociferous suffragette and Maxham's Combined Remedy pictured a felon who looked suspiciously like New York's Boss Tweed, walking out of jail.

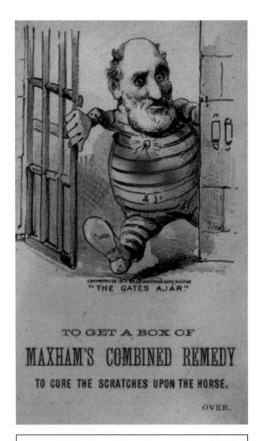

Above, a Bufford stock card from 1875 when Boss Tweed of Tamany Hall slipped out of jail. Below, a comment on new legislation that curtailed the special favors given by railroads to influential shippers.

Hagan's Balm has placed itself in a scene from the new Gilbert and Sullivan operetta, The Pirates of Penzance.

99

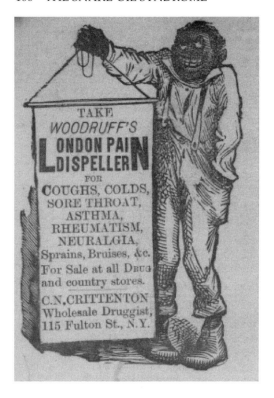

Three comic trade cards with the humor directed at blacks. Top left, a crude early stock card. Top right, a more winsome private card that was well lithographed in color.

The recently emancipated blacks were the focus of political resentment in the South and of economic concern in the North, where their increasing numbers were a threat to the holders of low-paying jobs. Professor James Harvey Young, who has written widely on the natural history of patent medicines, believes that nostrum advertising played a significant role in establishing racial stereotypes in the public consciousness during this period.[1]

Bilousine, Hartshorn's No. 18, Kendall's Spavin Cure, Parker's Ginger Tonic and many other trade cards gave currency to the image of the thick-lipped witless negro (Plates 64 and 65). One racial stock card, that was imitated by several printers, shows a black woman in the pose of the Statue of Liberty, sometimes holding a rooster. The usual title is "Liberty Frightening the World." Currier and Ives issued a variation of this picture.[2] An overtly political expression of the racial issue appeared on the back cover of a Sulphur Bitters almanac, which showed William A. Douglas, the famous black Abolitionist, with his white wife on his arm. The caption was "Golly! Is he going to take the Sulphur Bitters for his complexion?" (Plate 64).

The patent medicine era spanned not only the Civil War and the Reconstruction period, but also the waves of immigration that produced their own social pressures and prejudices. A number of ethnic groups were the butt of jokes in the advertising of this period (Plate 65). The Irishman with his shillelagh was lampooned by Pond's Extract ("Off to Donnybrook Fair") and the Germans by King's Twenty-five Cent Bitters ("I Say, Hans, Now I'se got just what I wants"). The Wells Medicine Company advertised its product, Rough-on-Rats, with a trade card illustrating the belief that Chinese ate rats, together with a doubly aimed slogan, "They must Go."

BRER THULDY'S STATUE
LIBERTY FRIGHTENIN DE WORLD.
To be stuck up on Bedbugs Island - Jarsey Flats, opposit de United States.

The cartoonist, looking at the newly enfranchised blacks in the 1880's, would not have intended the irony that we sense today in this mocking reference to civil liberty and the matter of race.

Most ethnic humor was on stock cards that a job printer could use for any advertiser. The stock card at right is the third in a series showing a rat pursued with fire tongs.

Without comment, Vegetine salted its newsheet, entitled *National Life*, with pictures of the Presidents.

The medicine proprietors were not shy about using political figures in their advertising (Plate 66). There were several series of stock cards picturing our presidents. Vegetine produced a fine illustrated booklet in 1879 entitled "The National Life", giving synopses of the presidents from Washington to Hayes. Johnson's Anodyne Liniment issued a handsome piece entitled "Madison to McKinley." Most of the pictures were black and white drawings, or sepia renderings with a photographic aspect. Almost all were stock cards with the product information overprinted upon them.

In the election of 1884, we see candidates pictured who are in the heat of battle (Plate 66). A full page cartoon in color, published by Sulphur Bitters, was entitled "The Presidential Barn Door Reel." It showed Benjamin Butler, Samuel Tilden and others flirting with the Democratic nomination of 1880. A fold-out card issued by Horsford's Acid Phosphate in 1888 showed both Cleveland and Blaine together with past national election statistics.

It seems unlikely that the cards picturing presidents or presidential aspirants were intended to denote a product endorsement. This advertising appears to be a bit of coattail riding by the nostrum proprietors or perhaps a kind of public service. The most elaborate advertising cards with political subjects amounted almost to "cabinet" photographs. Harter's Iron Tonic furnished cards that measured twelve by seven inches with formal portraits of Cleveland and his wife and Blaine and his wife (Plate 7). Mrs. Cleveland, who became the President's bride while he was in the White House, was a favorite advertiser's subject. In order to be perfectly fair, Harter's also produced a picture of Jefferson Davis and of Winnie Davis, "Daughter of the Confederacy" (Plate 66).

Patriotic images were a staple of all advertisers. In less sophisticated days, many made a very direct appeal to national pride by attempting to associate their product with familiar patriotic symbols. The medicine proprietors were no exception (Plates 67 and 68).

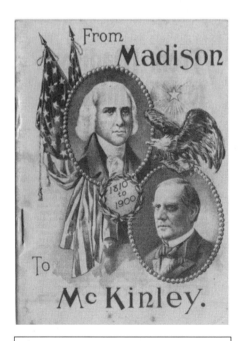

This brave title did not identify a series of presidential biographies. It simply referred to the life span of Johnson's Anodyne Liniment as a nostrum.

This political cartoon, captioned "The Barn Door Reel", graced the cover of a Sulphur Bitters Almanac. It shows Benjamin Butler, Samuel Tilden and others, flirting with the Democratic nonimation for 1884.

Plate 82. The butterfly at right was a cardboard toy with a tiny weight at each wing tip that could balance it on the head of a pencil.

Plate 83. At bottom are medicine advertisements in the form of bookmarks. They are cards except for that shown at far right, issued by Lydia Pinkham, which was real leather stamped with gold.

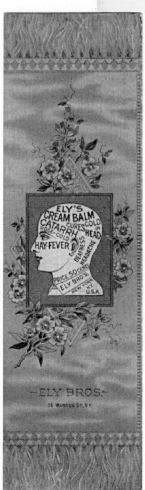

Plate 84. Two hidden-figure cards. It is claimed that 153 figures may be found within Dr. Abbey's "Toll Gate No. 4," above.

Plate 85. Below at left, a rebus issued by Dr. Seth Arnold's Balsam. The back of the card contained no solution. The reader was on his own. At right, a "marriage puzzle," furnishing ages and marital destiny, compliments of The Dr. Harter Medicine Company.

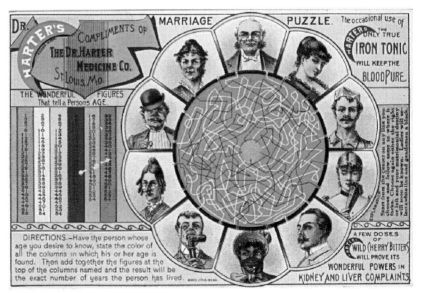

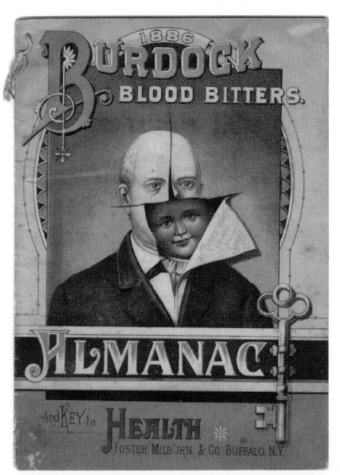

Plate 86. A representative group of medicine almanac covers. Note the image of the druggist on the August Flower cover, upper right, who is brandishing a booklet marked "Free Almanac," and has the same slogan on his open door.

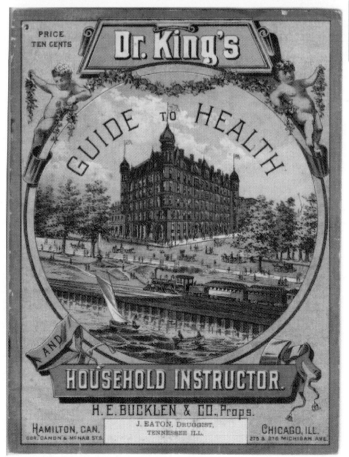

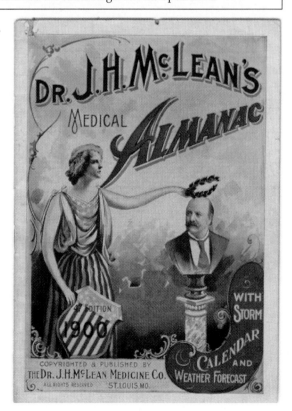

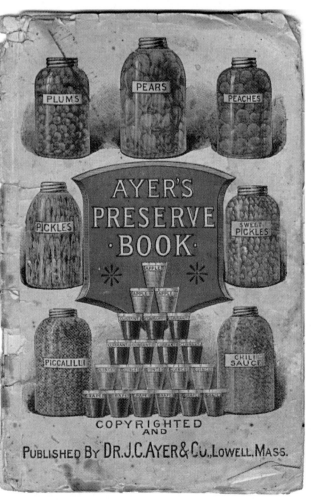

Plate 87. Following the almanacs, some of the larger medicine proprietors issued more specialized booklets. Dream books and cookbooks were especially popular.

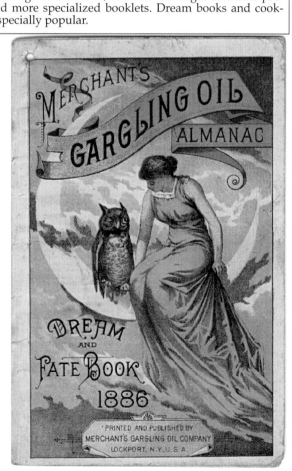

Plate 88. Top row: miniature almanacs of 32 pages, about two inches high, that advertised Piso's Cure for Consumption.
Middle row: die-cut booklets issued by Hood's Sarsaparilla in the shape of a silver dollar and a pansy.
Bottom row: booklets for children; animal fables from Pond's, classic tales from Malena, and the alphabet from Crook's Wine of Tar.

Plate 89. The calendars issued by the patent medicine proprietors ran heavily to babies. Three fancy examples distributed by the C.I. Hood Company are shown here. The calendar pages were apparently considered of minor importance.

Plate 90. The medicine calendars were never of the "girly" type later found upon garage walls. They were entirely suitable for the family kitchen.

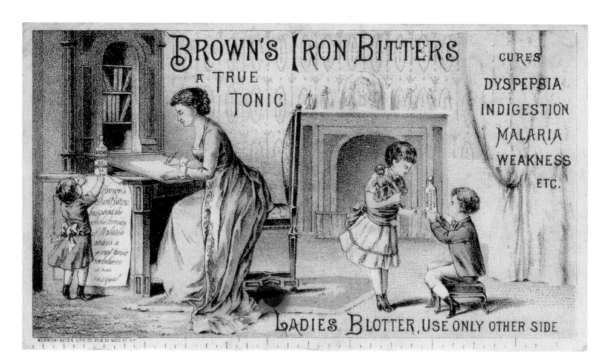

Plate 91. The ubiquitous medicine blotter, handy when the doctor was writing his prescription, has been a fixture of medicine advertising since the earliest days.

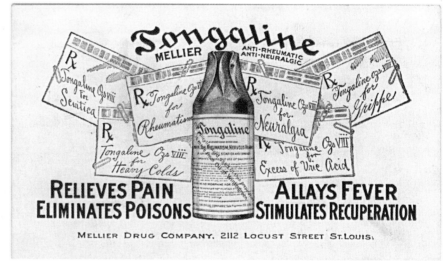

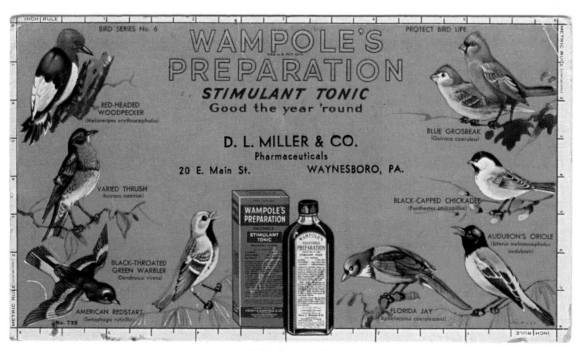

The cover of Burdsall's Almanac for 1876 shows Liberty, massed colonial troops and a virtual supply dump of Burdsall's medicine (Plate 6). Prior to World War I, the German Electric Company peddled its "magnetic" healing belts with a picture of "Liberty for a suffering world." Columbia graced the front of a booklet issued in 1908 by Doan's Pills. Hop Bitters distributed a trade card of our nation's flag with advertising across its red and white stripes. Mennen's showed a child seated on an enormous package of its product, waving an American flag. Congress Bitters used a picture of our Capitol building as its symbol.

Uncle Sam has been a popular fixture for well over a century. The Emmert Proprietary Company of Chicago published Uncle Sam's Almanac in 1881, advertising Uncle Sam's Nerve and Bone Liniment, among other products. Green's August flower, with its almanac cover for 1911, showed the fellow with whiskers still in there pitching for the medicine proprietors (Plate 67).

Battle scenes and pictures of soldiers were a favorite of nostrum advertising (Plate 68). The most frequent association was with our brave boys of the Grand Army of the Republic. There is no doubt that many who served in the Civil War gained both a need and a familiarity with patent medicines from their experience. Disease took as great a toll as the clash of arms and the deplorable state of army medical and sanitary facilities gave a healthy boost to the practice of self-dosage. It is no accident that the name of a great battlefield appears in Shiloh's Consumption Cure. Records show that the army bought quantities of some patent medicines, largely the bitters type.

The German Electric Company was not trying to prove its patriotism — this was only 1893. Columbia was a symbol almost as popular as Uncle Sam and one frequently used in medicine advertising.

That is not to say that America's other wars were ignored. Warner's had a popular product named "Tippecanoe" after the Indian battle of the same name, or possibly after its hero, General William Henry Harrison whose nickname it became. Harrison's campaign for President in 1840 used the log cabin as his symbol, to emphasize his humble and truly American background. Tippecanoe tonic was not only advertised with battle scenes (Plate 67). It was packaged in an intricately molded bottle resembling a rough log.

The Spanish American War was memorialized on dozens of almanac covers of which Doan's (Plate 68) and Peruna are fair examples. A Perry Davis booklet, issued at about this time, honored our navy. It was die-cut in the shape of a bottle made into a vessel of the Great White Fleet and, inside, pictured the various classes of U.S. warships. Hostetter's Bitters touched a strong patriotic interest by presenting on a postcard a map of the Panama Canal (Plate 5).

A Civil War image, highly favorable to the Union, that suggests Dr. Radcliffe's Seven Seals was not being sold in the South.

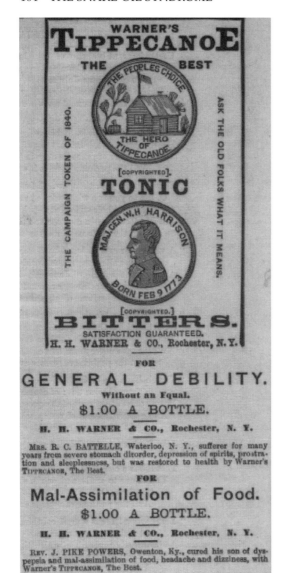

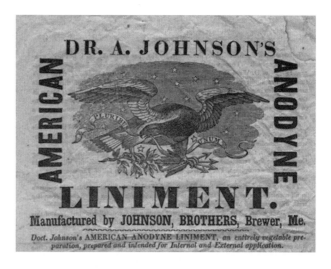

A variety of patriotic images used to sell patent nostrums. The eagle motif at top right is an early effort. The naval scene at bottom shows American might in the age of steam.

21.

Religion and Morals

Some nostrum proprietors sought an image of probity and respectability by pursing religious or semi-religious themes in their advertising (Plates 69-71). Patent medicine advertising was particularly heavy in religious newspapers and some owed their existence in large part to this revenue.[1]

A few depicted the clergy explicitly, among them Father John's Medicine, Carmelite Cordial and Antikamnia, a headache remedy that issued calendars of heavy cardboard showing nuns wearing the habits of their orders. These products were still on the market at the turn of the century. St. Jacob's Oil used as its trademark a monk in a red robe. He was found in various poses, among them that of the Statue of Liberty (Plate 3). Testimonials were secured routinely from the clergy of many faiths.

The earlier advertising of this sort concentrated principally upon the Quaker and Shaker sects. It may have aimed at a more general association with their reputation for thrift, common sense, and especially their temperance views. Both the Quakers and Shakers were said to have secret herbal lore. Mother Seigel's Syrup actually represented that it was manufactured and bottled by the Shakers, and filled its almanacs with pictures of daily life in their spartan communities (Plate 69). Advertising for the Quaker products (which included alcoholic bitters) featured sober gentlemen in broad-brimmed hats and apple-cheeked girls in poke bonnets (Plate 102).

Medicines that sought a religious flavor were sometimes named explicitly for a clergyman, either real or mythic. Father Arent and Father Matthew are two examples.

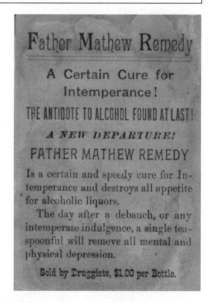

Carmelite Cordial and Quaker Bitters sought to tie themselves to a religious order and a religious sect, respectively.

The angel was a safe non-denominational symbol with useful overtones. Dr. Kaufman's aid to the Life of the Flesh was, of course, named Angeline.

Biblical scenes and characters were not overlooked. Jayne's Carminative Balsam was advertised on a number of trade cards with easily recognized Old Testament scenes such as Rebecca at the well and Moses in the bullrushes. Jayne's depicted the family gathered around the Bible for the evening scripture lesson ("Words of Comfort") and a mother teaching her child to pray (Plate 69).

Still earlier medicine advertising made reference to divine inspiration, either in the product name or by the liberal use of the angel motif. Thus we have Salvation Oil, Radway's Resurrection Pills and M.K. Paine's Balm of Gilead. Angels were used with particular effectiveness by Roger's Royal Remedies and Rudisch's Sarco-Peptones (Plate 70). Older advertising of this sort included Holloway's Pills, Dr. Kermott's Mandrake Pills and Tolu Rock and Rye. The angel symbol was a bit ambiguous. On the one hand it represented comfort for those in pain. On the other hand, the angel with a trumpet was a convenient reminder of final judgment, and a companion to the fearful skeleton advertising.

The remedy named Foe to Pain has here preempted a religious stock card, probably intended for a devotional message, and made it a billboard.

HUMPHREY'S GOOD SAMARITAN
Cures Rheumatism, Neuralgia, Pains in the Back, Chest or Limbs.
GIVES UNIVERSAL SATISFACTION.
Dr. CROSBY'S Secret Remedy for Habitual Constipation.

The Good Samaritan was a very useful biblical reference found in a number of trade cards and other medicine advertisements.

On the whole there was little in medicine advertising that did not comport with the high moral tone demanded by straight-laced Victorian convention. As a matter of record, however, women's fashions ran to a good bit of decolletage, even in less formal scenes like the girl leaning over the porch rail, who advertised Brown's Bitters (Plate 97). In one or two cases, there were revealing and covered-up versions of the same trade card. The Antikamnia Company, which issued the pictures of nuns, apparently felt quite comfortable with the exposed portrait entitled "Purity," which it published in 1909 (Plate 71).

There was of course a marketing reason why medicine advertising did not, like cigarette cards, run to pin-up girls. Quite simply, most of the household nostrums were purchased by proper matrons, while tobacco products were almost exclusively the province of the male sex. In any event bathing beauties appeared at the beach in full length fashions during the Victorian era, to such an extent that you were lucky if a naked ankle was exposed. Naturally, medicine advertising portrayed some girls who just came from the bath or were about to enter it. Parker's Hair Tonic gives us an example. Some of these might be regarded as cultural explications of the Grecian form of dress. Sachs Prudens' advertising may be viewed as an excursion into mythology (Plate 72).

The advertising materials that might truly be called risque were very rare indeed. There was the opportunity for an instant strip tease in the hold-to-light cards that changed the picture when the printing on the reverse was allowed to show through. Lash's Bitters presented, with a measure of restraint, a girl in front of a mirror in this situation, and a farmer's daughter, somewhat more compromised (Plate 73). There is also the teasing card with a series of panels entitled "The Five Senses." The story line was pirated by Ginseng-Gin (or vice versa) and issued under the title "In the Good Old Summer Time."

"Girly" images were found primarily on cigarette cards, which had a different gender market from that for most medicines.

The hold-to-light card was the natural vehicle for a strip tease. The lady here was revealed to be wearing completely modest undergarments.

Lash's Bitters, although not identified on the front, is the issuer of this story card, unusually risque for medicine advertising.

The scatalogical had a very small representation in the nostrum area but a child on the potty was in fact the logo of Cascarets. At right, almost actual size, is the back of a pocket mirror without a handle, a giveaway advertising item.

The temptation for the laxative manufacturers must have been great but a very few descended to the scatological level. Cascarets was one of these, adopting as its trademark a child on a potty and the slogan "All going out, nothing coming in." Pond's Liver Bitters offered a further propagation of this display.

This monument of poor taste was authored by The Pond's Bitters Company, of Chicago.

22.

Everyday Life

While advertisers who depicted fashions, sports, and children were not pursuing issues, they may be said to have followed a broad theme of identification with consumer aspirations. Many of the images in this category were idealized or sentimentalized. They did not generally portray the average American, either the farmer or the factory laborer, and very few were addressed in any serious way to the living conditions of the poor. They were sales images, cozy, comfortable and untroubling. They were not intended to be instruments of social protest. Viewed in this context, however, the printed ephemera of this period give us a brilliant window upon upscale America in the nineteenth century. They are an incomparable resource that has only lately been discovered by social historians (Plates 97-103).

Ladies' fashions were displayed in a fascinating spectrum across the patent medicine era (Plates 97-99). Female headgear went from the poke bonnet to the large brimmed hats of the 1880s and 1890s, dripping with feathers or trimmed with fur. The boas and long strings of pearls, common at the turn of the century, reflected the widening affluence achieved during the Industrial Revolution. The proprietors' advertising pictured them all. Girls' hair styles, for example, can be traced year by year in the stunning calendars published by Hood's Sarsaparilla. Ladies at home, in the parlor, on the veranda, or in the garden, appear in all their elaborate Victorian elegance.

Everyday scenes tended to picture an elegant upper class, untroubled by health or any other problems.

Gentlemen's clothing styles are less common in nostrum advertising but we can see a tall top hat, worn at a picnic, the formal suit of a business executive of the robber baron era, and a dandy in his quilted smoking jacket (Plate 100).

Genteel diversions and pastimes were also among the advertisers' images (Plate 101). We see a charming picture of a young lady bundled in furs being pushed across the ice in a quaint sleigh. Later scenes

reflect the more active, emancipated lady, dressed in her driving clothes, or playing golf. Summer sports for polite society included croquet, tennis and punting.

The medicine trade cards that portray sports are not portraits of athletic heroes but more general scenes of amateurs enjoying themselves. Baseball was treated in a comic fashion by Merchant's Gargling Oil, Hill's Golden Oil, and Wright's Pills. The Merchant's trade cards show ugly fat boys in the uniforms worn in the infancy of the game and bear titles like "The Hero of the Home Run" and "The Ladies Favorite" (Plate 14). Actually these are stock cards and they were also used to advertise Capadura Cigars.

Today "sports cards" mean pictures of baseball, football, basketball or hockey players, issued in endless series by the makers of bubble gum. In the late nineteenth century, the sports cards were largely issued by the tobacco companies and the athletes were baseball players or professional boxers. These cards were all "inserts," packaged with a product that had to be bought in order to obtain them. For some reason, few insert cards were distributed by the medicine proprietors. Medicine was not usually bought as repeatedly as chewing tobacco, and lengthy series of cards were probably not considered appropriate. In addition, avid interest in sports was usually confined to boys and men.

Children have always been an appealing subject for advertising material (Plate 103). There is an assurance of wholesomeness and mildness in the picture of a child, and a special appeal to Momma as a customer. Some of the most delightfully healthy babies grace the medicine trade cards. Children's adventures make good pictures that tell a story. A frequent device in Victorian advertising was to show children dressed as adults, in adult situations. Dr. King's Wonderful Discovery illustrated scenes from Shakespeare with children. Some of the medicine advertising materials were intended for entertaining the children themselves.

Malena, an ointment for chafes, burns and piles, distributed nursery stories and animal tales with colorful slick covers that could be washed. Other proprietors offered alphabet books and paper toys (Plate 92).

Images of children were heavily used in nineteenth century advertising, including nostrum advertising.

PART FOUR

The Media

Whoever shall give Notice of the said Horse to the said *Isaac Little*, or to the said *Peter Cullimore*, so that he may be recovered again, shall be well rewarded for the same.
DAFFY's Elixir Salutis, very good, at four shillings and six-pence per half pint Bottle : And good Hungary Water at One shilling and six-pence per Bottle. To be Sold by *Nicholas Boone* at the Sign of the Bible in *Cornhill*, near School-street. Where any that want a quantity of either, may be supply'd very Reasonably.
TWO Negro Men to be Sold on reasonable Terms : Inquire at the Post-Office in Cornhill, Boston, and know further.

23.

Newspaper Advertising

Advertising media, broadly defined as channels of commercial communication, were obviously fewer and less immediate in the nineteenth century. Before radio and television, the advertiser was forced to make more insistent use of the printed word in all its myriad forms, and of those promotional devices that his imagination could create. The nostrum manufacturers used everything at their disposal: newspapers, almanacs and pamphlets of various types, trade cards, calendars and other giveaway items, posters and outdoor displays including the medicine show.

Newspaper advertising was always extremely important to manufacturers of patent medicine. "The newspapers made the patent medicine business and the patent medicine business in turn supported the newpapers," one writer has said.[1] It has also been asserted that the newspapers as a whole made far greater fortunes out of the business than the medicine proprietors.[2] Newspapers were the primary means of mass communication as we know it, during the patent medicine era, and one would expect to find the nostrum proprietors making heavy use of them.

Between many products that were essentially without merit, advertising and marketing methods marked the difference between the successful and the unsuccessful. In the case of many nostrums it is fair to say that there was no demand at all for the product until it was created by advertising. The profits to be made and the competitive frenzy of the medicine industry prompted the expenditure of enormous sums for their day. The mass production of medicine, requiring ever larger markets, compelled the manufacturer to go directly to the consumer to establish his image surely and effectively. With surprising swiftness the advertising of certain medicines became national in scope.

The first known American newspaper advertisement for a medicine appeared in the Boston News-Letter of October 4, 1708.[3] By a hundred and thirty years later, the eastern newspapers were infested with medicine advertising in epidemic proportions. In 1839, almost half of the advertising space of the *New York Herald* was devoted to medicines, and by the end of another decade, this condition had spread to most western newspapers.[4] In 1847 there were some eleven million medicine advertisements in about two thousand newspapers.[5] The record for immediate saturation by one medicine

R. R. R. No 2.
A New Principle discovered in Medicine, Cure Old Diseases, Scrofula, Bad Humors, Syphilis, Frightful Sores, Ulcers, Fever Sores, Eruptions of the Skin.
RADWAY'S RENOVATING RESOLVENT.
A CURE FOR SORES.
This famous Remedy cures every kind of Sores, from the loathsome and putrid Ulcer, Fever Sore, Cancer, Syphilis, Scrofulous, Leprosy, down to the Pimple, Blotch, and Tetter. It quickly heals the most obstinate and angry Sores, and will leave the skin without a scar. It cleanses the system from all corrupt Humors—*purifies and enriches the blood.*
If you are covered with sores from head to foot, Radway's Renovating Resolvent will quickly heal them, and leave you a *sound and healthy body.*
If your bones, joints, or limbs are diseased in an any manner, or enlarged or drawn out of shape, or if they are shrivelled, crippled, or enfeebled, Radway's Renovating Resolvent will *resolve away the diseased deposits* that inflict their miseries upon you, and restore each member of your body to its natural and healthy condition.
CHRONIC DISEASES OF LONG STANDING.
Persons who have been afflicted with disease for years, will find R. R. Resolvent a certain cure. Scrofula in its worst forms, Syphilis in its most frightful and alarming character, have been cured by R. T. Resolvent.
PAINFUL ITCHINGS.
Persons who are trouble with Painful Itchings of their Legs, Arms, Feet, Head, and other parts of the body, will find instant relief by a dose of R. R.Resolvent.
Synopsis of Diseases Cured by R. R. Resolvent during the 1854, as reported to us:

No. of Cures.	Complaints.	No. of bottles used.
200	Scrofula	3 to 6 bottles.
60	Glandular Swellings	4 to 5 do
500	Hacking Dry Coughs	1 to 3 do
50	Cancerous Affections	6 to 8 do
200	Syphilitic Sores	3 to 6 do
4	White Swellings	2 to 5 do
50	Gout	1 to 3 do
600	Common Pimples	1 2 to 1 do
50	Fever Sores	2 to 6 do
20	Running Sores, all over the body	2 to 6 do
30	Bad legs, some of the Sores as large as the bottom of a tea saucer,	3 to 6 do
70	Salt Rheum	4 to 7 do
65	Very Ulcers	6 to 8 do
17	Females—Tumors in the Womb	1 to 6 do
200	Females—of the various complaints peculiar to the organs of the female sex	1 to 3 do
80	Scorbutic Eruptions	1 to 3 do
70	Bronchitis	2 to 6 do

1000 cases of different kinds of Sores, Eruptions, Swollen and Enlarged Joints, Hip Diseases, Rickets, Kernels in the Throat, Swellings of the Glands, Lumps and Knots in the throat, under the ears; Sores in the eyes, head, nose, mouth, gums, &c. Infants with sores on their heads, ears, faces, &c., have been cured by the miraculous efficacy of the R. R. Resolvent.
One bottle will prove to the afflicted sufferer that it will cure you, one dose will do you good.
LADIES IN TROUBLE.
If you have any difficulty in the Womb, R. R. Resolvent will set you right.

A newspaper advertisement from the Middlebury (Vermont) Register of November 21, 1855.

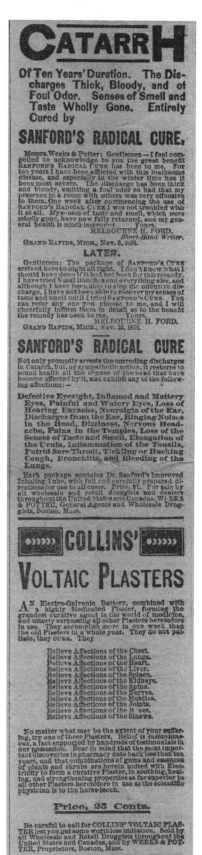

A column from the *Troy Daily Item*, June 4, 1879.

An advertising contract of the Cheney Medicine Co. in 1904. The "red clause" appears in two lines of bold type just above the company signature.

advertiser is probably held by Ripans Tabules, which bought six pages in each of the *New York Herald* and the *New York Journal* of April 16, 1899.[6]

Throughout the nineteenth century, medicines were first in volume of newspaper advertising, ahead of all other products. It was reported in 1899 that the largest proprietor spent $1,250,000 a year on newspaper advertising and the next largest $1,000,000.[7] A medium sized firm, such as the California Fig Syrup Company, spent as much as $500,000, of which about $300,000 went for newspapers and the balance was about equally divided between popular magazines, medical journals, outdoor advertising, and lithographed pamphlets or circulars.[8]

In time the country's newspapers as a whole came to share an economic bias in favor of patent medicines which served to keep their editorial columns understandably quiet as to the dangers of certain preparations. In later years many medicine proprietors put a clause in their lucrative advertising contracts with newspapers that permitted cancellation if any local law restricting the manufacture or sale of proprietary medicines should be adopted.[9] This provision was known as "the red clause" because it was sometimes printed in bright red type.[10] An appreciation of the weight of advertising revenue makes it easier to understand why the patent medicine problem was so long unarticulated and why general public awareness of it grew so slowly.

The earliest newspaper advertisements were apt to be placed by the local retailer who was simply announcing the names of medicines that he had in stock. The first ads of medicine manufacturers usually consisted of lists of diseases that the product promised to cure. At this stage, medicine advertising had all of the eye appeal of a present day "classified" column, or perhaps that of a simple New England tombstone. It was the larger companies, reaching for national coverage, who introduced the innovations.

Lydia Pinkham was among the first to supply local newspapers and print-shops with an engraved block or plate for printing her trademark. Happily for the printers, this consisted of a prim portrait of the lady herself in ruffled collar, and it was often the only picture of a woman that the printer had in stock. It is said that Lydia appeared as the "most recent likeness" of Sarah Bernhardt, Lily Langtry, Queen Victoria and even as President Cleveland's new bride.[11]

In time, newspaper advertising became more sophisticated but its importance was lessened by the emergence of the great national magazines. In general the use of magazines encouraged advertising of better quality, commensurate with more expensive paper and printing techniques, especially those for printing pictures.

The size and depth of the campaigns mounted by the medicine proprietors were directly responsible for the rapid development of advertising as a science. Nostrums provided the funds that enabled advertising men to apply and assess new techniques for the first time. When a fair sample was on hand, technical knowledge could be acquired by measuring the effect on sales of ad position (especially that of advertisements on magazine covers), the personality of the publication, the season, weather and concurrent news events. With sufficient budget, the ad men could study the appeal of various layouts, illustrations, headlines, ornaments and typefaces, when each was used for the same product.[12] In this manner, the patent medicine whose success was created by advertising, in turn served to nurture and mature the process by which it was sold.

In addition to using the ordinary daily newspapers, some of the larger medicine proprietors also published newsprint throw-aways of their own. They imitated the heading and format of a newspaper and used a spurious headline to catch attention. H.H. Warner is said to have originated the newsheet advertisement. One writer has called them "masquerade ads."[13] The headline might read "Entire Family Suddenly Stricken." The reader would discover that the only remedy for this and other dire calamities, and indeed almost the only topic of discussion in this publication, was Hood's Sarsaparilla or Warner's Safe Cure. While the newsheets did not run to as many pages as a daily, some of them achieved respectable bulk and used impressive mastheads and numerous line drawings.

Two advertising pamphlets in the style of periodicals. Typical was *Guide to Health* (1890), 16 pages of newsprint in tabloid form touting Dr. Kilmer's Swamp Root Kidney, Liver and Bladder Cure. *Minard's Magazine* (1903) ran to 32 pages with a cover lithographed in color.

The Evening Telegram

A PAPER FOR THE PEOPLE.

VOL. 5. NO. 2.   PRICE 2 CENTS.

State Capitol, Montpelier, Vt.

After the Grip.

Strength and Health Restored by Hood's Sarsaparilla.

"Two years ago I had a severe attack of the grip. I was left in a very feeble condition. I could not do any work during that winter and not much during the following summer season. About a year ago I had a second attack, but my condition was worse than at first. I was

Left With Heart Trouble

and was unable to do the least work, such as light chores about the house, without sitting down to rest. My breath was very short and I had great difficulty in breathing. I used different medicines, but did not improve. We have used Hood's Sarsaparilla in our family for a good many years previously, but did not know it was particularly beneficial for the grip. However, I thought I would try it and I

Improved From the First.

After taking eight bottles I was able to be out all the past winter and worked every day. Hood's Sarsaparilla has done me a great deal of good, and I gladly recommend it to others." A. J. MOULTON, Gouldsville, Vermont.

Hood's Starts the Blood Along.

"We have taken about a dozen bottles of Hood's Sarsaparilla in all and find it improves the appetite and seems to start the blood along and make anyone feel better all over." Mrs. O. E. BUNDY, Sutton, Vermont.

After Lung Fever.

"My little girl, Hattie D. Cole, had a severe case of lung fever two years ago, and she has had a very bad cough every since, until last spring she began taking Hood's Sarsaparilla and her cough is almost entirely cured. She took three bottles and is well and healthy." Mrs. S. C. COLE, Walden, Vermont.

Hood's Cures Rheumatism.

"For several years my husband was troubled with rheumatism in all his hands, sometimes as large as a half dollar, and his fingers would become numb. He has taken seven bottles of Hood's Sarsaparilla. His rheumatism has left him, and he has not had those purple spots for several months." Mrs. E. L. ABNNER, North Walden, Vermont.

Kidney and Liver Trouble.

"I am more than pleased with the good

Vermont's New City

Barre, the Centre of the Granite Industry

Now Supplied With All the Improvements of a Busy and Wide-awake Place.

Barre, Vt., March, 1895.—Unlike the early residents of Boston, the people of this green mountain town have not waited until the population of the place reached 40,000 before casting off the old-fashioned town government, but have taken a long step forward, and on March 5th entered the small but increasing list of Vermont cities.

Its history, unlike a majority of New England towns, belongs to the present generation.

Nov. 6, 1780, 19,000 acres of wild land, comprising the present town of Barre, was chartered to William Williams and 60 others, and to this tract of unbroken wilderness the name of Wildersburg was given.

In 1788 Samuel Rogers and Roger ... took up their families, moved into town from Massachusetts. From that time on the town prospered, emigrants from New Hampshire, Massachusetts and Rhode Island arrived and established homesteads where their descendants now live.

The first town meeting was held at the residence of Apollos Hale, March 11, 1793. The selectmen chosen were Nathan Harrington, Asapha Sherman and Joseph Dwight.

The freeman's meeting was held Sept. 3 of the same year, with the following voters: Nathan Harrington, Joseph Gould, Asapha Sherman, Benjamin Walker, Benjamin Richardson, Samuel Cook, Nathan Sherman, Sylvanus Goldsbury, Henry Gale, Gardner Wheeler, Reuben Benton, P. Richardson, Jacob Scott, Joseph Browning, A. Peck, Calvin Smith, Asa Dodge, Peter Gale, B. French, Reuben Carpenter, John Goldsbury, Jr., John Warren, Elias Cheney, Joseph Dwight, Nathan Harrington was chosen rep...

Name Chosen Long Ago

by Ezekiel Dodge ... for ... 60 pounds lawful money ... being the highland bidder ... named the town can ... The man who ... best be ... fitted by ...

In 1830 the town had 2015 people, in 1880-2060, in 1890-6790, and at the present time the population is estimated at 10,000.

This growth has brought with it abundant schools, churches and business enterprises. But ... house industry for which the town is ... famed in every section of the country is the quarrying and finishing of Barre granite.

What started the development of the granite business ... located from the central ... which was built in 1875 ... opened to travel with a grand celebration July 4, 1875.

The town gave $35,000 and a ... construction of the ... In 1888 the citizens subscribed $40,000 to build a road from the town centre to the granite quarries D. E. Sackwell, president of the Montpelier & Wells River company furnished the first train was run to the quarry, in December, 1888.

To show the marvelous growth of the granite industry, it need only be stated that its Millstone hill 70 quarries are in operation, and 800 quarrymen are given employment.

Water, electric lights, fire alarm, telephone communication, and all the modern equipments which are a guarantee of a bright and successful future for the new and widewake city.

Great Shipwrecks

A Ghostly Company Which the Elbe Has Gone to Join

Half a Century's Deadly Record

Ships Which Have Vanished Without Leaving a Trace.

The loss of the Elbe, with more than three hundred souls, has just struck terror into the hearts of the people, as only a great ocean disaster can. No other calamity of this nature ...

Miss Ellen G. Ellis,
Roxbury, Vt.

Good News

Reliable Reports From All Directions

The People Glad to Tell How They Have Been Encouraged and Cured.

Hood's Prolonged Her Life.

"Four years ago I had the grip which left me feeble, with no appetite and tired all the time. I was also troubled with catarrh and rheumatism. I began to take Hood's Sarsaparilla and commenced to gain at once. I am now well. I can eat and sleep well, and believe Hood's Sarsaparilla has prolonged my life." SUSAN P. SARTEE, 28 Loomis St., Montpelier, Vt.

Warded Off the Grip.

"I have been troubled with rheumatism for many years. In the spring of 1891 and '92 I suffered attacks of the grip which took a long time to recover my strength. In 1893 I had symptoms of the grip coming on and I began taking Hood's Sarsaparilla. All of these symptoms disappeared and the granite industry ... Hood's Sarsaparilla has helped my rheumatism and I am now quite well and strong." Mrs. J. T. FULLAKSFON, East Cambridge, Vermont.

Neuralgia and Inflammation.

"Eight years ago I was sick with neuralgia and inflammation and I did not work for four years to speak of, and I could get no help until I began taking Hood's Sarsaparilla, which has been of great benefit to me. My little son is troubled with catarrh and has been greatly benefited by Hood's Sarsaparilla." Mrs. WM. B. HENKINS, Lyndonville, Vermont.

Walked Three Miles.

"My grandmother is 85 years old and had not been out of the house for five months the day she was 85. She has taken four bottles of Hood's Sarsaparilla and last summer she walked three miles in one day and she goes four miles to church every Sunday. Her name is Mary Sullivan." HENRY SULLIVAN, Marshfield, Vt.

Hood's Gave Strength and Appetite. "Hood's Sarsaparilla has helped me ...

be caused by constipation and torpid liver. I continued to take Hood's Sarsaparilla and in several weeks the disagreeable feeling left me. I continued to take the medicine through the spring and escaped an attack of the grip. The pain in my arm was less severe and I could use my hands to a better advantage. I resumed taking the medicine the past spring and

Have Been Benefited by It.

The old adage, 'An ounce of prevention is worth a pound of cure,' has been proven in my case by my experience with Hood's Sarsaparilla." Mrs. J. T. FULLARSON, East Cambridge, Vermont.

Rheumatic Fever.

Also Severe Headaches Affect General Health

A Cure and Improved Health Found in Hood's Sarsaparilla.

"C. I. Hood & Co., Lowell, Mass.:

"Gentlemen:—I have been afflicted with a very severe trouble. About a year ago I had an attack of rheumatic fever and never fully recovered from that complaint.

Afterwards

"I Had Severe Headache

which lasted me for three weeks with hardly any let up. I began to be alarmed and thought I must do something for myself. I commenced to take Hood's Sarsaparilla and am happy to say that it completely cured my headache so that I have not had any trouble from that complaint since. I had kidney trouble which was also the effect of rheumatic fever.

The Human Blood

How It Is Composed—What It Is For

A Study of the Vital Fluid It Must Be Kept Pure If You Wish Good Health.

The blood is a red fluid circulating through the heart, arteries and veins of the human body, serving for the nourishment of all its parts and for the support of life. It is. Heartily, the vital fluid. It consists in the first place, of water, which contains various substances, and secondly of corpuscles, or little globes which float in this liquid. The blood is the product of the elaboration of chyle, and by means of, the arteries and veins it carries nourishment to every organ and thence of the body. From it the secretive organs obtain material for their respective secretions, such as saliva, bile, etc.

The little red globes in the blood are most important and they should be red in color. It is by keeping them in this condition and in a healthy state that the natural condition of the blood is maintained. When it is remembered that the blood circulates through all the great organs of the body and to all the extremities, reaching every part without any distinction as to its importance, it will be understood that the purity and vitality of the blood are essential to health.

If the blood contains impurities or if it lacks the richness and vitality which in a natural condition it possesses, all the organs must suffer the consequences.

Without vitality in the blood there will be a feeling of lassitude and an indisposition to work, a condition which is most readily understood when described as "that tired feeling."

When the blood is impure either through some taint which has been transmitted from former generations or because of the peculiar condition in which the person has been placed, it will not fail to scatter disease throughout the system. The result of such a condition will be scrofulous eruptions, rheumatism, indigestion, dyspepsia and a thousand other ills which came more

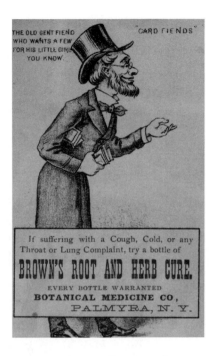

24. Trade Cards

In this survey of patent medicine advertising we pause to look in detail at the advertising trade card, perhaps the most vivid and artistic medium of all those used by the nostrum proprietors. During the last two decades of the nineteenth century these cards were issued in prolific quantities and enjoyed an extraordinary success as sales material.

The trade card, intended for business purposes, followed its cousin the *carte de visite*, already well established for social use.[1] Starting with modest sizes, the trade card grew larger but in general did not exceed five by three inches. It was intended to be given away by the retail merchant and pocketed by his customers.

We take for granted the vast amount of visual material spread before us today. In the 1870s, pictures were mostly black and white engravings, and the colored advertising card brought a new pleasure to an America in which small pretty illustrations were not available for free. Many a farm housewife stayed up late at night pasting trade cards into an album as a Christmas present or a birthday present for a child. Trade cards were also a convenient means of reaching that sizeable portion of the public that could not read. The popularity of the colored trade card in the 1880s amounted to a public craze.[2] "Card Fiends" was the title of a series of comic stock cards issued by Bufford that made fun of the collector. Eventually untold millions of trade cards were issued, exchanged and treasured.

In time, card collecting, in common with many leisurely forms of home-oriented recreation, was displaced by competition from other sources. The novelty of the trade card decreased, not only because of the glut of cards at its peak, but also because of the appearance of colored pictures in magazines and elsewhere. Once advertising and marketing reached a national scale, other forms of visual persuasion became more efficient. National newspapers with photo reproductions made good pictorial material commonplace. By 1900 the issuance of trade cards had declined very markedly.

Mrs. Pinkham knew where her cards were going. "Put this in your album," she said.

117

The forerunner of the trade card was the English "shop bill," used as early as the 1630's to render accounts and to advertise. William Hogarth drew this one in 1725 for a druggist at The Three Angels in Cornhill. *Courtesy The British Museum.*

Benedict Arnold was a druggist and bookseller in New Haven in 1762. His broadside, about 12 inches high, lists more books than drugs. *Courtesy The Toledo Museum of Art.*

As might be expected, the earliest cards used in this country were of a simple type, engraved or printed in black upon white and unadorned by pictures or designs.[3] They identified the merchant, his place of business and his trade, but usually did not identify any specific products. One of the few that did, a particularly desirable example, is the advertisement of Benedict Arnold, in his younger days a book seller and drug merchant. Later American cards used fancy script and some were embossed with a seal or a raised picture.[4] A few used colored inks. At the time of the Civil War we find trade cards of stiff paper on which a small photograph has been pasted. A card for Bicknell's Syrup is decorated with a tiny picture of Abraham Lincoln and his son in a frame embossed upon the card.

The trade cards with which most collectors are familiar today are those that were produced in volume, beginning in the late 1870s, when a number of technological advances were put together. The most important of these was lithography, invented in the late 1700s, which gradually overtook the established method of printing with engraved metal plates. Steel or copper engravings could produce very fine lines and intricate designs, but the plates wore out quickly and had to be recut. This method was slow and best suited to hand printing. Mass production of images only became practical with the advent of lithography, which substituted a heavy block of special limestone for the metal plate. The design was drawn on the stone with a greasy chalk and the surrounding stone etched away with a bath of nitric acid. Before each impression the stone would be moistened and inked. The ink would adhere to the etched design and transfer to the paper.[5] Lithography in color (chromo-lithography) was achieved by overprinting with a different stone for each color. Pastel shades and very sophisticated soft effects could be created in this manner. The lithographed posters of Toulouse-Lautrec are outstanding examples.

The Centennial Exposition of 1876, held in Philadelphia, was a major milestone in the development of a national market in this country and of new advertising techniques, in particular the trade card.

Plate 92. Examples of toys distributed by the patent medicine manufacturers, in this case the C. I. Hood Company of Lowell, Mass. There were 19 pieces in the set of paper dolls (at top) and they could be had for ten cents. At center are three of a series of 12 animal statuettes. The jigsaw puzzle at bottom was sent upon receipt of three wrappers from Hood's Sarsaparilla.

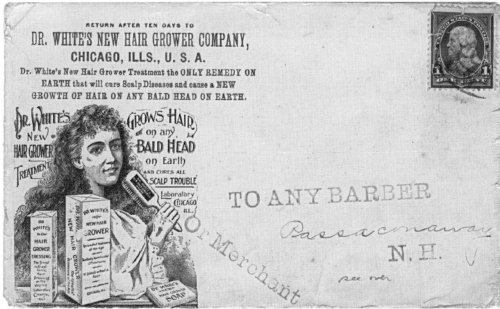

Plate 95. Posters for well-known patent medicines. The Vin Mariani poster, top left, was drawn in 1894 by Jules Cheret, a French artist who pioneered in this art form. *Collection William H. Helfand.* The Hood's poster, top right, came from an unknown artist but was probably also lithographed in France. *Courtesy The Philadelphia Museum of Art.* The Hamlin's Wizard Oil poster, below, was an American product the size of a barn. It depicts a medicine show coming to town. *Courtesy The Library of Congress.*

Plate 96. Songbooks were another popular giveaway item used by a number of nostrum proprietors. A few, like the makers of Beecham's Pills, distributed sheet music as well (top right).

Plate 97. The upscale fashions of the era were faithfully recorded in the patent medicine advertising. Here are examples of ladies' indoor and outdoor wear at the turn of the century.

Plate 98. The hats of elegant ladies ran to luxurious feathers and elaborate decoration. Burdock Blood Bitters, which frequently headlined its ads, "Invalid Ladies!" has pictured these four.

LOUISE PAULLIN.

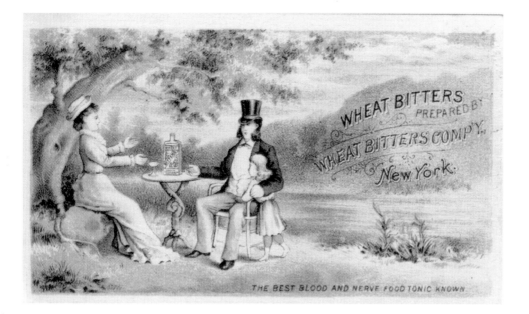

THE BEST BLOOD AND NERVE FOOD TONIC KNOWN

Plate 100. Gentlemen's fashions also received attention. These trade cards show us a top-hatted paterfamilias in the garden (from an early period), a gentleman at home in a morning coat with his more informally attired son, and a dandy in his smoking jacket for evening wear.

The economics of the stock card. Above, is a card copyrighted in 1876 that can be adapted for the use of any druggist; about one cent each. At left, a letter from Currier & Ives offers their stock cards of trotting horses at about two cents each. *Photo courtesy Col. L.C. Rosser.*

At the same time that printers perfected chromolithography, the papermakers began to produce light cardboard from woodpulp, bleached by chemical means, at a fraction of the cost of earlier heavier materials. The newly developed photographic camera offered an inexhaustible supply of images for reproduction. High speed presses, powered by steam, were introduced in 1865 and gave tremendous impetus to all types of printing. At the International Centennial Exposition of 1876, held in Philadelphia, the trade card received instant and widespread prominence as an advertising medium[6] (Plate 74). Louis Prang & Co. of Boston, a pioneer lithographer, gave away thousands upon thousands. Many of Prang's wares were "stock cards," designed with blank spaces in which local printers could insert the name and slogan for any customer's product.[7]

A rapidly expanding economy created an impelling need for cheap, attractive and easily distributed advertising, and the nostrum manufacturers proved to be a breed that appreciated its value. Medicine trade cards were essentially an American phenomenon. Attractive cards were produced contemporaneously in Europe, but during the Victorian era the volume was relatively small compared to the vast outpouring in this country. It seems that few European cards were devoted to the advertising of medicines.[8] Some stock cards made in France are found with overprints for American medicines, occasionally with a title in French. A number of these have a gold background of metallic ink, and this type is frequently referred to as a "French" card.

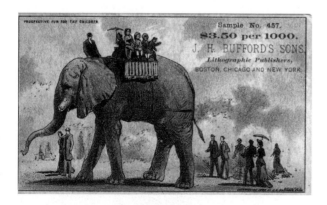

Cheaper cards. J.H. Bufford sold chromolithographed cards to the job printer at about 3 for a cent (left). The black and white drawing at right was priced at 10 to a penny.

Two excellent European trade cards issued by the maker of a nutritious meat extract. The "Leibig chromos" first appeared in 1872. They employed up to 14 colors. A German card at left; an Italian scene with French caption at right.

The advertising trade card often reflected considerable artistic ability, but rarely gave credit to the artist or designer. We can identify the typical drawings of a few prominent illustrators, among them the Brownies of Palmer Cox and the dainty misses of Kate Greenaway. The noted artist Winslow Homer created a few trade cards. The name of the printer or lithographer appears fairly frequently, in the bottom margin of the card. The major American lithographers were Louis Prang & Co. and J.H. Bufford & Co. of Boston, the Philadelphia firm of E. Ketterlinus, the Buffalo firms of Clay and Cosack, Richmond & Co. and Gies & Co., and in New York City, Napoleon Sarony, Major & Knapp, and Currier & Ives. Currier & Ives were first and foremost the producers of black and white lithographs and hand-colored pictures. They made only a few chromolithographed advertising cards, most of them comic stock cards. Although these are highly prized by print collectors, and expensive, they are by no means the best trade cards either from an artistic or technical standpoint.[9]

Cards by Kate Greenaway (above) and Palmer Cox (below). Few artists who drew trade cards can be identified.

One of the best Currier & Ives trade cards, copyright 1881. The firm was noted for its fine large lithographs of trotting horses.

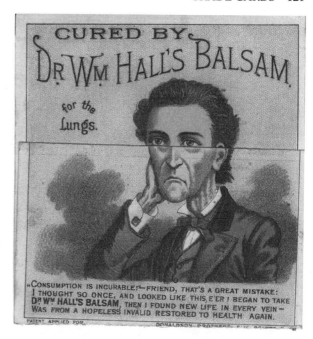

> The sufferers shown on these two metamorphic cards can be cured instantly by flicking open the card, if not by taking the medicine.

Patent medicines are represented in all types of advertising cards and in fact exemplify some of the rarest and most elaborate. The Greek word "metamorphic" is used to describe a picture that is capable of change. Donaldson Brothers, a firm located in the notorious Five Points District of New York, produced metamorphic trade cards with the picture printed across one or more flaps forming the face of the card. When a flap is folded downwards, for example, the composite picture is altered and a sad face becomes a happy one, a bad complexion is cured, or a white beard turns into a bushy black one (Plates 44, 75 and 76). Another trade card rarity, the "mechanical," has moving parts, the simplest having a sliding cardboard disc affixed to the center with a grommet. Brown's Iron Bitters issued a calendar card with a window in the disc that discloses different pictures as it is turned (Plate 74). The rarest mechanical cards are "pop-ups," with a paper component that rises when the card is unfolded or a tab is pulled (Plate 77).

A further variety is the hold-to-light card, which is printed on thinner stock than usual, and presents a

> A hold-to-light card with a typical subject. When illuminated from behind, even the cat opens its eyes.

> This curious card cannot be read until it is held up. With the printing on the back filling in the letters, it spells out the virtues of German Corn Remover.

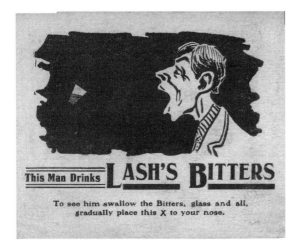

To achieve its special effect, Lash's Bitters was apparently willing to make the customer cross-eyed.

An attempt at cooperative advertising. This rare example is known as an Oak Hall card. The druggist has positioned himself at bottom center.

transformation of the picture when the printing on both sides of the card is seen together. A number of these show a baby, or a reclining girl. The eyes open when the card is held to the light. A card for Hood's Pills spells out the product name in the sky when additional stars appear (Plate 76). Several cards produce a symbol on the moon when held to the light. In a class by themselves are Beecham's Oracles, issued by the English pill manufacturer. These cards were printed on soft paper of which the center panel was impregnated invisibly with potassium nitrate. When one corner was ignited by a spark or a hot iron, the impregnated portion burned out and left a short message in rather crude script. These Oracles were a sensation in the Paris drawing rooms of the 1890s, according to a contemporary author who hailed Thomas Beecham as "the Sun King of the reclamé."[10]

Cobalt chloride was another chemical used to produce an interesting effect on several trade cards. It has the property of changing color from blue to pink in the presence of moisture. The card for Dr. Bull's Baby Syrup is impregnated with this chemical. The caption invites you to change the color of the baby's face from a strangled greenish hue to the ruddy color of health by blowing on the card. Lawson's Curative

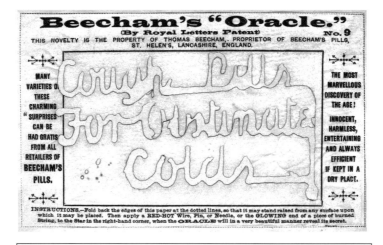

One of the famous Beecham's Oracles. The wonder is that the entire card did not go up in a puff of smoke when it was activated.

A card that was meant to be cut in pieces, and not for decoupage.

used this effect with two negro figures (Plate 79). There is a rare card advertising Wistar's Balsam of Wild Cherry which glows faintly in the dark from some luminous chemical (Plate 78). Perfume cards were in a number of instances printed on porous paper and impregnated with the scent being advertised. A few cards held sand applied with glue on which you could strike a match.

Some trade cards were cut in fanciful shapes by the use of special dies (Plates 80 and 81). Several proprietors issued butterfly die-cuts and some of these double as toys (Plate 82). They have tiny weights at each wing tip that permit the butterfly to be balanced on the head of a pencil. There are trade cards labeled "bookmarks." They are long narrow cards and often depict the silken fringe of the real article. Lydia Pinkham issued actual bookmarks of stamped leather (Plate 83).

The most numerous category of the special trade cards is probably that of the puzzle cards (Plates 84 and 85). Many of these were simple line drawings, often black and white or monochromes in red or blue. The most common contain a number of "hidden" figures, usually animals, that may be identified with more or less success when the card is viewed from various angles. In a caption, the reader is told

A charming die-cut card with the figures of the children lithographed in color. The back of the card shows the rear view of the same scene.

Below, an early puzzle card advertising a medicine named SSS, made by the Swift Specific Company. At right is a hidden-figure picture issued by St. Jacob's Oil that also contains a rebus on the obelisk within it.

PUZZLE CARD. find Cow, Rhinoceros, Owl, Kangeroo, Deer, Turtle, Squirrels, Face, Whale Lion, Elephant, Frog, Eagle, Vulture, Giraffe.

SOLUTION.
Seek you a cure, easy and sure
For aching sprains or hurts or pains,
Of every sort, in any part.
Be of good cheer, the secrets here ;
And if you heed what here you read,
Your pains you'll end, your ailments foil,
For you will send for ST. JACOBS OIL.

Seek for five months in the surroundings.

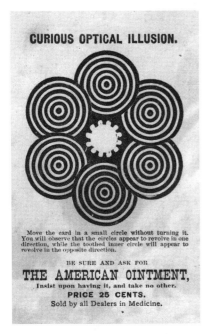

CURIOUS OPTICAL ILLUSION.

Move the card in a small circle without turning it. You will observe that the circles appear to revolve in one direction, while the toothed inner circle will appear to revolve in the opposite direction.

BE SURE AND ASK FOR

THE AMERICAN OINTMENT,

Insist upon having it, and take no other.

PRICE 25 CENTS.

Sold by all Dealers in Medicine.

what he is expected to find. The card for Dr. Abbey's Great Specific for Skin Diseases, entitled "Toll Gate No. 4," purportedly contains a hundred-and-fifty-three hidden figures (Plate 84).

A variety of the puzzle card is the rebus, and the best examples are those issued by Seth Arnold's Balsam (Plate 85). A few cards have a rebus on the back. You're too late, but one rebus card for Thomas' Eclectric Oil offered six free bottles to those who mailed in the solution before June 1888. There are also a few optical puzzle cards for medicines which offer black and white designs that fool the eye.

An optical puzzle, left, and a rare puzzle blotter, below.

The first American patent medicine advertisement appeared in an almanac in 1692. *Courtesy the New York Public Library, Lennox, Tilden and Astor Foundations.*

FREE ALMANACK,
FOR THE YEAR
1843,
And of American Independence the 67th:
Being the third after Leap Year!

Containing, besides the usual Astronomical Calculations, a variety of useful and entertaining matter.

Calculated for the Meridian of NEW-YORK, but will answer for any of the adjoining states or Canada.

ASTRONOMICAL CALCULATIONS BY GEO. R. PERKINS, *Professor of Mathematics, Utica, N. Y.*

Printed and Circulated Gratis, for reasons explained inside.

STEELE'S PRESS.

25.

Almanacs and Pamphlets

The Bible and the almanac were the only reading material available to most rural Americans in the 1700s and the almanac constitutes an important source of the raw material of social history in this country.[1] The treatise writers have concentrated on the eighteenth century almanacs, but those of the nineteenth century are of equal interest and importance.[2] Up to the time of the Civil War, a great many farmers were still beyond the reach of daily newspapers or other periodicals and many small printers issued almanacs for local distribution that reflect in rich detail the interests and attitudes of their day. The wit and charm of *Poor Richard's Almanac*, published in Philadelphia by Benjamin Franklin, has achieved lasting recognition and the ever-popular *Old Farmer's Almanac* is still published today.

The content of the earlier almanacs ran heavily to astronomical and weather information interspersed with proverbs, anecdotes, scraps of poetry and fragments of history. Most nineteenth century almanacs expanded their content with practical advice on crops and animal husbandry, and there followed almanacs devoted to a number of special subjects. What is thought to be the first almanac addressed to medicine, *The Physician's Almanac*, appeared in 1817. It contained general rules of health and simple home remedies. No medicines were advertised in it.

The medicine proprietors began with isolated advertisements in the general almanacs. The earliest advertisement of a medicine in the Colonies appears to be that for Aqua Anti-Terminales, an antidote against "Gripings of the Guts and Wind Cholick," sold by Benjamin Harris at the London Coffee House in Boston for three shillings the half pint. This remedy was advertised in *The Boston Almanac* for 1692, printed by the selfsame Benjamin Harris and one John Alden. Swaim's Panacea was up to six pages in the Farmer's and Mechanics Almanac of 1832. It was only logical that the major proprietors would soon publish their own almanacs on an annual basis. *The Free Almanac* for 1843, issued by Bristol's Sarsaparilla, and *Dr. B. Jayne's Medical Almanac and Guide to Health for Gratuitous Distribution* (1843) are thought to be the first almanacs wholly devoted to advertising one medicine and distributed without charge.[3]

Bristol's Sarsaparilla was the only medicine advertised in this almanac, one of the first two issued in this country by a medicine proprietor. *Courtesy The American Antiquarian Society.*

VINEGAR BITTERS ALMANAC
FOR THE YEAR
Adapted for Use throughout the United States.
1878
Containing Useful and Valuable Information.

Anatomical diagram with related signs of the zodiac. This was the conventional first page of all early almanacs and some later ones.

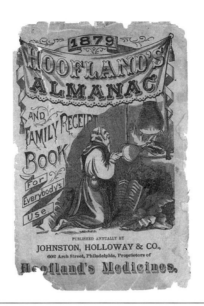

Three almanacs, above, with more elaborate covers typical of the second half of the last century. At far left, with Zoaves in the bottom panel, is a Civil War almanac of Plantation Bitters that does not even bear the medicine's name on the cover.

In time a profusion of medicine almanacs with handsome covers lithographed in color were distributed on the counters of the country store and the urban pharmacy (Plate 86). The quantity issued by the largest proprietors grew to enormous proportions. The makers of Ayer's Cherry Pectoral boasted that their almanac was second only to the Bible in circulation. An average year for the J.C. Ayer Company was about sixteen million but in 1889 they distributed more than twenty-five million almanacs, including copies in twenty-one languages.[4] It is thought that Hostetter's Bitters was second, with an average distribution of thirteen million copies per year.[5] The foreign-language copies were, of course, aimed at the newly arrived immigrants in this country as well as customers abroad.

At left, a listing of the foreign language editions of Ayer's for 1889 and an example below it of a Voegler's Almanac in German. Immediately below are two 20th century almanacs. Ayer's used this simple type of cover for over 70 years.

Among the most collectible of almanacs are the tiny "pocket editions" published by the E.T. Hazeltine Company to advertise Piso's Cough Cure (Plate 88). These little booklets of 32 pages measured about two inches high. The Colgate Company issued similar miniatures for their perfume and soap, with exquisite covers decorated by gold tracery. (See page 77.)

Following in the footsteps of the almanac came an abundance of other booklets and pamphlets large and small. They made no pretense of copying the monthly calendar format, and in a number of cases consisted of page after page of testimonials with line drawings of the purported grateful users who had written them.

A few medicine proprietors issued serious booklets on medical problems, as serious that is as you could expect from a high class pitchman. Dr. R.V. Pierce published the "Dime Series." Some of these cost 10 cents and some 6 cents, describing in graphic detail the symptoms of varicocele (enlarged veins of the scrotum), Bright's disease, locomotor ataxia, and other diseases that the reader was encouraged to discover in himself. Dr. Pierce was, of course, ready to help the sufferer with a full understanding of these problems, and to treat them either at his Invalid's Hotel and Surgical Institute (Plate 19), or through the products of the World's Dispensary Medical Association which included Dr. Pierce's Favorite Prescription, Dr. Pierce's Golden Medical Discovery and Dr. Pierce's Extract of Smartweed (which contained opium).

Two publications of Dr. R.V. Pierce and his World Dispensary Medical Assoc.

Dr. Pierce also published a hardcover book containing over a thousand pages of medical advice, product puffing, testimonials and advertising for the Invalids Hotel. It was entitled *The People's Common Sense Medical Adviser*. The first edition came out in 1875. The ninety-second edition, in 1918, claimed sales of almost three and a half million copies.The price appears to have fluctuated between $1.50 and 21 cents according to the edition and the promotion to which it was currently subject.

The volume of material distributed, in relation to the amount of the product sold, tells something about the economics of the medicine business. One trade card for Paine's, apparently addressed to the druggist himself, lists the following items that were supplied free with an order for twelve bottles costing a total of eight dollars: one hundred diary calendars, one hundred copies of the pamphlet *Great Things*, one "handsome sign" (probably a counter card) and three show cartons.

A number of proprietors distributed pocket memorandum books with a month's calendar and a blank sheet for notes facing each page of advertising. The most widely known is probably "Dr. Pierce's Pocket Memorandum Book

The retailer was deluged with printed matter for his customers including trade cards, pamphlets and calendars.

Notebooks for the customer's pocket, about 5 inches high, with calendar pages and product information.

Above, booklets distributed in the 1890's by medicine proprietors, on a variety of subjects. They usually contained a minimum of advertising.

Designed for Farmers and Mechanics and All People." Best Tonic, Bromo Seltzer and Paine's Celery Compound also issued these books.

In due course, as the public became increasingly saturated with hard-sell health material, the alert merchandiser wooed his customers' attention with booklets on many unrelated subjects of general interest, which might only have an advertisement for the product on the back cover.

Lydia Pinkham distributed 32-page booklets with as many as a hundred titles in several languages, on subjects ranging from first aid to beauty hints, candy recipes, marriage problems and female chauvinism (Plate 35). Dr. Miles' Nervine published pamphlets on stamp collecting, buried treasure, rescues at sea, and tales of the jungle.

Medicine booklets may be found in a number of categories that invite special collector interest (Plates 87 and 88). There are the fortune-telling variety, "dream books," "fate books" and horoscopes. These were issued by The Kickapoo Indian Medicine Company, Dr. Kilmer's Preparations, Kunkel's Malaria and Ague Powders, Dr. Harter's Wild Cherry Bitters and Hartman's Peruna, among others. Cookbooks were issued by Hood's Sarsaparilla, Mrs. Ransom's Hive Syrup and Tolu, Lydia Pinkham's, Sulphur Bitters and others. Warner's Safe Cure published a pamphlet dictionary in 1889 listing five thousand words. Malena, Horsford's Preparation, Castoria and Pond's Extract offered children's story books. The Malena series have particularly vivid and handsome lithography. Nichol's Extract of Bark and Iron published a drawing book for children and Warner's and Hood's distributed coloring books. The Hood's book came with a sheet of paint pigments and a tiny camel's hair brush. There were books of parlour games and joke books.

Medicine booklets that bring us into the radio age. These last three advertised Dr. Miles' Nervine.

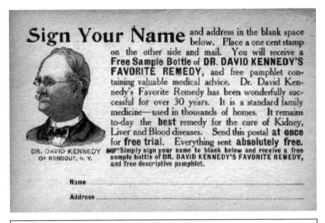

Free samples were widely used in later years by the patent medicine proprietors.

The "rewards," never claimed, were a favorite device of advertisers in the 1880's.

26.   Giveaway items

The gimmicks used to advertise patent medicines ranged across the spectrum of man's imagination, from trial samples to outrageous "reward" offers, paper toys, stamps and coins, and finally a variety of household articles. This advertising-in-kind has become an increasingly popular type of collectible today.

No word that can be used in advertising attracts more attention than "FREE." Down through the years the trial sample has been almost irresistible sales bait. The patent medicine proprietors worked the device for all it was worth. "Try them at my expense," urged Dr. L.D. LeGear and Dr. David Kennedy. Seven Roots Tonic offered coupons worth 25 cents each. The German Electric Company distributed "checks" worth $3 against the purchase of one of their medical devices.

A few nostrum firms in the early days offered "rewards" to disappointed users. Howe's Never Failing Ague Cure promised $500 to the person whom it in fact failed to cure. John Root's Bitters offered $1,000 to any person not cured of a list of diseases that included typhoid, brain fever and small pox. Pulvermacher's Electric Belt gave the idea a curious twist by guaranteeing $5,000 to the person who could prove that one of its competitors' contrivances had a curative effect! The reward device may have been done to death by the famous Carbolic Smoke Ball Case in 1892. The advertisement promised £100 to anyone who breathed the noxious fumes as directed for a period of weeks and was not cured. A Mrs. Carlill sued to recover the promised £100. The manufacturer argued that no contract existed on which the lady could sue because she had not furnished sufficient value on her part. In a landmark decision on this narrow point of law, the judge awarded the £100 to Mrs. Carlill, saying that the small purchase price and the countless futile inhalations were enough to make the offer a binding contract with whomever accepted it.[1]

A first! Mrs. Carlill sued for her reward after using a Carbolic Smoke Ball in vain. An English court awarded her the promised £100.

Among the most handsome paper items distributed by the nostrum proprietors were their calendars (Plates 89 and 90). They were generally not of the type that can be remembered on the wall of the country garage, with a sheaf of date pages hanging beneath a picture of a well-endowed girl in a bathing suit. The medicine calendars were of slick cardboard, perhaps twelve inches high at most. They were fully colored gems of the lithographer's art. A few had a grommet for attachment to the wall, but usually the calendar pages were only a few inches square and decoration was the main purpose.

A number of these calendars were "die-cut," that is, punched out in special shapes by the use of a knife-edged plate in the printing press. The pictorial matter covered a wide variety of subjects but children were a favorite calendar subject. The Hoods series were devoted exclusively to babies, young girls or pretty ladies. Scott's Emulsion, Dr. Miles' Nervine, and Schenck's Pills followed the same line.

The medicine blotter had its start in the last century. It was based upon a reasonable assumption. The prescribing doctor has his pen in hand (not a ball point) and needs to blot the prescription. What better place for a medicine advertisement? This giveaway item became a tradition and it is one that is honored by today's pharmaceutical manufacturers with the colorful glossy-backed modern variety (Plate 91).

Paper dolls were a delight to the Victorian-era child and they are greatly prized by collectors today. They were die-cut from light cardboard and had a minimum of advertising on the back. Among medicine manufacturers this advertising was favored by Dr. Jayne's Products, Hood's Sarsaparilla, Doctor Miles' Medicine, McElree's Cardui, Lyon's Kathairon and Mellin's Food (for babies) (Plate 92). One Hood's series consisted of barnyard animal "statuettes" about four inches high. Jaynes put out a circus series and also sheets of stand-up baseball players. Kickapoo issued an Indian Dale Camp consisting of twenty-two different pieces.

Three medicine calendars. A typical scene, at top; a die-cut whimsey, at left; and a calendar lithographed upon a blotter that was used to sell a toothpowder. It was also impregnated with a perfume made by the same manufacturer.

Imperium Granum, a dietetic cereal for children, distributed real dolls upon occasions. Hamlin's Wizard Oil put out a children's game in a cardboard box. Hood's and Piso's made some jigsaw puzzles that are first-rate collector's pieces (Plate 92). Among the adult toys, provided for the player by his favorite remedy, were dominoes from Warner's Safe Cure and Hood's Sarsaparilla, and cribbage boards from Lash's Liver Bitters and Priests' Indigestion Powder.

Berliner Magen Bitters supplied their own corkscrew for getting at the beverage. Lash's provided a large copper funnel with a spring-operated valve. These latter items were suitable for barroom use, a reminder that in the 1800s and 1890s the tonics known as "bitters" were often sold over the bar. They were certainly not the mildest drinks purveyed on such premises. Shot glasses can be found, etched with the names Rooster Bitters, Petzgold Bitters, Our Native Herbs and others.

At a later stage other medicine products catered to the soda fountain business with brightly enameled tip trays, among them the headache remedies Antikamnia and Hick's Capudine, and the mineral water sold as Red Raven Splits. If you needed a toothpick, there was a celluloid item in a convenient case emblazoned "Bouvier's Buchu Gin."

Hood's War game, played with special cards, celebrated the Spanish-American War. A set of Warner's dominoes, each advertising a different Warner product, and their wooden box.

Shot glasses were supplied by many purveyors of bitters and similar medicines. Left to right: Dr. Green's Blood Purifier, Harter's Iron Tonic, Adlerika Natural Bowel Cleanser, and Smith's Green Mountain Renovator.

Tin giveaways. A soda fountain tip tray, from the early 1900's, advertising Antikamnia, and an ash tray from the 1950's distributed by Hadacol.

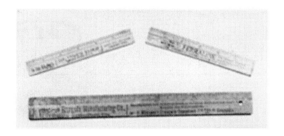

Household helps. Six-inch rulers from Dr. True's Elixir and Ferraline; a whole foot from Frangula.

Lydia Pinkham's gifts. Clockwise: sewing kit in a metal vial, a tape measure with her picture, a compact, and a needle and thread in a paper cover.

A number of handy items were provided for the home. Lydia Pinkham distributed an octagonal pad for hot dishes, covered with silver foil, that bore her likeness and several catchy slogans. She also gave away tape measures and sewing kits in several sizes and, as late as the 1920's, cosmetic aids such as cuticle sticks and compacts. Some of these items were obtained for ten cents and a coupon from the back of a Lydia Pinkham booklet. Cardboard fans bearing medicine advertising were common. Household rulers, some of them four or six inches only, were offered by Dr. True's Elixir, Mrs. Winslow's Soothing Syrup and the remedy called Frangula. Pepsin Bitters provided a match safe, a tin device that hung on the wall as a container for fresh matches and a receptacle for burnt ones. Glass paperweights may be found, embossed with the names of Goulding Spring Lithia Water and of Hunyadi Arpad, a popular mineral water imported from Budapest. Smith Brothers made an admirable replica in cast iron of their round black cough drops. The replicas weighed almost a pound.

An iron paperweight from Smith Brothers and one of glass from a medicinal spring water.

The medicine proprietor naturally supplied his retailers with a certain number of props for advertising display purposes. There were store banners, like that for Dr. McLean's Strengthening Cordial, which was made of felt twelve inches high and five feet long. They were tacked on the wall or hung from a shelf or perhaps a beam. There were stand-up figures die-cut from heavy cardboard. A hinged cardboard foot was attached to the back to keep the figure upright. Some of them were king-sized versions of figures shown on the proprietor's trade cards. Ayer's "Country Doctor"(Plate 103) and "Eliza and the Deacon" (Plate 16) are examples of this type of counter-card. They stood thirteen inches tall. A small panorama could be arranged with the cut-outs distributed by Morse's Indian Root Pills. They measured about ten inches by fourteen and represented an Indian campfire, a brave in a canoe, and the like. One of the largest display items was a paper mache elephant, complete with mahout and a banner, advertising Hamlin's Wizard Oil, which measured twenty-seven by thirty inches.

The best giveaways were probably used as premiums for the drug store owner who made a large purchase of the product, and they may also have been used to reward the givers of testimonials. In this category may be found barometers with faces bearing the name of Dr. McLean's Tonic Vermifuge, or Kickapoo Indian Oil. There are also clocks for the mantel or the back-bar, some of them very handsome indeed. (See page 95.) Clocks were given by Reed's Tonic, Mishler's Herb Bitters, Simmon's Liver Regulator and Duffy's Malt Whiskey (a reliable medicinal invigorant).

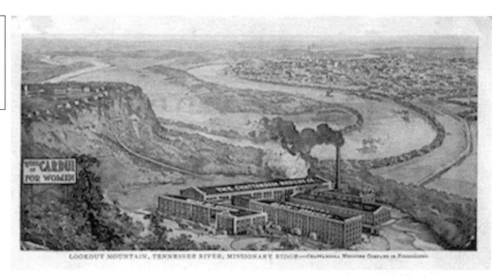

A patent medicine postcard. McElree's Wine of Cardui was a leading Southern medicine for women. Lookout Mountain was the site of a notable Civil War Battle.

Postcards advertising medicines were not plentiful during the patent medicine era. During the most prolific years of nostrum advertising, the trade card was king, and the commercial use of the postcard was not very widespread. The trade card could, of course, carry a long advertising message on the back, and never asked for the purchase of a stamp. Trade cards achieved a level of considerable artistry, both in design and execution. Delicate lithography was not suited to open handling in the mails and, as one would expect, the medicine postcards were generally of a simpler style and form of execution. Most have a geographical aspect. They show the factory where the product is made, or the headquarters building, or a drugstore in the case of a local product. The postcards attempting a hard sell of the product are rare.

In somewhat earlier years, advertising envelopes or "covers," in philatelic parlance, were used by a few medicine proprietors. It was common practice to decorate envelopes during the patent medicine era with elaborate embellishments including patriotic and other vignettes, often in color[2] (Plate 94). The advertising vignette might be supported on the back of the envelope by the slogan of the proprietor, and sometimes that of two or three other advertisers. There are also several rare types of patent medicine advertising that are of special interest to the philatelist.

There were two hundred and seventy-seven medicine manufacturers who used what were known as "private die proprietary stamps."[3] These were revenue stamps evidencing payment of a tax levied, in

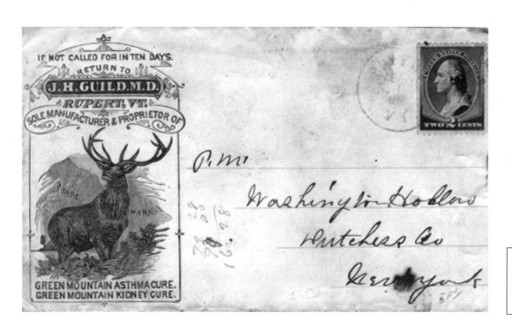

Postal covers were decorated in black and white and sometimes in color. This one was, of course, printed in green.

The trade card (right) advertises Atwood's Bitters. The girl is holding a picture of the company's private stamp, of which it is justly proud, but which is no longer required as a tax measure.

Private die tax stamps used by, left, Walker's Vinegar Bitters. The right-hand stamp advertises Drake's Plantation Bitters and 5 other Demas Barnes products.

addition to medicines, on cosmetics, perfumes, matches, playing cards and business documents. Stamp taxes of this nature were a time-honored fiscal measure of hard pressed governments. The British angered the American colonies with such a tax in 1775. America in turn imposed such a tax internally during the Civil War and succeeding decades (1862-1883) and again during the Spanish American War period (1898-1901). Most manufacturers used the revenue stamps issued by the government, of which there were several varieties and denominations over the years. Some cancelled them with their firm names. A limited number designed their own tax stamps, which the law permitted, and these are the "private die" specimens (Plate 93).

After tax stamps were no longer required by the revenue authorities, a few medicine firms retained their specially designed stamps as a bottle closure, or as part of a label.[4] The proprietor may have been as much interested in the suggestion of government approval of his product as he was in preserving the familiar image. Warner's Safe Cure and Ayer's Vegetable Cathartic Pills used such packaging.

Loose postage stamps were sometimes used for small change during the periods when coinage was scarce, but the stamps crumpled, stuck together, and were easily lost. John Gault of New York City patented an invention in 1862 that was intended to remedy these problems and provide advertising as well. It was known as "encased postage." An encased postage stamp is a rarity unknown to many advanced philatelists. It is a hybrid,

Right, Warner's made a great point of its paper seals, seeking to prolong the mystique of the tax stamp.

Plate 101. Sports for both the men and the ladies. After the turn of the century, the lady in the antique sleigh gives way to images of women newly engaged in more active athletic endeavors.

Plate 102. Four appealing children from the makers of patent remedies. These trade cards also touch variously upon the themes of reli-
gion, foreign lands, and ethnic comedy. Note the caption partly in
Spanish on the Scott's Emulsion card, indicating its use in the export
trade.

Plate 103. Pictures of babies made a direct appeal to the mothers who purchased the nostrums. The trade card for Dr. King's New Discovery, at bottom right, shows children in an adult situation, a frequent convention in advertising of this sort. Today, the scene from Shakespeare would be regarded as much too highbrow and obscure.

DANIEL BRUCE, SR., Druggist. 62 Broadway. Providence, R. I.

WHAT'S ON THE BACK?

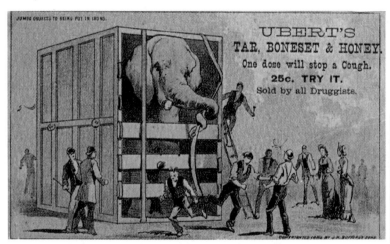

Plate 104. Animal images were a perennial favorite, especially for comic situations. The Ubert's trade card refers to Jumbo, an enormous African elephant brought to this country by P. T. Barnum and exhibited widely to great crowds.

Funny money. The Centaur Bank, and the Mustang Bank below, existed only in the imagination of their proprietors.

part stamp and part coin, usually round and of copper or brass, with a mica window through which a carefully folded stamp may be seen. A product or firm name was embossed on the back. The federal government put an end to this usage within one year but, in any event, the invention was impractical because the protective mica wore out too easily.

Four medicine proprietors were among forty or so firms who issued encased postage stamps. They were the makers of Ayer's Cathartic Pills, Brown's Bronchial Troches, Burnett's Cocoaine and Drake's Plantation Bitters. The denomination of stamps that were encased ranged from one cent to ninety cents, but it is probable that only one or two denominations can be found for any particular issuer, and that only a few stamps of the larger denominations were encased.[5]

How do you create an irresistible urge in the customer to pick up your advertisement? Easy. Just make it look like a hundred dollar bill. This device appealed to about thirty-five medicine proprietors who printed small handbills with facsimile banknotes of various denominations on one side.

These are rare and charming pieces. The format often followed that of a United States or Confederate bill, but most were black and white only, and on thin paper, which prevented too many from passing for the real thing. Some of the advertisements were in a column of text on the reverse of the bill, but frequently advertising was worked into the bill format, the vignettes, and the signature. The bill would be styled as an obligation of The Plantation Bank (Drake's Plantation Bitters) or The Centaur Bank (Centaur Liniment).[6] Whatever the denomination, it never entitled the bearer to more than one free bottle.

A few proprietors issued metal coins or tokens, among them French Cognac Bitters (copper), Cascarets laxative pills (brass) and Dr. Caldwell's Syrup of Pepsin (aluminum). The tokens were used far less than the banknotes.

The face of this bill was a reasonable replica of a Confederate banknote. The advertising for Morse's Indian Root Pills, below, appeared on the back only.

This is presented to you in order to impress on your mind the fact that

DR. MORSE'S INDIAN ROOT PILLS

Have been before the public for more than sixty years, and to-day are the most popular family Pill in the market. To those who have used them we need not say one word—they stand on their merit. To those who have not used them we simply say they are the best Pill that skill, money and experience can produce. They are a specific cure for most of the Blood, Stomach and Liver Diseases. They absolutely remove all Dyspepsia, Giddiness, Headache and are most useful in female disorders. Don't forget! DR. MORSE'S INDIAN ROOT PILLS.

W. H. COMSTOCK, Sole Proprietor, Morristown, St. Lawrence Co., N. Y.

Collectors in the numismatic field can also find genuine financial obligations issued by medicine proprietors in the days when currency was scarce and the laws permitted liberal use of "scrip" by merchants of all sorts. T.W. Dyott's Manual Labor Banking House was a financial enterprise of one of the early American nostrum manufacturers. Bank notes in many denominations, from 50 cents to $100, can be found for this institution. In fact, Dyott issued them so enthusiastically that he experienced not one but two bankruptcies as a result. The triumph and travails of this early giant in the patent medicine field illustrate graphically the days when there appeared to be no restraint, either medical or financial, on the patent medicine entrepreneur.

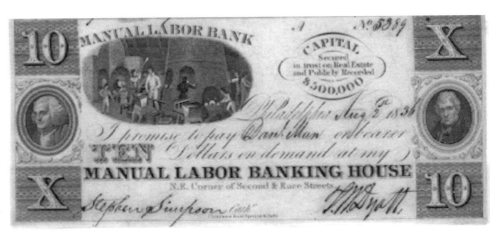

Insofar as Thomas W. Dyott had any money in his Manual Labor Bank, this was a genuine banknote. Dyott manufactured medicines and glass bottles.

27.

Containers

Packaging is a very important part of selling any consumer product today. It attracts the eye at the point of sale and it differentiates one product from its competitors. The design of the container and the appearance of the wrapper mattered more, in the case of the patent nostrums, as the methods of marketing them developed during the nineteenth century.

The rural pedlar of the early days sold his potions in any bottle that was available to him. The local pharmacist might improve the appearance of a bottle of standard shape from the wholesale house by adding a printed label of his own. When the medicine was produced in quantity it became worthwhile for a proprietor to have his bottles blown in a mold that would emboss them with his name and the name of his product. In time, some of the larger medicine proprietors began to use bottles with very elaborate embossing.

A few medicines, mostly those in that class of alcoholic tonics known as bitters, were sold in bottles of special shapes that are now called "figural bottles." These are very desirable examples of the glass blower's art. They include human figures, animals, a cannon, a lighthouse, and a number of barrels and log cabins.[1] These medicine containers approached the status of decanters, no doubt, when they stood on the back bar of the saloon.

Old and interesting bottles that are rarely found with labels. Clockwise from the top: Chaulmoogra, The East Indian Cure (for leprosy), Jayne's Carminative Balsam, Dr. McMunn's Elixir of Opium, Dr. Evan's Camomile Pills, and Opodeldoc.

Figural bitters bottles are among those most sought after by collectors. From the left: Old Homestead Wild Cherry Bitters, Dr. S.W. Robach's Stomach Bitters, Tippecanoe, and Brown's Indian Herb Bitters (the "Indian Queen").

Wooden pill boxes for sale to the manufacturer or druggist, as shown in a catalogue from the 1870's.

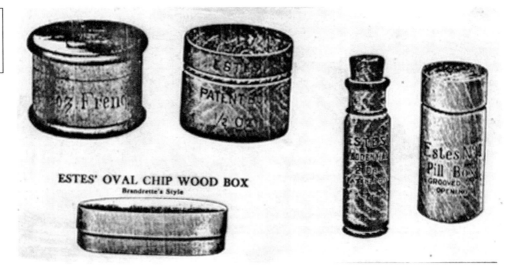

ESTES' OVAL CHIP WOOD BOX
Brandrette's Style

Medicine bottles are the subject of considerable collector interest. The details and delights of bottle collecting are too numerous to summarize briefly. The literature in this field is extensive and just a few of the many excellent books available are listed here in the section entitled Works Consulted. Bottle collector's magazines have encouraged research into the history of some of the lesser known medicine proprietors, as background for articles on their containers.

It is difficult to find examples of the more perishable forms of early medicine packaging, like the small round boxes of light wood or birch bark in which pills were sold, or the paper packets in which powders have been retailed by pharmacists for centuries. It is also difficult to find complete packages of nineteenth century medicines with their boxes or outer wrappings. These may be seen in pharmacy museums and some country store displays but lucky is the collector who has, for example, a full bottle of Dr. J. Hostetter's Stomach Bitters with St. George and the Dragon on a complete label, an intact lead foil seal and the carton with its printed wrapping. Many of the labels on old medicine bottles were elaborate and colorful.[2] The scarcity of these labels today is attributable to the fact that many old bottles now come from trash heaps. Some are even recovered from under water.

A Hostetter's bottle pictured in the 1910 almanac, still looking as it did in the 1860's.

Packaging Ayer's Pills, a task for cupids, apparently.

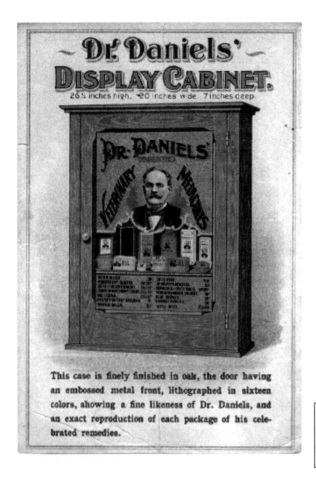

This case is finely finished in oak, the door having an embossed metal front, lithographed in sixteen colors, showing a fine likeness of Dr. Daniels, and an exact reproduction of each package of his celebrated remedies.

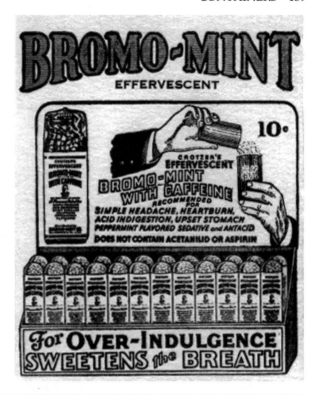

Package displays. Left, above, the cabinet furnished by Dr. Daniels in 1904. The different packages were red, pink, orange, yellow, green and blue. Above, right, a display carton, probably 1920's, advertised on a blotter that was distributed to retailers.

Tin containers were less commonly used for medicine products. Some pills and salves were put up in tins, and tin tubes were commonly used for the medicinal plasters, like mustard plaster, lead plaster, or capsicum plaster, which were sold in a roll. The more spectacular medicine tins were those used by the large wholesale drug houses like Parke Davis & Co. to hold crude drugs that were sold to the pharmacist in bulk. A few such tins have glass windows for viewing the contents.

Two lithographed medicine tins, not shown to scale. Taffy Tolu was an herbal remedy, not a candy.

Two tins with special features. The tin at left has a glass window for inspecting the product. Licorice was sold as a medicine for coughs, colds and sore throat. The tin shown in two views at right contains a pump for expelling the contents, usually an oil like glycerine. These were druggists' containers.

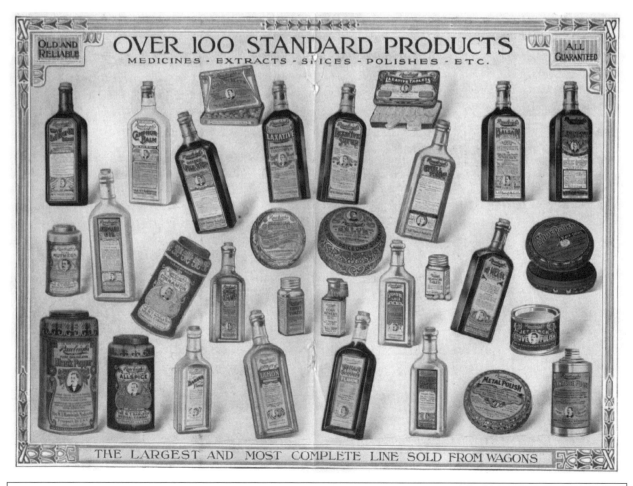

"Wait for my wagon. I am coming soon," said W.T. Rawleigh in the *Freeport Illinois Weekly Journal* in 1892. By 1918 he had branches in Memphis, Minneapolis, Oakland, Winnepeg and Toronto, but his advertising, like the back cover of his almanac above, still emphasized direct sale of these packages from a horse-drawn cart.

The rural fence rails read, in letters reversed by the murky tintype photography, "Hardy's Cures Headaches."

28.

Outdoor Advertising

Outdoor advertising reached obnoxious proportions during the nineteenth century. A British visitor wrote in 1882:

"America is daubed from one end of the country to the other with huge white-paint notices of favorite articles of manufacture, with an endless array of advertisements puffing off the medicines of pretentious quacks . . . it is one of the first things that strike the stranger as soon as he has landed in the New World: he cannot step a mile into the open country, whether into the fields or along the high roads without meeting the disfigurements . . . at length he becomes quite accustomed to the sight and is able to look upon it with complacency and expect "Bitters." "Gargling Oil," "Horse Powders," etc. at every turn of the path.[1]"

This is the corner of Park Avenue and 79th Street in New York City, about 1880. The message painted on the rock, "Henry's Carbolic Salve Bitters," was probably intended for riders on the New York Central Railroad whose tracks had just been placed underground at this point. *Photo courtesy Janet Lehr.*

A drawing from the July 1884 issue of *Cottage Hearth* illustrates the Centaur Company's proposed outdoor advertising. "Castoria," which that firm owned at the time, was to be emblazoned on the pedestal of the Statue of Liberty for one year. *Courtesy John E. Duncan.*

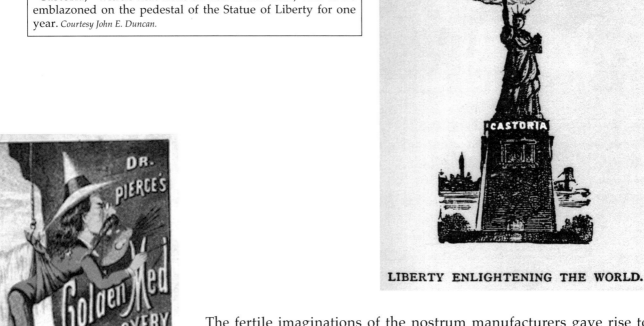

LIBERTY ENLIGHTENING THE WORLD.

Dr. Pierce's illustration of an attempt to decorate the cliffs at Niagara is probably apochryphal but it is certain that one of his competitors accomplished the feat.

The fertile imaginations of the nostrum manufacturers gave rise to some of the most outrageous outdoor advertising.[2] When funds were being raised in 1884 to construct a base on which to mount the new Statue of Liberty, the Centaur Company offered very seriously to donate $25,000 if they could emblazon "Castoria" across the top of the pedestal. The Voegler Company painted a huge ad for St. Joseph's Oil on a rock near Niagara Falls. The sign was removed after public protest.[3] Voegler's placarded a Mississippi River steamboat that was visible for many miles from the river banks. Several trade cards for Shiloh's Consumption Cure show paddlewheel steamers bearing the name of this renowned benefit to humanity but it is doubtful that they actually existed. Morton Wineburg, proprietor of Omega Oil, boasted:

> We have painted signs everywhere. Between Forrest Hills and the South Terminal Station in Boston we have 2,500 feet, or nearly half a mile, of sign boards, which breaks the record for the distance.[4]

The 65 foot steamer shown on this trade card was used solely to distribute material advertising St. Jacob's Oil to the river towns of the Mississippi, Ohio and other Western rivers.

On the urban scene the "sandwich man" made his appearance in the 1850s bearing large placards in front and behind. In 1900 there were between 1,000 and 1,200 employed in New York City alone and in a few places they are with us yet. There were no buses or taxis to carry product signs during the patent medicine era, but beginning in the 1830s merchants hired advertising wagons that toured the streets, ablaze with pennants and banners. The Bromo Seltzer Building in Baltimore probably deserves the prize for large-scale urban display. Its tower was crowned in 1911 by a rotating fifty foot replica of the familiar blue bottle which, when lighted at night, was visible for twenty miles.

It was not difficult to buy up walls and fences, as the manager of Tarrant's Seltzer Aperient revealed to his colleagues at the time. A year's rental could be procured with a subscription to one of the magazines in which Tarrant's was advertised. Tarrant arranged the subscription without cost to itself. The outside walls of drug stores were held in particular esteem by the medicine proprietors, or the walls of the building next door, if the pharmacist was reluctant.

Posters were used both outdoors and inside the store. One is tempted to say that the best were the small posters intended for indoor use but it is hard to be sure because so very few of the large outdoor posters have survived. There is one splendid barn-sized specimen for Hamlin's Wizard Oil in the Library of Congress that depicts an entire medicine show coming to town (Plate 95).

In France, the poster blossomed as an art form. Toulouse-Lautrec is perhaps the best remembered artist to work in this medium but it was another Frenchman, Jules Cheret, who was most responsible for the development of poster art and showed the way for the Englishman, Aubrey Beardsley, and the American, Edward Penfield. The prolific Cheret designed twenty-four posters for pharmaceutical products. The posters of the patent medicine era were lithographed, sometimes in flamboyant colors and bold outlines, often in delicate tones and designs. Only a few nostrums were represented in this type of artwork, but posters provide some of the most beautiful (and most expensive) patent medicine advertising that can be found.[5] An original French poster from the 1890s may sell today for thousands of dollars.

Dr. John F. True of Auburn, Maine, designed this advertisement himself. He began selling his Pin Worm Elixir in 1851.

The Emerson Drug Company, proprietors of Bromo-Seltzer, made their Baltimore headquarters into the extraordinary display shown above. At left is an advertising wagon, one of the firm's earlier more conventional efforts.

American posters for patent medicines, on the whole, did not rise to the level of technique or sophistication found on the Continent. At top left is an early example of an image wholly unrelated to the nostrum that it advertises. *Courtesy the Library of Congress.* Top right is a straightforward rendering of the package and owl logo used by the C.I. Hood Company. Bottom left is a fanciful elegant image used for a rather pedestrian horse liniment. Bottom right, an art nouveau design by Maxfield Parrish that shows a rare degree of artistry. *Courtesy The Philadelphia Museum of Art, gift of William H. Helfand.*

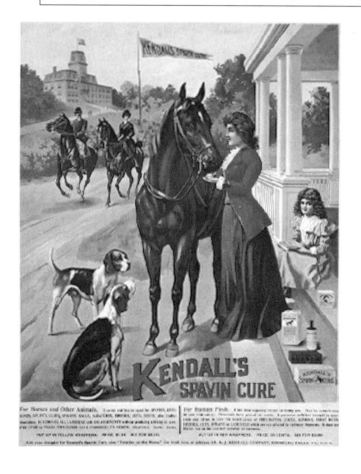

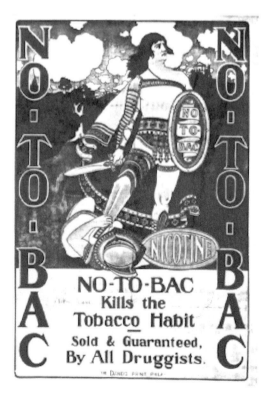

29. The Medicine Show, Music

There is one type of nostrum ballyhoo that has printed its mark indelibly on the American scene—the patent medicine show. Some people might say it provides the philosophical basis for many television commercials. Once upon a time, the traveling medicine show was as much a part of rural American life as the circus parade or the county fair, with each of which it shared a number of aspects.

The medicine show evolved slowly from humble beginnings. It began with the act of the single pitchman who attracted his customers with a banjo and pseudo-medical patter. One sample goes: "Meno secundo, stale tomatoes, saleratus, oxious, noxious, polly, pollygopsious, erysipelas!" This fellow worked the country towns in a wagon, where like as not he slept and also bottled his own goods. If sales went well, a fresh batch could be mixed by the edge of a stream just before pulling into the next town.

The more prosperous remedy peddler hired assistants and traveled with a group. The basic format of his show was the "doctor's lecture" punctuated every twenty minutes or so by a commercial and climaxed by the doctor's assistants passing through the crowd with baskets of his bottled nostrum. Their classic cry was "All sold out, Doctor!" The use of shills or accomplices was common, but the professional had many sly tricks to produce a sincere endorsement from the genuinely afflicted customer that he treated in front of the crowd. Later troupes actually included a bona fide doctor, usually some wretch in the last stages of alcoholism, to give them protection from charges of practice without a license.

James Whitcomb Riley, sometimes called "the poet of the common people", was for a season an assistant in a troupe that sold patent medicine. A letter records that he chalked one of his lesssor known verses on a blackboard, in the form of a rebus, to illustrate his spiel: "Why let pain your pleasure spoil, for want of Townsend's Magic Oil?"[1]

The larger medicine manufacturers put their own traveling shows on the road. Old Doc Hamlin's Wizard Oil, Shaker Soothing Syrup, Hood's Sarsaparilla, Lydia Pinkham's and Merchants' Gargling Oil, were all sold by medicine shows. The greatest name in medicine show business, however, was Healey & Bigelow, a partnership organized in 1881 that made the Kickapoo Indian remedies. The Kickapoos were a minor branch of the Algonquin tribe that helped the British capture Detroit in the French and Indian War. They also participated in the

Miniature songbooks of 16 pages, about 3 inches high, given away by the makers of Piso's Cure for Catarrh.

"A Balsamic Ditty" was not a song but a poem of 26 verses with an alphabetical theme, extolling the virtues of Wistar's Balsam of Wild Cherry. A companion ballad from the same proprietor, concerning an unhappy victim of consumption, was entitled "The Lay of the Lonesome Lung."

Kickapoo Indian Remedies of New Haven, Conn., sought a direct involvement with the redman through medicine shows and exhibitions. Left, an announcement of a druggist's window display in Rochester, N.H. Right, one of a series of trade cards depicting Indian life.

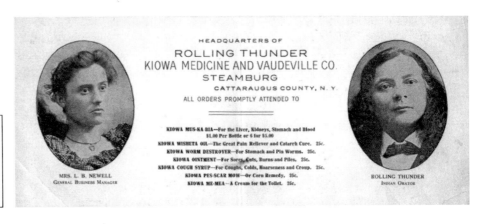

Black Hawk uprising of the 1830s. At the height of the company's success, Healey & Bigelow hired more than a thousand Indians from U.S. Government Indian Agents at $30 per head a month and their upkeep. Not one actual Kickapoo was involved. Some shows were simply rented out to a local promoter for a fee and a royalty on sales. His contract would specify the area and the products and had some aspects in common with modern franchising operations in the consumer field.

Indians were not chosen simply for theatrical reasons. In fact the Indian was romanticized far more in the East than in the West, where Indian fighting was much more recent. The Indian was a symbol of natural, herbal medicines and proven folkways, contrasted with dangerous, newfangled chemicals and expensive doctoring. The Indian theme was used by many medicines and persisted for decades.

Usually a Healey & Bigelow show consisted of a manager, six Indians, and six other performers. The Indians lived in teepees, and the show used a platform with a painted Indian panorama as a backdrop. Each of the Indians was introduced by name and grunted appropriately. The last Indian made a speech in "Kickapoo" translated by the showman,which led into the "doctor's lecture." There followed music by three performers accompanied by three Indians on tom-toms. The six others fanned out into the audience and sold the remedies. Healey & Bigelow also sought the goodwill of the local druggists, and an aftermarket for the product, by wholesaling it in conjunction with the show at forty percent of its retail price.

Above, Healey & Bigelow, agents for the Kickapoo shows, solicit business from retailers. Below, an ad for another medicine show company that illustrates its ties to vaudeville and general entertainment.

Public entertainment of any sort was hard to find in the rural America of the nineteenth century and free theater like the medicine show was a wonderful gift. While its message may not have been wholly believed, it was beloved, at least as much as our modern video fare a century later. The music provided at the patent medicine shows was band music to begin with, appropriate to the nostrum maker's loud brass instruments, but later it included popular ballads for public singing. For these occasions the patent medicine proprietor distributed song books (Plate 96). The older copies of Hamlin's depict on their covers the medicine man's wagon-load of musicians. They contained the words only—appropriate for the crowd at the tailgate. Later song books, like those advertising Thedford's Wine of Cardui and Merchants' Gargling Oil, set out the music as well as the words and were intended for use around the piano in the parlor.

The pages of these tattered pamphlets tell us what America was singing—not in the academy of music perhaps but in the town square or in the evening when a couple of fellows with handlebar moustaches were paying a call on Sis. Dr. Andral S. Kilmer must have been very fond of *The Old Oaken Bucket.* There are several almanacs and other pieces published by Kilmer's Swamp Root that feature this song on the back cover. Beecham's Music Portfolio (Plate 96) was distributed free by the agents for the pills of the same name, and Bromo Seltzer published handsome copies of sheet music about the turn of the century, with a minimum of advertising. There were 171 selections offered in this series. We find the Spanish-American War reflected by *"The Manila Quickstep," "Do They Think of Me at Home,"* and *"Columbia, My Country."*

The song with the biggest advertising pay-off was the proprietor's very own ditty—if he could get anyone to sing it. The Song of Lydia Pinkham has entered history, recognized even when performed by a modern night club comic:

> "Ah we'll sing of Lydia Pinkham
>   And her love for the human race.
> How she sells her Vegetable Compound
>   And the papers they publish her face."

This famous number was set to the old hymn tune "I Will Sing of My Redeemer," with several dozen verses added by admirers, some printable and some not (see page 56). It was a gentle parody, originated by some boys of the Dartmouth College Glee Club in the 1880s. It amused Lydia, who welcomed the exposure, and pasted in her own album the songs and jokes that displayed her name in print.[2]

The medicine show was not limited to indian affairs. Hamlin's Wizard Oil offered brass band concerts and sometimes a circus.

After the turn of the century, patent medicine music moved indoors, so to speak, with songbooks more adapted to singing by young ladies in the parlor.

The lyrics of "The Bridge" (some verses omitted) concern a customer who was contemplating suicide until he learned of Kline's Elixir Vitae.

"The Singing Hutchinsons" were neighbors of Lydia Pinkham in Lynn, Massachusetts, and their song-books, published in 1852, included a satiric ballad entitled "Calomel" that castigated the medical profession for harsh medicines and high fees, sentiments that Lydia fully shared.[3]

More commercially inspired were "Down Where the Paw-Paw Grows" (Courtesy of Munyon's Paw-Paw), Musica-Medicus (copyright 1886 by Kilmer's Swamp Root) and "The Bridge" (Kline's Elixir Vitae). From an earlier day, we have "Morison's Pills" in eight verses.[4] Consider the song honoring "Rough on Rats," a widely touted product of Wells Richardson & Co. that was usually co-advertised with Well's Rough-on-Corns, Well's May Apple Pills, and Well's Buchu-Paiba. It would have taken Cole Porter to find a rhyme for the last product. Contemporary patent medicine music is, on the whole, somewhat shorter. Our television audiences are forced to be satisfied with:

> Plop, Plop
> Fizz, fizz,
> Oh what a relief it is!
> *(Alka-Seltzer - 1976)*

Today the writers of singing commercials rarely get a visible screen credit. It was not always so. Vin Mariani ran an endorsement by Charles Gounod, one of the leading French composers of the 19th century, noted particularly for his opera, Faust. Under a picture of Gounod appeared a signed bar of music and a dedication to A. Mariani. Devotion to this product is sometimes ascribed to the fact that it contained an appreciable amount of cocaine dissolved in wine.

PART FIVE

General Information

Glossary

The following words, as **used** in names of patent medicines, usually have the meaning set out below:

Ague—fever accompanied by chills and sweating at regular intervals, as in malaria.

Alterative—a drug intended to produce changes in metabolism or to modify circulation in certain parts of the body. A non-technical term.

Analgesic—a pain killer that does not produce loss of consciousness. Example: aspirin.

Antacid—a medicine to reduce stomach acidity.

Anodyne—a pain reliever, particularly a narcotic.

Antikamnia—from the Greek, "opposed to pain".

Anticephalgine—a headache remedy. A non-technical word.

Antipyretic—for preventing or reducing fever.

Antithelmintic—for expelling worms from the intestines.

Aperient—a laxative.

Aromatic—to stimulate and remove gas from the digestive tract.

Astringent—for shrinking mucous membranes or exposed tissues, and for reducing discharge; more generally, for contracting any soft tissue, as in cosmetic lotions.

Balm—a healing ointment; also generally any aromatic preparation. A non-technical term.

Balsam—containing a resinous substance, usually aromatic, from certain plants and trees. May be liquid, semi-liquid or solid. Examples: Balsam Copaiba, Balm of Gilead. Includes the oleoresins which are fatty or essential oils holding the resin in solution. Examples: capsicum, cubeb, ginger.

Bitters—alcoholic preparation of an herb, leaf, fruit, seed or root used as a mild tonic for the appetite and digestion. Frequently laxative.

Cachet—rice flour wafer containing a powder.

Canchalagua—a bitter herb of the genus Centaurium, which includes gentian (a tonic and stomachic).

Carminative—for eliminating gas from the digestive system, to relieve colic or flatulence. From the Latin, "to cleanse or disentangle".

Cataplasm—a poultice.

Catarrh—inflammation of mucous membrane usually producing discharge, swelling and congestion, for example, of the nasal passages in the common cold.

Cathartic—a purgative or laxative.

Catholicon—a panacea or cure-all; from the Greek "universal".

Caustic—a substance that destroys living tissue.

Cerate—a preparation for external application that melts above body temperature, consisting essentially of wax (sometimes a resin) mixed with oil or lard and medicinal ingredients.

Cholagogue—for increasing the flow of bile from the liver.

Cordial—an invigorating or stimulating medicine. From the Latin word for "heart".

Decoction—extract made by boiling a plant in water, usually 5 parts of drug and 100 parts of water; from the Latin "to cook".

Demulcent — a medicine that counteracts irritating or stimulating substances; an emollient.

Desicant—a medicine that reduces secretions and discharges.

Diaphoretic—for increasing perspiration.

Diuretic—for increasing the flow of urine.

Ecbolic—promotes uterine contractions.

Electuary—a medicated paste, usually containing sugar or honey, used in veterinary practice and administered by smearing on the tongue, teeth or gums.

Elixir—a sweetened aromatic preparation containing alcohol . Used for flavoring as well as medicinal purposes.

Embrocation—a liniment, lotion. From the Greek "to moisten and rub."

Emetic—for producing vomiting.

Emmenagogue—for producing menstrual discharge.

Emollient—for softening the skin or soothing mucous membranes.

Emulsion—mixture of two liquids that are not completely miscible, such as oil and water. One of the liquids is dispersed in droplets in the other, usually with the aid of an emulsifying agent.

Epispastic—a blistering agent.

Errhine—for increasing nasal secretions.

Essence—an extract or concentrate made from a plant or other natural substance.

Expectorant — for increasing the discharge of mucous from the respiratory tract by coughing and spitting.

Extract—a concentrate, usually a solution in alcohol but, more generally, any substance made by distilling or evaporating a solvent that has been applied to another substance or material.

Febrifuge—for reducing fever.

Hematinic—to improve the quality of the blood.

Homeopathic—based on treatment of a disease by giving tiny doses of a remedy that would produce in a healthy person symptoms of the disease being treated.

Infusion—liquid extract of a drug steeped or soaked, usually in water.

Linctus—preparation for licking or sipping.

Liniment—a preparation thinner than an ointment for rubbing on the skin; may be liquid or semi-liquid, oily, alcoholic or soapy.

Lithontriptic—for dissolving kidney or bladder stones. From the Greek "stone crushing."

Mydriatic—to dilate the pupil of the eye.

Myotic—to contract the pupil.

Nervine—a nerve tonic or a preparation intended to soothe the nerves.

Ointment—a semi-solid preparation for application to the skin with a base of fatty or greasy substance such as lard, lanolin (wool fat) or petroleum.

Opodeldoc—a soap liniment with the properties of a rubefacient or an anodyne.

Panacea—a cure-all. Remedy for all diseases and conditions. From the Greek "all healing."

Pectoral—relating to diseases of the chest.

Petrolatum—a greasy substance distilled from petroleum oils. Chemically related to paraffin wax, but semi-solid in consistency.

Plaster—material spread on gauze and applied to skin, usually stiffer consistency than an ointment and adhesive to the body. Examples: mustard plaster, capsicum plaster, lead plaster. Term also applied to"sticking plaster" for closing superficial cuts, the forerunner of "adhesive tape" and the "Band-Aid."

Reparation—for restoring wasted tissue.

Resolvent—for dispersing liquid oozed from the skin, especially discharges from inflammations or lesions.

Rubefacient—for stimulating or inflaming the skin.

Salve—any healing ointment.

Sanative—beneficial, having the power to cure or heal.

Saponaceous—soapy.

Sarsaparilla—an infusion, extract or syrup made from a plant of the Smilax family.

Sialagogue—for increasing the flow of saliva.

Soporific—inducing sleep.

Specific—directed towards a particular illness or part of the body.

Sternutatory—increases nasal secretions.

Spirits of ____ : an alcoholic solution of a volatile substance.

Stomachic—stimulant for the stomach.

Sudorific—producing perspiration or heavy exhalation.

Syrup—a medicinal preparation using a concentrated sugar solution as a base.

Tincture—a solution of a medicinal substance in alcohol, alcohol and water, or alcohol and ether.

Tonic—a medicine to increase body tone by stimulating tissue nutrition; intended to invigorate and refresh.

Topical—for local application.

Troche—a cough drop or, more generally, any medicinal tablet or lozenge, usually circular or oval.

Unguent—a salve or lubricant, especially one for sores or burns.

Vermifuge—expels parasitic worms, especially those of the intestine.

Vesicant—a blistering agent, used as a counter-irritant.

Wine of ____: a pharmaceutical preparation using purified wine as a vehicle. Examples: Wine of Iron, Wine of Tar.

Notes

Part One

1. What is a Patent Medicine?
[1]Lyman F. Kebler, "United States Patents for Medicines during the Pioneer Years of the Patent Office," *Journal of the American Pharmaceutical Association* 24 (1935):489.

2. What Was in Them?
[1]American Medical Association, *Nostrums and Quackery,* 2nd ed. (Chicago: American Medical Association Press, 1912) I, pp. 513-514.
[2]Josephus Goodenough, *The Favorite Receipt Book and Home Doctor,* 1904 rev. ed. (New York: Avenel Books, 1982), p. 627.
[3]*Ibid.,* p. 632.
[4]Arthur J. Crane, "Therapeutic Thaumaturgy," *American Mercury 3,* No. 12 (1924), p. 423.
[5]American Medical Association, *Nostrums and Quackery* (Chicago: American Medical Association Press, 1912); Harvey W. Wiley, *1,001 Tests of Food, Beverages and Toilet Accessories, Good and Otherwise,* (New York: Hearst International Library, 1916); Charles Solomon, *The Traffic in Health* (New York: Navarre Publishing Company, 1937); John Phillips Street, *The Composition of Certain Proprietary Medicines* (Chicago: The American Medical Association Press, 1917); Peter Morell, *Poisons, Potions and Profits* (New York: Knight Publishers, 1937).

3. One Born Every Minute
[1]Charles E. Rosenberg, "The Therapeutic Revolution: Medicine, Meaning, and Social Change in Nineteenth-Century America'. *Perspectives in Biology and Medicine* 20 (1977),485, 487.
[2]*Ibid.,* p. 490.
[3]Samuel Thomson, *New Guide to Health or The Botanic Family Physician,* Boston: E.G. House (1822),43.
[4]The Thomsonian Recorder, Vol. IV, No. 17 (1836),187.

[5]Alex Berman, "The Thomsonian Movement and its Relation to American Pharmacy and Medicine," *Bulletin of the History of Medicine*, 25 (1951),405-428, 519-538. Susan E. Fillmore, "Samuel Thomson and His Effect on the American Health Care System," *Pharmacy in History*, Vol. 28, No. 4 (1986),191.

[6]For the stories of these drugs, simply told, see Morton Silverman, *Magic in a Bottle* (New York: The MacMillan Company, 1941).

[7]A well-expressed overview of medical theories and treatments of the time is found in Sarah Stage, *Female Complaints* (New York: W.W. Norton and Company, 1979), pp. 45-62.

[8]Oliver Wendell Holmes, *Homeopathy and its Kindred Delusions* (Boston: W.D. Tichenor, 1843).

[9]For an exposition of various types of patent medicines and their purported medical justifications, see J. Worth Estes, "The Pharmacology of Nineteenth-Century Patent Medicines," *Pharmacy in History*, 30, No. 1 (1988),3-19.

[10]William Radam, *Microbes and the Microbe Killer* (Albany: Knickerbocker Press, 1890).

[11]American Medical Association, *Nostrums and Quackery*, 2nd ed. (Chicago: American Medical Association Press, 1912), I, pp. 68-75.

[12]Bailey Radium Laboratories, *Radium Water* (East Orange, N.J., 1926), pp. 6-11. Malorye Allison, *The Radioactive Elixir*, Harvard Magazine, Jan.-Feb. (1992), 73-75. Roger M. Macklis "Radithor and the Era of Mild Radium Therapy," *Journal of the American Medical Association*, Vol. 264 (August 1990), p. 614.

4. Nineteenth Century Huckstering

[1]John K. Winkler, *John D. Rockefeller, A Portrait in Oils* (New York: Vanguard Press, 1929), p. 12.

[2]James Harvey Young, *American Self-Dosage Medicines* (Lawrence, Kansas: Coronado Press, 1974), pp. 3-6.

[3]Frank Presbrey, *The History and Development of Advertising* (New York: Doubleday, Doran and Company, 1929), p. 297.

[4]Frank Rowsome, Jr., *They Laughed When I Sat Down* (New York: Bonanza Books, 1959), p. 45.

[5]"Proprietary Specialities," *Scientific American* XLIV, No. 13 (1891),194-195.

[6]Jean Burton, *Lydia Pinkham Is Her Name* (New York: Farrar Strauss and Company, 1949), p. 209.

[7]Philip Loring Allen, "Dosing the Public as a Business," *Leslie's Monthly Magazine* XIX (1905):575.

[8]Nathaniel C. Fowler, *Fowler's Publicity* (New York: Publicity Publishing Company, 1897), p. 135.

[9]*Ibid.*, p. 138.

[10]Lee J. Vance, "Evolution of a Patent Medicine," *Popular Science Monthly* 39, No. 1 (1891), p. 83.

[11]George Presbury Rowell, *Forty Years an Advertising Agent* (New York: Printer's Ink Publishing Company, 1906), p. 371.

[12]James R. Chiles, "Civic Pride, Old West-Style," *Smithsonian* Vol. 20, Number 12 (1990), p. 100.

[13]*Home of August Flower and German Syrup* (Woodbury, N.J.: G.G. Greene, 1889).

[14]Gerald Carson, "Sweet Extract of Hokum," *American Heritage* Vol. 22, Number 4 (1971), p. 24.

[15]Presbrey, p. 296.

[16]The story of H.H. Warner is well told by Edward C. Atwater, "Hulbert Harrington Warner and the Perfect Pitch: Sold Hope, Made Millions," *New York History* LVI (1975), pp. 154-190.

[17]New York Graphic, May 10, 1888, p. 536.

[18]American Medical Association, *Nostrums and Quackery* (Chicago, 1921) II, p. 211.

[19]*Rochester Democrat and Chronicle*, February 28, 1889, p. 6.

[20]*Rochester Union and Advertiser*, January 19, 1884, p. 2.

[21]*Rochester Democrat and Chronicle*, January 28, 1923, p. 1.

[22]*Warner's Safe Cure Almanac* for 1892, pp. 24-25.

[23]*New York Times*, October 14, 1894, p.21; January 28, 1923, Sec.2, p.6.

5. Boom and Decline

[1]Frank Rowsome, Jr., *They Laughed When I Sat Down* (New York: Bonanza Books, 1959), p. 55.

[2]*Ladies Home Journal*, Vol. 22, No. 10, September 1905, p. 15.

[3]*Ladies Home Journal*, Vol. 21, No. 12, November 1904, p. 18. A letter in the Pinkham files at Schlesinger Library, Radcliffe College, confirms the sale of customer information.

[4]Herrick, Arthur Donald, *Drug Products* (New York: Revere Publishing Company, 1942), p. 15.

[5]Natenberg, Maurice, *The Legacy of Dr. Wiley* (Chicago: Regent House, 1957), pp. 47-57.

[6]Federal Food and Drugs Act 34, Stat. 768.

[7]Gunning, Robert, "Hypocrites Highball," *American Mercury*, November 1942, pp. 722-729.

6. Patent Medicines, Twentieth Century

[1]James Harvey Young, *The Medical Messiahs* (Princeton: Princeton University Press, 1967) contains an excellent history of regulatory developments, updated by the same author in *American Self-Dosage Medicines* (Lawrence, Kansas: Coronado Press, 1974).

[2]See Floyd Martin Clay, *Coozan Dudley LeBlanc* (Gretna, La.: Pelican Publishing Co., 1973).

[3]J.D. Radcliffe, "The Hullabaloo About Hadacol," *Readers Digest*, July 1951.

[4]*Rutherford v. United States*, 399 F. Supp. 1208 (W.D. Okla., 1975).

[5]See FDA Administrative Record, *Laetrile*, Docket No. 77 N-0048, Federal Register, Vol. 42 (1977), p. 39773

[6]The details of Laetrile's evolution are set forth in James Harvey Young, "Laetrile in Historical Perspective," in *Politics, Science and Cancer: The Laetrile Phenomenon*, ed. Gerald F. Markle and James C. Petersen (Boulder, Colo.: Westview Press, 1980).

[7]*Time*, June 20, 1977, p. 48.

[8]Lee Edson, "Why Laetrile Won't Go Away," *N.Y. Times Magazine*, November 27, 1977, pp. 41-49, 104-110.

[9]American Cancer Society, *Cancer Quackery — Laetrile*, np. nd., pp. 13-14.

[10]*Time*, May 11, 1981, p. 55.
[11]Alan E. Nourse, M.D., "Quack Cancer Cures," *Good Housekeeping*, September 1983, p. 58.

Part Two

7. The Cures
[1]Dr. Keeley's story is well told by Sam and Kate Hiller, "Have You Dug a Keeley Bottle?," *OBX Magazine*, May 1973, pp. 4-8.
[2]Josephus Goodenough, *The Favorite Medical Receipt Book and Home Doctor*, 1904 rev. ed. (New York: Avenel Books, 1982), p. 622-623.
[3]Sears Roebuck & Co., *The Great Price Maker (Catalogue No. 116)* 1906 ed. (1906; rpt. Secaucus, N.J.: Castle Books, 1976), p. 830.
[4]Conan Doyle, "The Sign of Four" in *The Complete Sherlock Holmes* (New York: Garden City Publishing Company, Inc., 1938), p. 91.
[5]Joel L. Phillips and Ronald D. Wynne, *Cocaine, The Mystique and the Reality* (New York: Avon Books, 1980), p. 92.
[6]Monroe Martin King, "Dr. John S. Pemberton: Originator of Coca-Cola," *Pharmacy in History* 29, No. 2 (1987), p. 87.
[7]American Medical Association, *Nostrums and Quackery*, 2nd ed. (Chicago: American Medical Association Press, 1912), I, pp. 487, 530, 533, 534, 537, 543, 546, 553, 562, 563, 573.

8. Bitters
[1]Very extensive illustrated and annotated lists of bitters bottles have been published by Richard Watson, *Bitters Bottles* (New York: Thomas Nelson & Sons, 1965) and *Supplement to Bitters Bottles* (Camden, New Jersey: Thomas Nelson & Sons, 1968) and by Carlyn Ring, *For Bitters Only* (Wellesley Hills, Mass.: The Pi Press, 1980).
[2]Other writers have given different percentages for alcoholic content. See, for example, Charles Solomon, *The Traffic in Health* (New York: Navarre Publishing Co., 1937), p. 123 and John Phillips Street, *The Composition of Certain Potent and Proprietary Medicines*, American Medical Association, Chicago (1917). One explanation for the differences may lie in the years during which the various analyses were made. Another may be the manufacturers' own poor quality control.

9. Sarsaparillas
[1]The most exhaustive survey of this group of products is Phyllis Shimko's *Sarsaparilla Encyclopedia* (Aurora, Oregon 1969).

10. Women's Medicines
[1]For a perceptive review of the sociological background, see Sarah Stage, *Female Complaints* (New York: W.W. Norton & Company, 1979), Chapter 3.
[2]Jean Burton, *Lydia Pinkham Is Her Name* (New York: Farrar Straus & Company, 1949), p. 107.
[3]Edward Bok, "How the Private Confidences of Women Are Laughed At," *Ladies Home Journal* 21, No. 12 (1904), p. 18.

12. Veterinary Medicines
[1]*Warner's Telephone Book Almanac for 1893*, p. 23.

Part Three

16. Fear Advertising
[1]Phillip Loring Allen, "Dosing the Public as a Business," *Leslie's Monthly Magazine* LIX (1905), p. 575.

18. Testimonials
[1]*Printer's Ink 2*, No. 8 (1899), p. 17.
[2]Robert Gunning, "Hypocrites Highball," *American Mercury*, November 1942, p. 722.
[3]Stewart H. Holbrook, *The Golden Age of Quackery* (New York: MacMillan Company, 1959), p. 241.
[4]Quoted in James Harvey Young, *The Toadstool Millionaires* (Princeton: Princeton University Press, 1961), p. 188.
[5]Frank Rowsome, Jr., *They Laughed When I Sat Down* (New York: Bonanza Books, 1959), p. 60.
[6]Mark Sullivan, *Ladies Home Journal* XXII, No. 2 (1960), p. 18.
[7]*Advertising in the United States* 7 (Dec. 1900), p. 17.
[8]*Printer's Ink*, No. 8 (1899), p. 3
[9]For the history of Mariani, his product and his advertising, see William H. Helfand, "Vin Mariani," *Pharmacy in History* 22 (1980), pp. 11-19.
[10]Angelo Mariani, *Coca and its Therapeutic Applications*, 2nd ed. (New York: 1892), pp. 30, 50.

20. Public Issues
[1]James Harvey Young, *The Toadstool Millionaires* (Princeton: Princeton University Press, 1941), p. 141.
[2]Frederick A. Conningham, *Currier and Ives Prints* (New York: Crown Publishers, 1970), p. 159. Used with overprint by Mansfield Medicine Company and R.C. Brown & Co. Copyright 1884.

22. Religion and Morals
[1]Frank Presbrey, *The History and Development of Advertising* (New York: Doubleday, Doran & Company, 1929), p. 294.

23. Newspaper Advertising
[1]Stewart H. Holbrook, *The Golden Age of Quackery* (New York: Collier Books, 1959), p. 33.

[2]Frank Rowsome, Jr., *They Laughed When I Sat Down* (New York: Bonanza Books, 1959), p. 54.

[3]James Harvey Young, "Patent Medicines: The Early Post-Frontier Phase," *Journal of The Illinois State Historical Society* (Autumn 1953), p. 290.

[4]James Harvey Young, *The Toadstool Millionaires* (Princeton: Princeton University Press, 1961), p. 7; Lawrence A. Johnson, *Over the Counter and on the Shelf* (Rutland, Vt.: Charles E. Tuttle Co., 1961), p. 116.

[5]Clarence Hornung, *Handbook of Early American Advertising Art* (New York: Dover Publications, 1953), p. X.

[6]*Printer's Ink* 27, No. 5 (May 3, 1899), p. 27.

[7]*Advertising in The United States* (Boston: The American Statistical Association, 1900), pp. 7, 17.

[8]*Profitable Advertising* 8, No. 11 (1899), p. 606

[9]James Harvey Young, *The Toadstool Millionaires*, p. 211.

[10]Edward Bok illustrated his crusading article in *Colliers* magazine of November 5, 1905 with examples of this sort of pressure.

[11]Gerald Carson, "Sweet Extract of Hokum," *American Heritage* 22, No. 4 (1971), p. 24.

[12]Rowsome, p. 59

[13]Frank Presbrey, *The History and Development of Advertising* (New York: Doubleday, Doran and Company, 1929), p. 294.

24. Trade Cards

[1]Ambrose Heal, *London Tradesman's Cards* (London: B.T. Balsford, 1925), p. 63.

[2]Mary E. Moore, *They Called It the Card Craze*, Northampton, Mass. n.p., n.d.

[3]A number of these cards are illustrated in Landauer, Bella C., *Early American Trade Cards* (New York: W.E. Ridges, 1927).

[4]A representative selection of these are shown in Landauer, Bella C., *Some Embossed American Trade Cards* (New York: Harbor Press, 1941).

[5]On the development of lithography generally, see Clarence Hornung, *Handbook of Early American Advertising Art* (New York: Dover Publications, 1935), pp. XLI-XLIII.

[6]Henry T. Peters, *America on Stone* (New York: Doubleday, Doran & Co., 1931), p. 60.

[7]Katharine Morris McClinton, *The Chromolithographs of Louis Prang* (New York: Clarkson N. Potter, Inc., 1973), p. 85.

[8]Leslie G. Matthews, *Antiques of the Pharmacy* (London: G. Bell & Sons, 1971), p. 102.

[9]c.f., Bella C. Landauer, "Some Trade Cards with Particular Emphasis on the Currier & Ives Contribution," *New York Historical Society Quarterly Bulletin* 17 (1934), pp. 79-83.

[10]John Grand-Carteret, *Vieux Papiers, Vielle Images* (Paris: a le Vasseur, 1896), Chapter XXII.

25. Almanacs

[1]Milton Drake, *Almanacs of the United States* (New York: The Scarecrow Press Inc., 1962); a checklist and census of almanacs.

[2]Clarence S. Brigham, "An Account of American Almanacs," *Proceedings of The American Antiquarian Society* (October 1925), p. 196.

[3]Ibid., p. 197.

[4]Ayer's issued two special hardcover volumes, for 1889 and 1892, containing all the foreign language editions for those years.

[5]James Harvey Young, "The Patent Medicine Almanac," *Wisconsin Magazine of History* XLV (Spring 1962), p. 159.

26. Giveaway Items

[1]*Carlill v. Carbolic Smoke Ball Company* (1893), 1 Q,B, 256. For a contemporary account see *Spectator*, July 9, 1892, p. 62.

[2]See Mathias Koref and Richard F. Riley, "Corner Cards and Advertising Covers of the Merchant's Gargling Oil Company," *The American Philatelist* 96 (1982), p. 889.

[3]A series of articles on these stamps appeared from 1936 to 1957 in *Weekly Philatelic Gossip* and a few other stamp magazines. They are collected in Henry W. Holcombe, *Patent Medicine Tax Stamps* (Lawrence, Mass.: Quaterman Publications, Inc., 1979).

[4]George B. Griffenhagen, *Private Die Proprietary Medicine Stamps* (Milwaukee: American Topical Association, 1969), pp. 70-78.

[5]Specialized Catalogue of United States Stamps, 1984 (New York: Scott Publishing Co., 1983), p. 600.

[6]John A. Muscalus, *Paper Money Pertaining to Druggists, Medicines and Medical Practitioners* (Bridgeport, Pa.: Historical Paper Money Research Institute, 1969).

27. Containers

[1]See Albert C. Revi, *American Pressed Glass and Figural Bottles* (New York: Thomas Nelson and Sons, 1964).

[2]A number of labels are illustrated in Adelaide Hechtlinger, *The Great Patent Medicine Era* (New York: Grosset & Dunlap, Inc., 1970), pp. 150-155.

28. Outdoor Advertising

[1]Wallis Gore Marshall, Through America, or Nine Months in the United States (London: Sampson, Law, Marston, Searle & Livingston, 1882), p. 111.

[2]Clarence P. Hornung, *Handbook of Early American Advertising Art* (New York: Dover Publications, 1953), p. xxxi; Frank Rowsome, Jr., *They Laughed When I Sat Down* (New York: Bonanza Books, 1959), pp. 48-49.

[3]Frank Presbrey, The *History and Development of Advertising* (New York: Doubleday, Doran and Company, 1929), p. 500-501.

[4]"How Omega Oil Has Won Success," *Profitable Advertising* 9, No. 9, (1900), p. 631.

[5]William H. Helfand, "The Pharmaceutical Poster," Pharmacy in History 15 (1973), p. 67.

29. The Medicine Show

[1]Marcus Dickey, *The Youth of James Whitcomb Riley* (Indianapolis: The Bobbs-Merrill Co., 1919), p. 198.

[2]Sarah Stage, *Female Complaints* (New York: W.W. Norton and Company, 1979), p. 42.

[3]*The Hutchinson Family's Book of Words* (New York: Goodwin & Baker, 1852), p. 41.

[4]Quoted by William H. Helfand in "James Morison and His Pills," *Transactions of the British Society for the History of Pharmacy* 1 (1974), p. 125.

Works Consulted

General

Adams, Samuel Hopkins "The Great American Fraud." *Colliers Weekly,* Vol. 36, Oct. 7, 1905, p. 14; Oct. 28, 1905, p. 17; Nov. 18, 1905, p. 20; Dec. 2, 1905, p. 16; Jan. 13, 1906, p. 18; Feb. 17, 1906, p. 22. (1905 and 1906; rpt. New York: Collier & Son).

Helfand, William H. "The Pharmacy in the Popular Arts." *Pharmacy in History*, Vol. 28 (1986), p. 75.

Holbrook, Stewart H. *The Golden Age of Quackery.* New York: The MacMillan Company, 1959.

Johnson, Lawrence A. *Over the Counter and on the Shelf.* Rutland, Vermont: Charles E. Tuttle Co., 1961.

Lyman, Rufus A. *American Pharmacy.* Philadelphia: J.B. Lippincott Company, 1945.

Natenberg, Maurice. *The Legacy of Dr. Wiley.* Chicago: Regent House, 1957.

Wilson, Stephen. *Food and Drug Regulation.* Washington, D.C.: American Council on Public Affairs, 1942.

Young, James Harvey. *American Self-Dosage Medicines.* Lawrence, Kansas: Coronado Press, 1974.

Young, James Harvey. *The Medical Messiahs.* Princeton: Princeton University Press, 1967.

Young, James Harvey. *The Toadstool Millionaires.* Princeton: Princeton University Press, 1961.

Advertising

Allen, Philip Loring. "Dosing the Public as a Business." *Leslie's Monthly Magazine,* Vol. LIX (1905), p. 575.

American Statistical Association, *Advertising in the United States,* Vol. 7. Boston, 1900.

Carson, Gerald. *One for a Man, Two for a Horse.* New York: Bramhall House, 1961.

Carson, Gerald. "Sweet Extract of Hokum." *American Heritage* 22, No. 4 (1971), p. 24.

Fowler, Nathaniel C. *Fowler's Publicity.* New York: Publicity Publishing Company, 1897.

Hopkins, Claude C. *My Life in Advertising.* New York: Harper & Brothers, 1927.

Hornung, Clarence P. *Handbook of Early American Advertising Art.* New York: Dover Publications, 1953.

Presbrey, Frank. *The History and Development of Advertising.* New York: Doubleday, Doran and Company, 1929.

Rowsome, Frank Jr. *They Laughed When I Sat Down.* New York: Bonanza Books, 1959.

Rowell, George Presbury. *Forty Years an Advertising Agent.* New York: Printers Ink Publishing Co., 1906.

Sullivan, Mark. "The Inside Story of a Sham," *Ladies Home Journal* XXII, No. 2 (1906), p. 14.

Early Medicines

Bender, George A. *Great Moments in Pharmacy.* Detroit: Northwood Institute Press, 1967.

Bigelow, Jacob. "On Self-Limited Diseases," in *Medical America in the Nineteenth Century: Readings from the Literature.* Baltimore: Johns Hopkins Press, 1972.

Brown, Alice Cooke. *Early American Herb Recipes.* New York: Crown Publishers Inc., 1966.

Haggard, Howard W. *Devils, Drugs and Doctors.* New York: Harper & Brothers, 1929.

Jameson, Eric. *The Natural History of Quackery.* London: N. Joseph, 1961.

Kebler, Lyman F. "United States Patents Granted for Medicines during the Pioneer Years of the United States Patent Office." *Journal of the American Pharmaceutical Association* 24 (1935), p. 486.

Riznik, Barnes. *Medicine in New England 1790-1840.* Sturbridge: Old Sturbridge Inc., 1965.

Shyrock, Richard H. *The Development of Modern Medicine.* Philadelphia: University of Pennsylvania Press, 1936.

Young, James Harvey. "Patent Medicines in the Early Nineteenth Century." *The South Atlantic Quarterly,* October, 1949, p. 69.

Young, James Harvey. "Patent Medicines: The early Post-Frontier Phase." *Journal of the Illinois State Historical Society,* Autumn, 1953, p. 290.

Patent Medicine Products

Adams, Samuel Hopkins. *The Great American Fraud.* New York: P.F. Collier & Son, 1905.

American Medical Association. *Nostrums and Quackery.* Chicago: The American Medical Association Press, Volume I, 1911, Volume II, 1921, Volume III, 1936.

Ashley, R. *Cocaine: Its History, Uses and Effects.* New York: St. Martin's Press, 1975.

Chase, Stuart and Schlink, F. J. *Your Money's Worth.* New York: The MacMillan Company, 1927.

Cramp, Arthur J. "Therapeutic Thaumaturgy," *American Mercury* 3, No. 12, 1924.

Crittenden, Ann and Ruby, Michael. "Cocaine: The Champagne of Drugs." *New York Times Magazine,* September 1, 1974, p. 16.

Edson, Lee. "Why Laetrile Won't Go Away." *N. Y. Times Magazine,* November 27, 1977, pp. 41-49, 104-110.

Food and Drug Administration Administrative Record. *Laetrile,* Docket No. 77 N-0048 (1977).

Food and Drug Administration. *Laetrile, Commissioner's Decision on Status,* Federal Register Vol. 42, (1977), p. 39773.

Goodenough, Josephus. *The Favorite Medical Receipt Book and Home Doctor.* 1904. rev. ed. New York: Avenel Books, 1982.

Gunning, Robert. "Hypocrite's Highball," *American Mercury* 3, No. 12 (1924) .

Harding, T. Swann. *The Popular Practice of Fraud.* New York: Longmans, Green & Co., 1935.

Herrick, Arthur Donald. *Drug Products.* New York: Revere Publishing - Company, 1942.

Kallet, Arthur and Schlink, F.J. *100,000,000 Guinea Pigs*. New York: Vanguard Press, 1932.
Lamb, Ruth DeForest. *American Chamber of Horrors*. New York: Farrar & Rhinehart, 1936.
Morell, Peter. *Poisons, Potions and Profits*. New York: Knight Publishers, 1937.
Phillips, Joel F. and Wynne, Ronald D. *Cocaine: The Mystique and The Reality*. New York: Avon Books, 1980.
Phillips, M. C. *Skin Deep*. New York: Vanguard Press, 1934.
Radcliffe, J.D. "The Hullabaloo About Hadacol," *Readers Digest*, July 1951.
Salomon, Charles. *The Traffic In Health*. New York: Navarre Publishing Company, 1937.
Smith, Andrew F. "Tomato Pills Will Cure Your Ills," *Pharmacy in History* 33, No. 4 (1991), pp. 169-177.
Smith, Elmer. *Early American Home Remedies*. Lebanon, New York Applied Arts Publishers, 1968.
Walsh, James J. *The Story of the Cures that Fail*. New York: Appleton & Company, 1923.
Wiley, Harvey W. *1,001 Tests of Food, Beverages and Toilet Accessories, Good and Otherwise*. New York: Hearst International Library, 1916.
Young, James Harvey. "The Hadacol Phenomenon," *Emory University Quarterly*, June 1951.
Young, James Harvey. "Laetrile in Historical Perspective," *Politics, Science and Cancer: The Laetrile Phenomenon*. Ed. Gerald F. Markle and James C. Petersen. Boulder, Colo.: Westview Press, 1980.

Patent Medicine Proprietors
Atwater, Edward C. "Hulbert Harrington Warner and the Perfect Pitch: Sold Hope; Made Millions." *New York History* LVI, No. 2 (1975), p. 159.
Auburn, Stephen. "Piso's Cure," *Old Bottle Magazine* 5, No. 10 (1973), p. 9.
Auburn, Stephen T. "Samuel Pitcher, Charles Fletcher, and Castoria," *Old Bottle Magazine* 11, No . 1 (1978), p. 7.
Bok, Edward. "How the Private Confidences of Women are Laughed At," *Ladies Home Journal* XXII, No. 12 (1904), p. 18.
Burton, Jean. *Lydia Pinkham Is Her Name*. New York: Farrar Straus and Company, 1949.
Campbell, Lucille A. "William R. Warner, The Sugar-Coated Pills," *Old Bottle Magazine* 6, No. 9 (1973), pp. 14-15.
Clay, Floy Martin. *Coozan Dudley LeBlanc*. Gretna, La.: Pelican Publishing Co., 1973.
Engel, Sally. "An Historic Old Company" (The B.J. Kendall Company), *The Western Horseman*, July 1971, p. 94.
Fritschel, Don. "Silas Smith and His Green Mountain Renovator," *Old Bottle Magazine* 10, No. 12 (1976), pp. 8-10.
Greenfield, Samuel F. "Katonka, The Great Indian Medicine," *Old Bottle Magazine* 1, No. 10 (1975), pp. 10-11.
Hiller, Sam and Kate. "Have You Dug a Keeley Bottle?," *Old Bottle Magazine* 6, No. 5 (1973), pp. 4-8.
Holcombe, Henry W. *Patent Medicine Tax Stamps*. Ed. George B. Griffenhagen. Lawrence, Massachusetts: Quaterman Publications, 1979.
"How Omega Oil Won Success," *Profitable Advertising* 9, No. 9 (1900), p. 627.
Humphreys, F. *Homeopathic Mentor or Family Advisor in the Use of Humphrey's Homeopathic Remedies*. New York: Humphrey's Homeopathic Medicine Co., 1918.
McKearin, Helen. *Bottles, Flasks and Dr. Dyott*. New York: Crown Publishers, Inc., 1970.
McKelvey, Blake. *Rochester, The Flower City*, 1855-1890. Cambridge: Harvard University Press, 1929. (H.H. Humphrey, Asa T. Soule).
O'Connell, Annette. "St. George and the Dragon," *Old Bottle Magazine* 5, No. 10 (1972), pp. 6-7.
O'Shea, Nancy. "Perry Davis Pain Killer, It Must Have Worked!," *Old Bottle Magazine* 10, No. 10 (1977), p. 9.
The Lydia E. Pinkham Medicine Company Papers. The Arthur and Elizabeth Schlesinger Library on the History of Women in America, Radcliffe College, Cambridge, Massachusetts.
Rosser, M.L. "The Smith Brothers Really Existed," *Collectors News*, March 1975, p. 25.
Seeliger, Michael Williams. *H.H. Warner, His Company and His Bottles*. Madison, Wisconsin, n.p., 1974.
Shaw, Robert B. *History of the Comstock Patent Medicine Business*. Washington: Smithsonian Institution Press, 1972.
Shiell, Jeanne R. "The Kickapoo Indian Saga," *Old Bottle Magazine* 3, No. 3 (1970), p. 8.
Shiell, Jeanne R. "Warner, The Man with the Safe Cure;" *Western Collector*, February, 1968, p. 41.
Skinner, Ralph B. "The Dr. True's Elixir Story," *Lewiston (Maine) Journal*, May 15, 1971, p. 1.
Spear, Alan. "Merchant's Gargling Oil," *Old Bottle Magazine* 4, No. 4 (1971), p. 20.
Stage, Sarah. *Female Complaints*. New York: W.W. Norton and Company, 1979.
The Story of Malt-Nutrine. St. Louis: Anhauser-Busch, Inc. 1952.
"The Thomsonian Movement and its Relation to American Pharmacy and Medicine," *Bulletin of the History of Medicine* XXV (September-October 1951), pp. 405-428, 519-538.
Thompson, Samuel. *New Guide to Health or the Botanic Family Physician*. Boston: E.G. House, 1822.
Waddy, George. "The Fabulous Dr. Fenner of Fredonia, New York," *The Antique Trader* (Dubuque, Iowa), October 22, 1972, p. 60.
Washburn, Robert Collyer. *The Life and Times of Lydia E. Pinkham*. New York: G.P. Putnam & Sons, 1931.

Trade Cards
Burdick, Jefferson R. *The American Card Catalogue*. New York, 1960; rpt. Franklin Square, N.Y.: Nostalgia Press, 1967.
Conningham, Frederick A. *Currier & Ives Prints*. New York: Crown, 1970.
Dow, George Francis. "Trade Cards," *Old Time New England* 26 (1936), 115 and 27 (1939), 10.
Freeman, Larry. *Louis Prang: Color Lithographer*. Watkins Glen, New York: Century House, 1971.
Heal, Sir Ambrose. *London Tradesman's Cards*. London: B.T. Balsford, 1925.
Helfand, William H. "Art and Medicine in Professional Communications," *Adler Museum Bulletin* Vol. 9 (1983), p. 15.
Huber, Mary Means. "Essex Country Trade Cards," *Essex Institute Historical Collection* 98 (1962), p. 154.
Jay, Robert. *The Trade Card in Nineteenth-Century America*. Columbia, Mo.: University of Missouri Press, 1987.
Kaduck, John M. *Advertising Trade Cards*. Des Moines, Iowa: Wallace-Homestead Book Company, 1976.
Lasher, Faith. "The Victorian Persuaders," *American Collector*. March 1973, p. 20.

Landauer, Bella Clara. *Early American Trade Cards*. New York: W.E. Rudge, 1927.
Landauer, Bella Clara. *Some Embossed American Trade Cards*. New York: Harbor Press, 1941.
Landauer, Bella Clara. "Some Trade Cards With Particular Emphasis on the Currier and Ives Contributions," *New York Historical Society Quarterly Bulletin* 17 (1934), p. 79.
Landauer, Bella Clara and Weiss, Harry B. "Some Trade Cards of American Engravers," *American Book Collector* 4 (1933), 250-255,308-311; 5 (1933), 16-18.
Lewis, John. *Printed Ephemera*. New York: Dover Publications, 1962.
Marzio, Peter C. *The Democratic Art: Pictures for the l9th Century America*. Boston: David R. Godine, 1979.
Maust, Don. "The American Trade Card," *The Antiques Journal*, June 1967, p. 46.
Means, Mary Elizabeth. *Early American Trade Cards*. Diss. American Antiquarian Society, Worcester, Mass., 1958.
McClinton, Katharine Morris. *The Chromolithographs of Louis Prang*. New York: Clarkson N. Potter, 1973.
Peters, Harry T. *America On Stone*. New York: Doubleday, Doran & Co., 1931.
Renoy, G. *Bruxelles sous Leopold Ier—25 ans de Cartes Porcellaine*, 1840-1865. Bruxelles (1979).
Rickards, Maurice. *Collecting Printed Ephemera*. New York: Abbeville Press, 1988.
Weinroth, L.A. "Advertising Cards: Sedate and Educational or Humorous and Colorful," *AdvertisingAge*, Sec.2, December 7, 1964, p. 88.

Almanacs, Posters and Other Paper Materials
Boston Philatelic Society. *An Historical Reference List of the Revenue Stamps of the United States Including Private Die Proprietary Stamps*. Boston: 1899.
Brigham, Clarence S. "An Account of American Almanacs," *American Antiquarian Society* (October, 1925).
Broido, Lucy. *The Posters of Jules Cheret*. New York: Dover Publications, 1980.
Burdick, Jefferson R. *Pioneer Post Cards*. New York: Nostalgia Press, Franklin Square, 1956.
Carline, Richard. *Pictures in the Post*. Folsom, Pa.: Deltiologists of America, 1972.
Drake, Milton. *Almanacs of the United States*. New York: The Scarecrow Press Inc., 1962.
Griffenhagen, George B. *Private Die Proprietary Medicine Stamps*. Milwaukee, Wisc.: The American Topical Association, 1969.
Havens, Meredith. "Almanacs of Yesteryear," *The Antique Trader*, (February 26, 1974), p. 29.
Hechtlinger, Adelaide and Cross, Wilbur. *The Complete Book of Paper Antiques*, Ch. 12. New York: Coward McCann & Geoghegan Inc., 1972.
Hechtlinger, Adelaide. *The Great Patent Medicine Era*. New York: Grosset & Dunlop, Inc., 1970.
Helfand, William H. "The Pharmaceutical Poster," *Pharmacy in History* 15 (1973), p. 67.
Helfand, William H. "Affiches Pharmaceutiques 'fin de siecle'," *Revue d'Histoire de la Pharmacie* 21 (1972), p. 163.
Helfand, William H. *La Pharmacie par l'Image*. Catalogue of the Exposition of the International Congress of Pharmaceutical History, Paris, September-October, 1973.
Helfand, William H. *Medicine & Pharmacy: 100 Years of Poster Art*. Albany: New York State Museum, 1981.
Holcombe, Henry W. *Patent Medicine Tax Stamps*. Lawrence, Mass.: Quaterman Publications, Inc., 1979.
Koref, Mathias and Riley, Richard F. "Corner Cards and Advertising Covers of the Merchant's Gargling Oil Company," *The American Philatelist* 96 (1982), p. 889.
Margolin, Victor; Brichta, Ira and Brichta, Vivian. *The Promise and the Product; 200 Years of American Advertising Posters*. New York: MacMillan Publishing Co. Inc., 1979.
Muscalus, John A. *Paper Money Pertaining to Druggists, Medicines and Medical Practitioners*. Bridgeport, Pa.: Historical Paper Money Research Institute, 1969.
Sagendorph, Robb. *America and Her Almanacs*. Boston: Little Brown & Co. Boston, 1970.
Slabaugh, Arlie R. *Encased Postage Stamps, U.S. and Foreign*. Chicago: Numismatic Publications, 1967.
Specialized Catalogue of United States Stamps, 1984. New York: Scott Publishing Co., 1983.
Staff, Frank. *The Picture Postcard and Its Origins*. New York: Praeger, 1966.
Young, James Harvey. "The Patent Medicine Almanac," *Wisconsin Magazine of History* XLV (Spring 1962), p. 159.

Bottles and Tins
Agee, Bill. *Collecting the Cures*. Waco, Texas: Texian Press, 1969.
Bartholomew, Ed. *1001 Bitters Bottles*. Fort David, Texas: Bartholomew House, 1970.
Bartholomew, Ed. *1200 Old Medicine Bottles*. Fort David, Texas: Frontier Book Co., 1970.
Blasi, Betty. *A Bit About Balsams*. Louisville, Kentucky: Farley-Goepper Printing Company, 1974.
Devner, Kay. *Patent Medicine Picture*. Tombstone, Arizona: The Tombstone Epitaph, 1968.
Ferraro, Pat and Bob. *A Bottle Collector's Book*. Sparks, Nevada: Western Printing and Publishing Co., 1966.
Griffith, David. *Decorative Printed Tins*. New York: Chelsea House, 1979.
Hammond, Robert and Dorothy. *Collectible Advertising*. Des Moines, Iowa: Wallace-Homestead, 1974.
Munsey, Cecil. *The Illustrated Guide to Collecting Bottles*. New York: Hawthorn Books Inc., 1970.
Petit, Ernest L. The Book of Collectible Tin Containers. Manchester, VT.: Forward's Color Productions, Inc., 1967.
Putnam, H.E. *Bottle Identification*. Duarte, California: n.p., 1965.
Putnam, P.A. *Bottled Before 1865*. Los Angeles, California: Rapid Blueprint Co., 1968.
Revi, Albert C. *American Pressed Glass and Figural Bottles*. New York: Thomas Nelson and Sons, 1964.
Ring, Carlyn. *For Bitters Only*. Wellesley Hills, Mass.: The Pi Press, 1980.
Shimko, Phyllis. *Sarsaparilla Bottle Encyclopedia*. Aurora, Oregon: n.p., 1969.
Toulouse, Julian Harrison. *Bottle Makers and Their Marks*. New York: Thomas Nelson, Inc., 1971.
Umberger, Art and Jewel. *It's a Sarsaparilla*. Tyler, Texas: Corker Book Company, 1968.

Watson, Richard. *Bitters Bottles*. Camden, New Jersey: Thomas Nelson & Sons, 1965.
Watson, Richard. *Supplement to Bitters Bottles*. Camden, New Jersey: Thomas Nelson & Sons, 1968.
Wilson, Bill and Betty. *Nineteenth Century Medicine in Glass*. Amador City, California: Nineteenth Century Hobby & Publishing Co., 1971.

Medicine Shows, Music
Freeman, Graydon Laverne. *The Medicine Showman*. Watkins Glen, N.Y.: Century House, 1957.
Helfand, William H. "Ephemera of the American Medicine Show." *Pharmacy in History*, 27, No. 4 (1985), p. 183.
Helfand, William H. "James Morison and His Pills," *Transactions of the British Society for the History of Pharmacy* 1 (1974), p. 125.
LeBlanc, Thomas J. "The Medicine Show," *American Mercury* 5, No. 18 (June 1925), p. 232.
Matthews, Leslie G. "Pharmacy in Song," *Pharmaceutical Journal* (1957), p. 480.
McNamara, Brooks. *Step Right Up*. Garden City, N.Y.: Doubleday & Company, Inc., 1976.
McNeal, Violet. *Four White Horses and a Band*. New York: Doubleday and Company, Inc., 1947.
Stout, Wesley. "Alagazam, The Story of Pitchmen High and Low," *Saturday Evening Post*, October 19, 1929, p. 12.
Wright, Richardson. *Hawkers and Walkers in Early America*. New York: Frederick Ungar Publishing Co., 1965.

NOTABLE COLLECTIONS that include patent medicine material

American Antiquarian Society, 185 Salisbury Street, Worcester, Massachusetts 01600. Telephone 617-755-5221.
Jerrerson R. Burdick Collection, Metropolitan Museum of Art, Fifth Avenue and 82nd Street, New York, New York 10128 (Print Room). Telephone 212-535-7710.
Downs Manuscript Collection, The Henry Francis duPont Winterthur Museum, Winterthur, Delaware 19735. Telephone 302-656-8591.
Bella Clara Landauer Collection, The New York Historical Society, 170 Central Park West, New York, New York 10024. Telephone 212-873-3400.
Library of Congress, Print and Photograph Collection, Madison Building, Room 339, First and Independence Avenue S.E., Washington, D.C. Telephone 202-287-6394.
Thelma S. Mendsen Card Collection, The Henry Francis duPont Winterthur Museum, Winterthur, Delaware, 19735. Telephone 302-656-8591.
Lydia Pinkham Collection, Schlesinger Library, Radcliffe College, 10 Garden Street, Cambridge, Massachusetts. Telephone 617-495-8647.
Margaret Woodbury Strong Museum, 1 Manhattan Square, Rochester, New York 14607. Telephone 716-263-2700.
Warshaw Collection of Business Americana, National Museum of American History, Smithsonian Institution, Washington, D.C. 20560. Telephone 202-357-1300.